# Women Living
# CONSCIOUSLY

*Real Stories of Women
Living on Purpose,
with Passion, Empowered*

Powerful You!
PUBLISHING
Sharing Wisdom ~ Shining Light

Women Living Consciously
*Real Stories of Women Living
on Purpose, with Passion, Empowered*

Cover Design by Jodie S. Penn
Editor: Sheri Horn Hasan


Published by: Powerful You! Inc. NJ USA
www.powerfulyoupublishing.com

Library of Congress Control Number: 2012934845

Sue Urda and Kathy Fyler– First Edition

ISBN: 978-1-4675-2176-5
First Edition May 2012

Self Help / Women's Studies

Printed in the United States of America

# Dedication

*This book is dedicated
to each and every woman who has
awakened her spirit to the
possibility of a more conscious
life, love and self.*

# Table of Contents

## PART THREE: CONSCIOUS CAREER

## PART FOUR: CONSCIOUS SPIRITUALITY

# Foreword

To live consciously is to live truthfully. To live truthfully is to live in a state of openness, exposure, vulnerability, humility, power, and grace. To live as a conscious woman is to live life in and from divine freedom.

So when did we stop speaking the truth? When did we start denying our most basic feminine qualities? When did we start fearing the essence of who we were born to be?

The answer is simple – It happened when we started looking for our consciousness (our connection, our essence, our truth) outside of ourselves in a culture that has been built upon unconscious thoughts, poor decision-making and complete inaction.

Why did we start looking for this consciousness? The search began the moment we felt it slipping away. Because, you see, you were born conscious, aware, powerful, strong and intuitive. You were born with an innate knowing of who you are and what you were born to be. And along the way, because of life's circumstances, that knowing was driven from your awareness and pushed down into the deep crevices of your heart; patiently waiting for you to find a way back to the truth of who you are.

Now, this truth, this essence, of who you are has always been here and will always be. There is not a situation terrible enough or a person dark enough to ever destroy it. That is an absolute impossibility because "this that you are" is connected to "all that there is". And "all that there is" holds the universe together by giving birth to us all and taking us back to where we began. This that you are is bigger than your wildest dreams and will carry you to your greatest heights the moment you choose to start telling the truth to yourself about how you feel, what you want, what you have lost, what you yearn for, who you are angry with, what is missing, what needs to be let go of, why it hurts, what is needed, what can't be said, what must be said and who must be forgiven.

It is in the truth telling that you will find "HER"... the part of you that is waiting to be dug up from underneath all of the layers of other people's rules, views and value systems, and your unexpressed hurt, pain, judgments and constant devaluing of what you have to offer to the world. And when there is a willingness to find her, your entire being (mind, body and spirit) will begin clearing the pathways for her to be seen, heard and revealed to you once again.

When you hear the resonating words of another, your body will give you  signs that it is time to start really paying attention, for there is an opening happening. The hair on the back of your neck will stand on end, the skin on your arms will pucker with bumps and a small tear may escape from the corner of your eye. These are all signs that she is throwing pebbles at the window of your soul in the attempt to wake you up to the knowing that there is something deeper. And she will call to you, to now allow your own words that have been shaken from their cage to be heard.

You will know you have reached her when you feel your body respond to your own words with an aching so deep that your bones begin to hurt. Then you will know that the secrets that have been buried deep within your marrow are beginning to break free in order to be revealed.

It is time for her to be heard, she needs her story to be told. She can no longer bear the burden of holding on to the pain of the past out of fear of rejection or persecution. She knows that your need to keep her a secret is your greatest pain and she has acted out at times, in desperation, with the hope that you will turn and face her, take her by the hand and show the world that together you are strong and cannot be beaten.

Know that her initial words of truth may be woven together like the strands of a tattered old blanket. So take a moment and listen, then pull those words back and look underneath and see what the deeper truth might be. And if you are truly courageous, allow yourself to pull back layer after layer and discover an even deeper truth still.

For this is who you are. You are a precious angel of truth that has been shrouded by layers upon layers of emotion and the deeper you go the richer your reward.

You will see her, this magnificent essence of consciousness that you are, in the stories that you and others will share about where you have been and where you are bound to go. You will hear her in the words that are read, that resonate so deeply that they cause you to remember who you truly are, what you are made of, and where your home has always been—deep within your own heart.

And once you have found her, be warned that you will most definitely keep her—for she comes with a bounty of creativity, passion, health, vitality, joy, relationship, depth, and meaning that is

driven by an undeniable knowing that she knows wh... s...
vibrant, she is conscious, she is alive, she is living an... She is

Over the last 15 years, I have had the immers...
working with thousands of individuals on a one-to-on...
private coaching practice, and in large group settings, ... of
mind, body, healing workshops throughout North An...
witnessed one person after the next go through ... have
transformations as they told their stories, felt what th... life
feeling, spoke the words that needed to be sp...
themselves and others and let go of years of pain and
held them back from everything that they longed for.

They all came searching for the answers while want...
defend, or play victim to the circumstances that had
them. However, once they had the chance to take resp...
the part that they played, and realized that they wei...
behaviors and were simply just someone doing the b...
could, then the rest would just fall away naturally. Av...
blame and defense and in came an effortlessness and p...
of being. And that truth of who they were, that essence,
consciousness that had been hidden away for so long was a
felt, experienced completely and set free to be all that is possi...

Upon reflection, I too have been changed from the insid...
from being in the courageous presence of these amazing individu...
I was able to see parallels in our lives, dreams, emotions an...
desires. Their stories held the mirror up for me to gaze upon and I
was offered the choice whether to dive in and meet them in the core
of it or hold back and watch from a spectator's perspective. Well, I
dove right on in and cried my own tears as they cried theirs. I shook
from the raw intensity of my own emotion as they shook with theirs.
I relaxed back in to my body as they once again felt what it felt like
to be back within theirs. That is the power of choosing to do the
work and be conscious—we show others what is possible and they
too wake up the consciousness that lies within us all. It is as if we
are all connected by this invisible energy and all it takes is one
person to open the door, clear out the cobwebs and turn on the light
for the same chain reaction to happen in others.

Choosing to live in this way is choosing to live consciously; and it
begins with taking back the reigns of your life by noticing where
your life is on autopilot and needing to be lived more truthfully,
tangibly and honestly. It is about setting new intentions for a better
today and tomorrow and then making daily decisions from a place of
awareness that serve that intention. It is about living the life that

osed to just settling for what has been given.

...scious life is not as easy as stepping into an old
...ol pajamas. It is a lifestyle choice where you must put
...seemingly uncomfortable and unfamiliar situations that,
...re difficult and challenging. You must be committed to
...integrity everyday and be vigilant in its pursuit. And it is
...hieved by staying present to the moment, speaking and
...he truth about what's in the here and now and letting go of
...r no longer serves.

...some, they choose this lifestyle, and for others it chooses
...Either way, living consciously is simply the single most
...rtant thing that you can do for yourself and those around you.

...am grateful for the words shared within the following pages by
...nen with whom I will probably never meet yet feel a deep kinship
...th. I have read their words, I have felt them deep within my soul,
...ey have moved me and I will forever be changed by the profound
...eauty, depth and bravery being offered up as a guide toward my
own inner clearing and conscious awareness. Because no matter
how much work you have done (and I have done a load) the
opportunity to deepen and expand in the essence of who you are will
forever be a part of this thing that we call life.

NOW is the time... She's calling to you to move forward, to live
this life consciously and truthfully from a place of openness, to be in
exposure, to feel the vulnerability, embrace the humility, and step
into your innate power and grace. She needs you to risk feeling
what it feels like to speak the truth, stand emotionally naked and
allow your being to be torn apart and brought back together again
by the depth of your emotions.

This divinely feminine—YOU—is longing to soar beyond the
imaginary boundaries of your past and live life from the absolute
freedom that you have always been.

Call off the search; for the answers do not lie outside of you.
Begin now to welcome yourself home. Welcome home!

~ Kristine Lackey
Evolution Unlimited

# Introduction

Awake. Alive. Aware. This is consciousness. The women who share their stories in this book have made a choice to live consciously in their lives. They have chosen to follow their inner guidance system and do as the Serenity Prayer suggests...accept the things they cannot change, change the things they can and engage their innate wisdom to know the difference.

This does not mean they deny the struggle and pain that sometimes comes to us as we move through life—tempting as it may be. Nor do they try to forget the not so great memories of the past—although this may be a welcome reprieve. Instead, they choose to allow whatever it is to become a part of them, weave the lessons into the fabric of their lives, and move forward as more colorful and 'whole' individuals. They have chosen to find the good and focus on it, they see the silver linings rather than the dark clouds—and now they share them with you.

These women are exceptional in every way...and they are no different than you. They were born into this life as children of our Infinite Creator and they are here for a higher purpose. Again, they are just like you. You too have a higher purpose—you have a calling. If you don't know what it is, simply ask and be open to receive—your calling, your higher purpose, will be revealed. It may even become clear to you within these pages.

As you read these stories, you may wonder what inspired these women to share such personal awakenings, intimate relationships and, in some cases, deeply-held secrets that many others would never reveal. Why would they risk being scrutinized, studied or perhaps even 'create a stir' among their families, friends and colleagues?

If you ask them some will say that they couldn't keep it in any longer, others will tell you that they were divinely guided, and some will say they wrote as a tribute to a loved one. *All of them* will affirm to telling their story so that you might learn from it and it will ease your way.

And so these stories are here for you.

The amazing and beautiful authors in this book will overwhelmingly agree that, in the telling of their stories, they each found an unexpected and sometimes life-changing gem awaiting them. As the words flowed through them to the pages, they often recognized a stronger, more powerful woman than they thought they knew. Many of them experienced a catharsis, a release, an opening— and they are grateful for the renewed sense of self. In the telling of their stories, they released themselves to be freer and more alive, awake and aware, they released themselves to live more consciously. They released themselves to simply *be*.

As you read these pages, allow yourself to be immersed in the words. As you feel the feelings of these courageous women, know that you too have courage beyond your mind and circumstances. The experiences and lessons shared are immeasurably healing, so open not only your mind, but also open your heart to them. You may be surprised at your own awakening through these words.

There is no particular order to these stories or sections enclosed herein. You may choose to read them front to back, choose a title that interests you or randomly open to a page and trust that this story is exactly the one calling to your spirit.

May you be blessed abundantly and may your earthly journey be filled with great joy and loving moments, and mostly, may you heed the calling to live your life consciously!

*With great love and deep gratitude,*

*Sue Urda*

# PART ONE

# Conscious Wellness

*"Love is always the answer
to healing of any sort."*
*~ Louise Hay*

# The Soul Can Only Whisper
## Marcia Ann Calantonio

I gasp as searing pain flashes across my lower left abdomen. The pain comes in waves, and I place my hand on my stomach, clutch the area like a corset, and clench my jaw. I imagine the comforting warmth of my hot pack, and know I'll be able to get some relief when I get home in about an hour. It's a misty chilly morning and I'm up early doing my morning feed at a nearby farm for twenty-three horses.

I love to be around horses, and volunteer to do this work three mornings a week. I also love the stillness of the morning as the birds chirp and the barn cats rub up against my leg. The horses chomp on their hay and grain, and give me love in return. For a few minutes in my day, I break away from my frenetic pace, stand in stillness, and tune into myself.

But today my body is screaming in pain. The familiar nagging discomfort is escalating with a fury. I'd experienced diverticulitis, an infection in my colon, six times in the past two years, and usually I'd just grin and bear it.

Today I just want to finish the feed and water the horses. The far paddocks necessitate me pulling two hoses joined together about two hundred feet down and back up the hill to the water troughs. Normally there's a hose reel to make this task easier.

Today, no such luck. As I approach the hose reel, my bound up and knotted emotions meet their match. There before me on this Monday morning is the aftermath of young girls who had fun with the hose over the weekend and didn't put it away properly.

Have you ever played tug of war with two hundred feet of garden hose? Tangled and bound up tight, the job requires multiple stops and rewinds. To pull the entire expanse of hose over and through, and back again to free it up, costs me forty minutes and a lot of focus in order to straighten out each loop of knotted hose.

This is hard to do one-handed, as I clutch my stomach with the other. Tense all over, my muscles ache. My emotions bubble up and over, and since no one is around to witness my outburst, I release my anger in a scream. As I let off steam, I hear myself say, "No, no, don't be angry, they're only children." *Yes, they are children,* I think to myself, *but they need to be responsible and accountable for their actions, and I need to set healthy boundaries...*

Home again and I can't heat my hot pack up fast enough. I'm brave, but I can't ride out this pain. Within two minutes of sitting still, I realize I need to call 911. God has been trying for so long to get my attention, but I keep looking at outer circumstances instead of within for the cause of my pain. And today it's the hose's fault.

The paramedics wheel me in through the emergency room, and my visit there turns into an eight day hospital stay, complete with intravenous antibiotics to combat a raging infection. I'm allowed no food or water by mouth, but I'm too sick to even care. Just make the pain go away!

I miraculously escape emergency surgery to remove the part of my colon that has shut down flat as a pancake, never to work again. It lost the ability to move digesting food in and through for about the last ten inches. My surgeon sends me home with a PICC line in my arm for intravenous antibiotics and nutrition for the next ten weeks and only clear liquids by mouth. The goal is to get me healthier before my surgery so it will be successful.

### Let Go and Let God...and Get Out of Her Way!

I'm not allowed eat or drive. I have to connect tubes up to this port in my arm to get nutrition that's infused twelve hours a day by a pump. I need antibiotics three times a day. Weak as a kitten and stopped nearly dead in my tracks, vulnerability sets in and I feel completely out of control. I can't even take care of myself! Tears of fear and frustration flow freely.

I remember thinking, *Why is this happening to me? What's the purpose?* I tried to connect the dots between the past events in my life to see what caused this. The inside of my body and the outside world are a dead match. It's obviously time to be still and heal from within.

About three weeks into my healing, as I begin to feel stronger, I have an epiphany that this experience is not just about me. Can this *be*? My daughter—at odds with me about college choices for months—is again my lovable daughter. My son, whom I'd nursed back from near death a year before from a MRSA bloodstream infection, makes sure I take my medicine properly and plays nurse. My youngest son is learning to be responsible and to take care of himself. And my boyfriend shows his love as he takes care of me around the clock.

I am a vehicle to help those in need—my family. They are learning to serve others; I am creating accountability, responsibility, and healthy boundaries.

Ten weeks at home is a long time to contemplate my options and to tap into what I believe is God's greater vision for me. I promise myself that if I wake up on the other side of my surgery, I will live my life the way I want to, and become happy and whole. It will be my rebirth. After all, I will eat food and move it through the "new me" for the first time—just like a baby. A newborn soul knows who she is and what she wants.

On February 23, 2009, I entrust myself to the skilled hands of the surgeons and anesthesiology team to support my life during the five hour abdominal surgery to remove my worn out anatomy, and with it, my dead emotions. When I wake up, I'm patched up "better than new." My loved ones are all there to greet me. I'm so grateful that God *does* have a special plan for me!

Twelve weeks after surgery I have healed, and am released to go back to doing what I love. My heart guides me to pursue my interior decorating business full time, and to delve deeper into the intuitive language of the horses while I am their caretaker.

An established business offers me the opportunity to become a decorator assistant. On the very day I am to sign a contract to seal this partnership, I am abruptly stopped. I foolishly lift a heavy bag of horse feed while giving the horses their afternoon meal at the barn that day. As I lean forward to lift the bag, *excruciating* pain rips across my abdomen.

Four days later, after not being able to keep even water down, I vomit green bile, and *know* I am dehydrated. Back at the emergency room, I figure I'll receive intravenous fluids and return home revived and rebalanced. Instead, the doctor tells me I have a small bowel obstruction and may need emergency surgery.

### Third Time's a Charm

Apparently my small intestine constricted, kinked, and twisted like a pretzel. Nothing was moving in me or through me. Rather, it was stuck in a vacuum.

Within one hour of hospitalization, I pleaded with God, *WHAT are you trying to tell me this time?*

And very clearly I hear the answer: *This is not the path your soul wants to take.*

It resonates in my heart. So, who am I? What do I want? How can I serve?

Suddenly, I get it! Innately artistic and creative with my hands, I lacked healthy expression of my thoughts and feelings. For many years, I shoved down all my feelings and thoughts, and when they wanted to move up—to be expressed through my voice—I shoved them down some more and told them, *"shhh! don't you dare!"* Some were too scary to go back and separate the truth from the illusion, and to speak about them seemed just too daunting. Unfortunately, what remained was the sticky toxic resonance of thirty-five years of quelled emotions.

Must I experience another eight days and eight nights with no food or water? Not even an ice chip? The uncomfortable tube stuck up my nose and into my stomach determines me to cure my problem by walking the halls—around and around and around—for days on end, like a horse on the track! Walking helps the intestinal tract remain active, and we all hope for a miracle!

The chalky barium I have to drink for a procedure on the seventh day proves to be the catalyst I need, as it relaxes and soothes my intestine enough to untwist it. My body reacts and rebalances—without logic or reason, like *magic*! Within the hour, I am in the flow. Miraculously, I escape emergency surgery *again!*

What became obvious to me is that I have not always lived in the flow of life. Being in the flow happens when I allow my thoughts and feelings to be expressed freely and authentically; this is true creative expression.

It took three hospitalizations totaling twenty-one days over six months of my life to understand the needling in my body and the whisper of my soul. These days, as I rekindle my love affair with the *real, authentic me,* I take huge leaps of faith and bank on my inner wisdom to follow my passion and purpose. I let go all that no longer serves me.

I love being The Barefoot Decorator of Inner Bliss Designs, standing in the green grass connecting sole to soul with spirit and earth, tapped into creator's expression. My clients connect to their inner wisdom and the divine sequence of the universe to create energetically supportive living spaces that reflect who they really are.

Partnering with the horse, I facilitate the deeper connection between true nature and inner beauty. Horses have a natural ability to pick up on our thoughts and feelings, and mirror them back to us for reflection. I share the language of horses and teach energy balancing activities to create authentic living.

That tangled and twisted two hundred foot garden hose set into motion a new beginning for me. It served as a metaphor for my own emotional knots, which were pleading for self-healing. Today I focus on self-love, respect, gratitude, and kindness, both given and received. My inner and outer worlds feel balanced, and true creative expression flows freely. Every day is the *only* day.

**ABOUT THE AUTHOR:** Marcia Ann has been vibrantly sharing beauty for 30 years. She is an award-winning floral designer, interior decorator, visionary, motivational speaker, and writer, who can intuitively connect others to their inner wisdom and to the divine sequence of the Universe. Marcia Ann reveals her client's true beauty as a unique energetic blend of nature since the moment they were born. She then uses this individual blueprint as a tool to create beautiful and balanced lives that mirror who they really are. Partnering with horses, she also facilitates the Sole to Soul Experience™, an energetic experience to facilitate authentic living. She lives in Poolesville, Maryland with her 3 children.

Marcia Ann Calantonio
Inner Bliss Designs
www.innerblissdesigns.com
marcia.ann@innerblissdesigns.com
240-393-1877

# Finding My Way Back Home
## Jodee Chizever

What a motley crew are we, traveling down the road in our van, surrounded by New Mexico's red, brown, and magenta rocks, sage everywhere you look. There's Brad, the handsome quadriplegic with his long brown hair and beautiful blue eyes, full of sadness and anger, and Kim, her flowing blond hair and sweet angelic face marred only by the fear and distrust in her bright blue eyes.

And Laura, short dark hair and brown eyes, who projects her butch lesbian toughness onto the world with every move she makes, but who's one of the kindest women in the group. There are ten or so of us in the Life Healing Center's van in Santa Fe. Once a week we're allowed to go on excursions outside of the center with our counselors/aides—the people paid to keep an eye on us.

The Life Healing Center—where people wind up who've suffered severe trauma—is the place that helped put me back together and saved me. I'd suffered from depression since I was twelve. In therapy off and on since, I'd done a lot of digging and healing. Recently, I'd found myself again in a very deep, dark place, but this time—mired in darkness—I truly fell apart.

I'd recently graduated from New York University with my master's in public administration and worked as the director of a refugee assistance program at a non-profit organization in Brooklyn, New York. Twenty-six years old and living in Manhattan; from the outside it all looked good and yet I remember taking the subway to work one day and thinking it would be easier if I just stepped off the edge and onto the tracks.

I'd look around at all the people on the subway, and those walking to and from work, and think they all looked so happy. I made up stories about their lives—that they were the opposite from mine. All I wanted to do was cry—cry from the bottom of my soul that my life wasn't working. I felt like the Energizer Bunny; I just kept going and going, but inside I felt dead. I'd worked *so* hard to get to this place in my life. I'd lived with a learning disability and still graduated from NYU! That was huge for me. Yet, it didn't fulfill me. The world did not all of a sudden become a brighter place—it remained the same shade of grey...

Because I've always been a spiritual being, I found my way to an amazing women's group with individuals who felt like sisters in many ways. This was when I began to realize that the fires of hell tormenting me—a.k.a. my depression—were a direct result of all the secrets I'd kept buried deep within. The women in my group achieved such amazing healing, and yet, my secrets were still eating me alive.

I was Humpty Dumpty on the wall and I finally fell off. Broken into too many numerous and assorted parts, I wasn't sure if I was ever going to come back. It was scary and I needed to find a place to heal. My research led me to this place in New Mexico that had a spiritual outlook on healing, and I found myself with a group of other fractured souls all trying to heal.

At the Life Healing Center for just under a month, I planned to extend my time there for another month. It was almost the holiday season, and I'd just begun to feel safe, to know that I had time, and to cope with my budding awareness of the fact that my unconscious mind could no longer contain within it those buried secrets of mine. To preserve my own sanity, it was time to shed light onto that deep, dark hole into which I'd submerged the horrific realities of my past. Unconscious denial was no longer a safe place, and it had cost me too much already.

Lights sparkled at the Center, and we created a family. This would be my first Thanksgiving without fighting—amazing! In my family, dinners were an exercise called "who can we get to cry?" A week didn't go by without someone running from the dinner table in tears from the nagging and "joking" in which it seemed everyone participated. Growing up, this didn't seem so bad, it was how we bonded. Until, inevitably, it was my turn to become the butt of the joke.

On major holidays this energy expanded. Dinners then became a loud free for all, with everyone wanting a say and a way to make someone else the focus of ridicule or shame. Then there was the fighting that happened even before a holiday began. I don't remember what the fighting was all about, except that it usually focused on little things that needed to be done to make the holiday "perfect." But the reality of the holiday's imperfection would crash down upon us mid-fight, and one of us would end up in our bedroom crying again. The amazing part was how we *never* spoke about it afterwards, as if it all miraculously just disappeared...

### Kiva and Sage

I am not sure exactly where they brought us that day, but I know it was an ancient native site with dwellings in the caves and the profound energy of spirit. I look around and take a deep breath. I am home. Something tingles and pulls. I survey the brown earth and again notice the sage everywhere. Everyone goes off independently, and I walk in a different direction with one of the counselors.

There in front of us appears a space with a ladder going down into the earth. The counselor tells me it's a *kiva* and encourages me to check it out. I don't know why she brought me there and I have only a vague idea of what a *kiva* is.

I step down the stairs and immediately the energy is very powerful. I get to the bottom and it's totally brown—with dirt all around. This circular space deep inside the earth has a bench around it, and two or three spaces for a ledge built into the dwelling. I have since learned that a *kiva* is used as a sacred space by the native people in this area. It is where the elders hold council to plan for the future of their tribe, and where ceremonies occur.

So here I am, alone inside this *kiva*. How intense the energy is! I can feel the beat of energy and Spirit all around me. Then my Spirit Guide Tah-Ne appears. It has been a while since I felt his presence. Filled with love—and intensity—he appears neither in regalia nor how I imagine a native elder to be. Instead, he's dressed just in brown pants and a pale blue shirt, and has long brown hair. I feel him right next to me, and he takes my hand.

"You are going to be okay," he tells me. "You are loved. We know how hard this has been for you. Know that you are safe now. You are safe. Take this space in and take in the feeling. This is your safe space—deep inside the earth. You are taken care of, and we are always here for you." Tears run down my cheeks, yet I don't push them away. I just sit there feeling his hand in mine. Safe.

I sit there for a long time—I don't want to move and change this moment. I wish I could stay there my whole life! But alas, that is not life, and I get up. My counselor does not ask questions and we leave the *kiva* slowly. It's at this moment that I *know* I will be okay. That I will heal. There have been other moments in my life that I have felt Spirit and I've been compelled to continue forward, and there will be more to come, and yet it is this one that allows me to know with certainty that I will make it.

I wish I could say that from that day forward my depression lifted dramatically and all my demons magically disappeared. They did not. And yet I was strong enough to continue on. I was strong enough to face the darkness and know that there was light on the other side.

I stayed at the Life Healing Center for another month. The day I was scheduled to go home was a scary one. The Center makes each person sign a document saying they will not try to kill themselves. I refused to sign it. I knew going back to my life would be difficult and I didn't feel ready.

My counselor came in and sat down with me. She assured me that I was strong enough and reminded me of all the work we'd done. But it was what she said next that shifted it for me. "Jodee, there is something in you that exudes caring and leadership," she said. "I wouldn't be at all surprised if you wind up making a big difference out there and helping other people shift their lives."

*YES!* I'd always felt that, and here was someone else who saw it too! And so I returned home. I was right—home felt harsh and unsafe and I didn't like it at all! I had some bumps, but through it all I felt my guides were with me and that I'd somehow get through. And I did.

I returned to work. My employers and co-workers thought I'd been at a rehab clinic. Somehow it's more acceptable to say that you're a drunk or a drug addict than to say you're a person that suffers from depression. I hope my writing this helps to change that.

I continued in my field for a number of years and then followed my calling to become a shamanic healer. Now I make a difference in many people's lives by helping those who need healing, just as I once did. I work out of my basement, decorated with beautiful soft brown clay paint. Here I've created my own *kiva, a* place where I feel safe and help others to feel safe, too.

When I look back at that day in New Mexico, I'm reminded of the healing properties of sage—just a bluish green bush and a weed to most people who live in the west. So innocent and sweet on the outside, but so powerful when used as an herb; its purifying energy is sacred to many native American Indians. Able to balance and cleanse the body and mind of negative energy, sage played as intricate a part in ancient healing ceremonies as it does in current ones. Now, when I close my eyes and see sage everywhere, I know I am home.

**ABOUT THE AUTHOR:** Jodee Chizever is called The Everyday Shaman. She began her Spiritual Path at a very young age and has studied with teachers around the Globe. She is the woman on the spin bike next to you at the gym who that night will be holding Sacred Ceremony. She is the mom with 2 kids in the suburbs who works with your Spirit Guides to assist you with releasing core issues, and the modern day woman who carries not only a cell phone, but the tools and wisdom of Ancient Shamanic Healing to help people remember that there is more to their lives than what they see!

Jodee Chizever
Shamanic Healer
www.marahlight.com
jodee@marahlight.com
732-406-1922

# My New Best Friend
## Donna DeMild

My parents began to have trouble in their marriage when I was five years old. My home went from a place of warmth and comfort to a cold and lonely environment infused with underlying fear and uncertainty. Often I felt like a person in a dark, damp alley, alone and unable to see what lurked in the shadows.

During and after the turmoil of the divorce, I learned the dependability of food. Always there, never angry, never sullen—food always cheered and comforted me when I felt sad, nervous, lonely, confused, angry, anxious, or bored. Best of all, it didn't judge me—it celebrated my victories and rewarded my accomplishments.

I watched other family members use food that way; it was totally acceptable. Like a baby with a pacifier and a blanket snuggled safely and warmly in her parent's arms, food soothed me no matter what emotion I felt. Nothing made me feel better than a slice of hot apple pie topped with delicious vanilla ice cream!

Sunday family dinner was the big "feast" day in my Italian/Russian household. Dinner began at two o'clock, consisted of several courses, and continued into the evening. Good or bad, everything was discussed—we seemed to eat to resolution. Food left on your plate was considered an insult and a sin. After all, there were starving people in the world!

Quiet, withdrawn, and innocent, I was the fat kid in school. I tried to be friendly but was often rejected. I had only one friend I trusted, the rest were fair weather friends always vying to be one of the cool kids. I kept trying until the hurt and rejection became so strong that I started to believe everything they said about me.

I remember my fourth grade teacher took us out one day to play kickball. Last to be picked, I resolved to try my hardest to kick the ball well. This would show them—I wasn't a fat nothing! As I ran to meet the ball to kick it, my feet slid and the ball got caught between them. I fell hard to the ground into a split. Everyone gasped, giggled, laughed, and called me names.

Horrified, I managed to hold back my tears, until I heard the teacher say: "I think that may have registered as an earthquake!" Quietly I asked to go to the nurse, called my mother, and begged her to pick me up.

I weighed one hundred and thirty-five pounds by fifth grade. When the nurse came to get me every Friday—she monitored my weight loss weekly—the other kids laughed and ridiculed me. Again, I figured that whatever they said about me had to be true.

I grew angry and bitter. I was a failure, though I kept trying to get out—like a fly that continually bangs itself on the window—because I knew deep inside I wasn't meant to be obese. Anger, depression, and bitterness became a constant internal struggle. I knew I had a higher purpose.

I attempted to lose weight any way I could. By the time I was in junior high school, I took Dexatrim—it was big back then—thinking it would jump-start my metabolism and help me lose weight fast. When I reached high school, I graduated to speed, little blue pills, yellow jackets, red ones—whatever I could get my hands on.

I remember my mother doing a bedroom sweep because she thought something was up. I had two pills left, so I took them. Up all night, I was totally wired—heart palpitations and all—until I crashed the entire next day. I never thought about my health or that anything fatal could happen. When you're seventeen, you feel invincible.

### What's Eating Gilbert Grape?

In 1990 I married a fantastic man who loves me for who I am. Blessed to have Sam in my life, frequently I felt undeserving. Always, I waited for the other shoe to drop. I questioned him constantly about why he was with me, and never really believed his answers. Sometimes I'd push him, testing to see if he'd stay. My insecurity and lack of self esteem led to a lot of arguments—half the time I worried that, at any given moment, he'd leave me for someone else, other times I tried to push him away.

Conceiving was difficult but our first child Jade was born in 1992. Her birth renewed our strength and bond as a couple. I delivered our son Nicholas in 1994, needed oxygen, and almost required a cesarean section due to the stress to both of us, but in the end was able to tough it out.

I gained seventy-five pounds during my pregnancy with Jade; only thirty-five with Nicholas. Now pushing three hundred plus pounds at five feet, seven inches tall, I fell into a deep depression. Drastic dieting was out, I had the kids to consider, but still the more conventional methods didn't work.

The kids were now seven and nine—I felt so out of place on play dates, couldn't physically keep up with them, tired easily, and forced myself to be involved with the school for the kid's sake. Embarrassed to go out, I'd see the other moms glance sideways at me and whisper, and then look away if I made eye contact. Other kids just came right up to me, and blurted "you're fat!," or asked me "why are you so fat?" I knew this hurt my kids. I was out of control and felt stuck in quicksand, ready to surrender and just give up.

At the end of my rope, I began to research weight loss surgery. One night as I sat on the playroom floor well past midnight and cleaned up after the kids, I finally found the courage to tell Sam how I really felt. Tired of fighting a losing battle, I truly felt I had nothing to offer my kids or him, and that this surgery was a last resort. It was either this surgery or I just go away.

I explained I wasn't giving him an ultimatum, just telling him how miserable, disgusted, and ashamed I felt, and that I loved my family way too much to sabotage their lives with my problem. I dreaded becoming an embarrassment like Bonnie, Gilbert Grape's depressed and morbidly obese mother who refused to leave her house and was ridiculed when she did, in the movie *What's Eating Gilbert Grape?*

"I've decided to have weight loss surgery," I told Sam once I knew I was a candidate for the surgery.

"Where is this coming from?" he asked, confusion in his eyes. "I love you—you're beautiful to me the way you are."

"I hear what you are saying, but *I* don't love me this way," I told him. "I can't function like this. I feel like I have nothing to offer you as a partner, or to contribute to our kids' lives."

Sam looked at me, floored. "But you always look so happy, doing your thing around the house, being with us. And what if something happened—if you died on the table? You're willing to risk leaving me alone with the kids?"

"I feel like I'm dying inside, anyway. If I don't have surgery, I might as well just leave. I feel it's my only hope."

"Wow, I never knew you felt that way, even though I know you've struggled with your weight," he replied. "I'm just nervous and scared, I don't want anything to happen to you—it seems so extreme."

Soon he acknowledged that I literally "ate my feelings" and always seemed to be in control, taking care of everybody with a big smile—and he finally understood. "I'll support you in your decision, whatever you need me to do. I just want you to be happy," he told me. We visited the surgeon together and attended several support group meetings prior to my surgery. He remains my strongest supporter.

### The New Me!

Sam and I took our children on vacation to Disney World two weeks before my scheduled surgery. Boy oh boy, if I had a shred of doubt in my mind about whether the surgery was right for me, this vacation took care of that! I couldn't get on a lot of rides with my kids, so I watched as Sam took them. Sweaty all the time and uncomfortable in shorts, I was the official bag holder. I tired quickly, and became irritable walking around the endless amusement parks.

I tried to keep up a good front, but Sam was onto my game. Seeing my pain and frustration, he sat me down and told me everything was going to be alright; soon I'd be able to participate, just hang on.

Surgery day came and, with Sam on one side holding my hand, the surgeon on the other, they wheeled me as far as he could go. Sam kissed me, and told me he'd be waiting for me as the surgeon took my hand and wheeled me through the doors. Tears rolled down my face.

*Please God, let me get through this surgery, I promise I won't mess up! I'll make the most of my life, find my purpose, and live up to my potential using all the gifts and talents you've given me!*

I awoke from surgery sore, but joyous. I knew I wouldn't let God—or myself—down. He'd fulfilled his end of the deal, now it was my turn. From day one I was out of bed, and walking around the nurses' station, up and down the hall—moving and loving it!

My life has never been the same since. Not hungry—the smell and look of food actually made me nauseous, I was happy on a liquid diet my first week. I continued to walk and quickly picked up my pace; the treadmill was my friend. I turned exercise into my new vice; walking calmed my nerves and relieved my stress.

Putting *me* first was tremendously hard, but it's what helped me most to achieve my one hundred and seventy pound weight loss—and maintain it. It wasn't *all* about the weight, it was about how I hadn't loved or cared for myself in so many facets of my life. I'd allowed myself to be a victim and relinquished control of my choices and my future.

I continued to grow and learn about myself every day, and I realized what a tough critic of myself I'd been all those years! As I satisfy and love myself—and become my own best friend in order to live a healthy and fulfilled life—I continue in my mission to help fellow bariatric patients and others with weight struggles to achieve a lifestyle change, personal growth, and the kind of empowerment that comes from becoming one's own best friend.

**ABOUT THE AUTHOR:** Donna DeMild specializes in bariatrics, and her passion and support make her a leader in the weight loss surgery community. Donna, an International Coaching Federation certified life coach, and certified bariatric support group leader, is also a licensee/facilitator of the *Success Habits Principles* and *Back On Track* Programs, designed to educate fellow patients on lifestyle change for ultimate success. An eleven year post-weight loss surgery patient herself, Donna successfully dropped 170 pounds. Donna is a patient advocate for fellow patients and is a member of the Obesity Action Coalition and a pending member of American Society for Metabolic and Bariatric Surgery. Donna lives in New Jersey with her husband, two children, and three dogs.

Donna DeMild, LPBLC
BodySmart,LLC.
www.bodysmartllc.com
ddbodysmartllc@yahoo.com
732-218-7610

# The Power of a Promise
## Shane Devine Forbes

Happiness lit my face like a ray of gentle sun—I knew the spring thaw was finally melting the troubles of our painful separation, and I was overjoyed that Tom was on his way back home to stay. I'd set out early that May morning for an appointment at the beauty shop and emerged with a stylish new hairdo.

What's a new "do" without a new dress, I mused, as I danced into the dressing room of a favorite boutique. I left wearing a rose-colored calico number bought in happy anticipation of the romantic dinner my husband and I planned to share later that evening.

High on the hill of North Elm Street, the chapel bells chimed the noon hour and, when the light turned green, I stepped off the curb into what suddenly seemed like a separate reality. Everything around me—cars, pedestrians, and pets—all moved as if in a slow motion movie. *How odd,* I thought.

Later that day, around five o'clock, the phone rang and my dear friend Sue, who was staying with us, picked it up. By the alarming tone of her voice and the few mumbled words I heard her utter into the receiver, I knew that the unimaginable had happened. It was my brother-in-law calling to say that Tom was in critical condition as a result of a serious highway accident earlier in the day.

Without warning, a loud, gut-wrenching, desperate scream came from deep within, as I yelled "NO!", and tears swelled and poured down my face. I sobbed and bellowed my unbelieving denial as if I might change something, anything, relating to this cruel news.

Sue drove, as if in her own private speed portal like a bat out of hell, along Route 2 from western Massachusetts to Newton-Wellesley hospital, making it in forty minutes. When we arrived at Tom's bedside, I was unprepared for the harsh reality of his condition. Unconscious and on life support, he looked radiant: young, strong, handsome, and peaceful. I held his hand and spoke to him softly, promising with all my heart that our precious son, Ethan, would receive all the love, guidance and encouragement he would need to grow up strong and true. He lightly squeezed my finger, and then his brain wave monitor went flat. A kindly social worker took me aside to talk about organ donation, but I found it hard to focus on such matters.

I began to wonder why Tom's family hadn't called me sooner. Then, a young familiar-looking woman, around my age, tired and distraught, walked into the family waiting room. She hugged my in-laws, one by one, while my heart sank. Why was she here?

I soon learned that she was in the car with my husband—on their way to spend the weekend together in Boston—when the accident happened. Amidst the shock and sadness of my sudden loss, and the difficult decisions that only I could make on my husband's behalf, I came face to face with the bitter truth that Tom had never intended to come home to me that evening.

My life changed suddenly and dramatically that day. No time for goodbyes, no answers to so many profoundly difficult questions, no more communication with the man I once called my best friend, my musical partner, my husband, my heart and soul. Life as I knew it was over and I was left standing on the precipice of the great unknown, holding my precious little five year-old son's hand firmly in mine.

Pockets empty, and the wolf at the door, we were bereft, left to face a precarious future. Tom had let our life insurance policies lapse just a few weeks before his death. Looking back, I wish I could say that I immediately pulled myself together and got on with my life, but I didn't.

### Picking Up the Pieces

Inconsolable, I cried every day for the first year of widowhood, and every other day the second year. After the third year, I cried only several times a week, while anniversaries, birthdays, and especially Mothers Day brought the searing grief and tangled heap of unanswered questions back to the surface with a perplexing vengeance.

Many times I asked myself "why did this happen? Where do I go from here? How do I carry on?" To be honest, most of the decisions I made in the years that followed were guided by my desire to set a good example for Ethan. Even as I struggled to put all the pieces of my shattered life back together, loving and protecting my treasured child gave me the most compelling reason to keep on going.

In the months following Tom's death, I dedicated myself to mothering and applied my musical talents in ways that helped me feel connected to a larger purpose, as I grappled with my grief. I now sang for special events, primarily those with an emphasis on world peace, and the reduction of nuclear danger.

One of my high points, just a few months after Tom's death, was when I was a featured singer on stage with Coretta Scott King and *Sweet Honey in the Rock* at the twentieth anniversary celebration of Martin Luther King's historic 1963 March on Washington. I opened the program with *America the Beautiful,* and sang a song that Sue Walsh and I had written, an informal anthem of the Nuclear Freeze movement, called *Save the Children,* to three hundred thousand like-minded people on the Washington Mall. We were all determined to make the world a better place, and singing in this kind of context helped me feel that I was doing all I could for Mother Earth and for our children and their future. With tireless help from my friend Sue, who always found a way to make me laugh, however challenging, I did as much singing as I could.

A year later I decided to resume my college education and get my bachelor's degree—but mostly because I hoped it would inspire Ethan to work diligently toward similar goals of higher education. In the fall of 1984, I was accepted to the Ada Comstock Scholars program and attended Smith College with a full scholarship.

A theatre major, I shaped my class schedule so that I could greet Ethan at the door when he arrived home from elementary school every day, determined that he would not come home to an empty house. Instead, the wafting scents of simmering stew and warm homemade cookies made our dining table a cozy and fun place to engage in homework projects together.

### "Children Are Our Most Valuable Resource" - Herbert Hoover

Perhaps an earlier stint with *Mothering Magazine* had prepared me more than I knew at the time for the hardships of single parenting that became my lot a handful of years later. In 1975, in the spectacular sunshine and starlight of Ridgway, Colorado, I worked along with the Vorhys sisters and several other women, to imagine and birth this beautiful publication. The magazine was intended for a new generation of parents, united by the vision of raising their families naturally and organically, and rooted in the wisdom that comes from the earth.

The first few magazine issues featured articles on natural home birthing, midwifery, breast-feeding, organic foods, home schooling, and the dangers of childhood vaccinations. Back then, the back-to-the-land message of *Mothering Magazine* was down-right radical! I eagerly recruited folks to write articles, wrote some myself, and helped envision the magazine that now, some thirty-seven years later, has fostered a conscious parenting movement that has helped make the birthing and parenting experience healthier, happier, and more holistic for parents and children alike. My humble contribution to this project gave me the validation I needed to place mothering at the center of gravity in my life.

Eventually, when Ethan turned fourteen, he went away to George School, a Friends boarding school in Newtown, Pennsylvania. A year later, I got a job there as alumni director and joined the school community. It was a daily joy to share Ethan's high school days with him!

However, what I didn't realize was that my health was still deteriorating, even after treatment for chronic fatigue syndrome (CFS.) Not well understood, CFS is now recognized as a real illness, after many years of medical skepticism. Its crises are brought on by unremitting stress over time, and there were, obviously, several major traumatic events that had piled up in my life: Tom's death and all that followed; then the death of my dear brother Shawn, for whom I'd provided round the clock care during the last three months of his life. Finally, fulfilling my responsibilities as alumni director brought me to the brink of total burn-out and my second collapse at the end of 1999. Life as I had been living it was over, and a long rehabilitation awaited me.

All along, I had held out hope that I would someday meet a wonderful man with whom I could share my love and my life. Through a very unlikely series of synchronicities, I met Charlie—the love of my life—whom I eventually married. Kind and generous, he's done everything in his power to help me recover—since the fateful morning we met at the local Starbucks—from the debilitating effects of CFS.

It was great good fortune that led me to the Clymer Healing Center near Quakertown, Pennsylvania, where the renowned naturopathic doctor Dr. Gerald Poesnecker was working on precisely my problem, chronic fatigue syndrome. Under his expert care, I slowly began to get well. Beyond that, without the unconditional love and strength of my husband and my now grown son, plus the positive power of my will, I would never have recovered.

My bouts with tragedy and illness have made me quite

sympathetic to people suffering from stress and pain, whether from sickness, trauma or other causes. I combine that sympathy with my intuitive understanding of people and what they are feeling, and this helps my clients begin to heal themselves.

Over the years, I've increased my knowledge as I studied and experienced many natural healing therapies. Seven years ago, I opened an integrative wellness practice–*Try Wellness*–that blends holistic systems with advanced energy technologies, including INDIGO Biofeedback, active dowsing, and stress management coaching.

It's taken quite a few years to feel whole again. The many pieces of my once shattered life have been reassembled into the beautiful mandala comprising all that I am now: business owner, public speaker, artist, healer, singer, writer, ordained minister, mother, grandmother, wife, and friend. Filled with gratitude for all that I've come through, I now live a creative, inspired, soul-lit life, and every new day carries the blessings and power of a promise kept.

**ABOUT THE AUTHOR:** A certified Indigo Biofeedback Specialist, Shane loves to help people with a wide variety of needs find their way back to extraordinary emotional and physical health. Her passion is in helping her clients experience profound health breakthroughs by training them to release the stressors that underlie all disease. Shane founded the Try Wellness™ program in 2007, based around her vibrant biofeedback practice in Langhorne, PA. Shane is also a singer, artist, minister, and author. Her singing, like her healing work, draws on a deeply spiritual and intuitive connection to the heart. Her CDs are available at www.shanemariedevine.com

Shane Marie Devine Forbes
www.try-wellness.com
health@try-wellness.com
215-588-3888

# The Heart Knows
## Kathy Fyler

Something jolted me awake. My heart raced like crazy and fluttered uncomfortably in my chest. I felt as though my whole body was vibrating. I tried everything I knew to slow my heart—I coughed, turned onto my side, sat up, stretched, even pounded on my chest—but nothing calmed the rapid beating of my heart. It raced faster than I could even count. *"Oh my God, is this it?* I started to panic. *"Am I going to die?"*

I realized I needed help. The ambulance arrived, and I was rushed to the hospital and whisked straight into the emergency room. Several nurses arrived and attached wires and tubes to my body. They discovered I was experiencing an arrhythmia called atrial fibrillation--a misfiring of the electrical system of the heart that caused it to beat erratically—around one hundred and eighty beats per minute. They administered an intravenous drug called Cardizem, and thankfully my heartbeat returned to normal. A few hours later I was able to go home.

The episode shocked me, despite the fact that I'd had open heart surgery twenty-two years earlier at the age of twenty-six. Now, forty-eight and healthy, I felt vulnerable for first time since then. I ran everyday on the beach, and felt strong and vibrant. *Will this happen again?* I worried. *Could the a-fib be an indication that something is seriously wrong with my heart? Is this condition going change the theme of my life?* I realized that only time would tell.

Months went by and then a year and I was beginning to feel pretty confident that the episode had been a one-time event. I was in the clear. I could relax.

Then it happened again. One day, out enjoying myself with friends, suddenly and without warning I felt the familiar, scary, mile-a-minute fluttering. *"No, it can't be!"* I thought, and ended up again at the emergency room for another dose of Cardizem. It worked quickly and I was "fixed" a second time. Three days later the third bout of a-fib reared its ugly head. This time I wound up spending two days in the hospital. This "a-fib" was not a random thing.

The doctors recommended I take a drug to prevent the a-fib from recurring and told me I would be on it forever. Not thrilled about the prospect of committing to a medication for the rest of my life, I was determined to find a different, more holistic approach to restore my physical body to vibrant health. For now, though, I'd use the medication as a bridge and safety net.

Meanwhile, I began to take an inventory of my life. Eager to know the root cause, I began to research whether what was showing up as this rapid heartbeat was a reflection of how I was living.

I started by looking at my stressors. The year 2010 was a rough year financially. When I thought about it, I realized 2009 hadn't been a great year either. Our business, slowed perhaps by the economy, wasn't growing as fast as we had planned. Also, we were forced to cancel a large event we'd planned (to which a large sum of money had been committed) because the number of registrations needed hadn't materialized in time.

I knew that if I wanted to calm the chaos, I had to transform my thoughts. As I reflected on how I'd gotten through similar times previously, I realized how many great things I've manifested in my life.

### Reflections

In high school, things came easily to me. An honor student and gifted athlete, I played the piano with grace and ease. I was fearless because it seemed like anything I believed I could do, I did.

I studied nursing in college, entered easily into my career, and continued to advance from floor nursing to the intensive care unit (ICU). When ready to transition to a corporate job, offers were plentiful and I was able to pick the best fit for me. Still fearless, I moved from my home in Connecticut to New Jersey.

As I continued to grow in my business, personal, and spiritual life, I became an avid student of personal development. I absorbed as much as I could from many teachers who guided me in meditation, yoga, self love, business growth, and the importance of vision and goals.

When I was forty, I read *Effortless Prosperity* by Bijan Anjomi—a spiritual book based on the teachings of *A Course in Miracles*. One of the daily lessons was about manifesting and it stated simply that all you have to do is ask the universe for what you want. You must state it exactly, clearly, in the present tense and first person. Currently house hunting, I knew that I needed additional funds, so playing along; I asked the universe for $500,000.

At that time, I owned a sign and display company. The phone rang at the office the next day, and one our largest clients ordered five hundred neon signs. The order totaled $500,000! The most amazing part was that our average order was normally much closer to $15,000—nowhere near the $500,000 for which I'd asked. *This really works!* I thought, as I jumped up and down and danced around the office! I began to study and experiment with this even further and with greater passion.

After attending a seminar on feng shui—the eastern practice of harmonizing space and placement to ease and enhance the flow of energy and life force—I learned that if you want to bring something into your life, you have to make room for it. I decided that it was time for an additional car. I looked at my garage and realized that, based on these principles, I wasn't going to manifest a car if there was no space for it. So I took a couple of days and cleaned out the garage. I threw away or donated lots of things and created the void for the universe to fill. It looked so clean and fresh—perfect for a new car!

The very next day, my dad called. He was buying a new car and asked if I wanted his old one. How quickly it worked! In just one day, I'd manifested a car! But I learned from this event that I'd missed an important step to manifesting: I must be *very clear* when describing what I want. Although I totally appreciated, and was grateful for, the car that my dad gave me—a thirteen year-old Honda with two hundred thousand miles and no air conditioning—I'd really wanted a brand new, fully-loaded SUV!

Upon reflection, I realized how many other things I'd manifested in my life. Some of them were crystal clear to me when they happened, others not so much—perhaps I needed more time to see the real essence of what was happening and why.

The next teacher in my life was Brian Tracy. I listened to a set of tapes titled *Million Dollar Habits* in which he strongly encouraged listeners to create goals. Following his instructions, I wrote my desires on paper, dated it, sealed the envelope, and put it away in a drawer. I didn't look at them again. The year was 2001.

One of my goals was to help women entrepreneurs. This was a passion of mine because I knew the struggles and joys of being a female entrepreneur and what it was like to grow a business "by the seat of my pants." If I could do something to help other women in the same position, I would be very happy. I wasn't sure how to do this, I just knew I wanted to.

While still involved in the sign and display company, we had a great deal of success, but I felt like there was something missing-- that there should be more to my career and life than making neon beer signs. We were growing, doubling our sales for the last few years, but I wanted more. I wanted to make a difference. Our company simply did not do this for me.

I wanted to fill the great big void in my heart with something more fulfilling but I didn't know how to sell or leave our company. Our employees and customers counted on us, and we had a long-term plan to eventually sell or open it up to other family members, but this seemed so very far in the future. I felt stuck.

In 2002, a catastrophic turn of events forced us to close the business suddenly. There was nothing we could do to save it. It was gone, and somehow, miraculously, all of our workers were taken care of one way or another. I realized once again I had manifested what I asked for; and again I learned that I must be even more intentional and specific when I put forth my desires to the universe.

Shortly thereafter, I attended my very first networking meeting. I had no idea what to expect or even what a network meeting was. All women, mostly entrepreneurs promoting their businesses, everyone was there to help and support each other. *This is wonderful,* I thought. *This is what I want to do!* But the real *aha!* moment occurred when I realized I'd manifested this! My goal of assisting women in business—that I'd set for myself and tucked away in the drawer—was coming to fruition. Powerful You! Women's Network was born.

### *Calming the Chaos*

From my current perspective, it's so easy to see how I'd allowed my imagination to run wild with fear. Eerily similar to the frantic racing in my heart, this fear slowly and consistently crept into my life and often raced through my mind.

When times got tough and money was tight, I forgot the many lessons I learned and the power I held to manifest anything and everything I desire. I knew I had to get back to the basics that had served me so well throughout my life.

Today, meditation, yoga, and joy are a daily regimen for me. I focus and refocus my mind many times throughout the day to stay clear, in the present moment and on path.

I am so happy to be off of medication and to feel the slow, strong, steady beat of my heart. As I practice calm and peace each day, I've not only calmed the chaos, I've found clarity and ease. One with all of life, I know that I continue to manifest whatever I think about. Now, my heart knows that I am truly the conscious co-creator of my life.

**ABOUT THE AUTHOR:** Kathy Fyler's diverse career includes being a Critical Care Nurse, Project Manager for a technology firm, and owner of a $5 million manufacturing company. In 2005, Kathy felt a calling to make "more of a contribution to what matters most in this world". Using her experience and passion for technology and people, she co-founded Powerful You! Women's Network and Powerful You! Publishing to fulfill her personal mission of assisting women in creating connections via the internet, live meetings and the published word. Kathy loves to travel the country connecting with the inspiring women of Powerful You!

Kathy Fyler
www.powerfulyou.com
www.powerfulyoupublishing.com
info@powerfulyou.com
973-248-1262

# What Would *You* Do?

## Cindy Giles

I'm the type of person who makes lists and crosses things off: grocery store; dry cleaner; drive to volleyball; call surgeon to remove tumor from breast. I lead a structured life, predictable and a little boring—but clearly that was about to change.

It was the beautiful Friday afternoon of Memorial Day weekend in 2006 when I got the call. I didn't cry, I wasn't angry—I just felt numb. I'm not sure what the reaction should be when you discover that you have cancer, but at the time it just seemed like something else I had to deal with—hurry here, hurry there, hurry up, and get this "thing" over with too.

The first week of my breast cancer diagnosis felt surreal, like living in the twilight zone. My predictable boring life was no longer predictable. Rather, it was uncommonly busy—filled with events that surprisingly revolved around me. On Wednesday, my plans to lunch with friends got traded for a meeting with my surgeon to talk about removing the tumor from my breast. On Friday, I celebrated my forty-eighth birthday with blood tests, x-rays, and a breast MRI, followed by dinner near Northwestern Hospital.

On Saturday, as my twelve year-old daughter Anne and I were driving to her volleyball tournament, a car in the other lane zigzagged across lanes and the driver seemed out of control. I pulled off the road quickly, just as the swerving car slammed into the side of my car. Fortunately, no one was hurt, though my car sustained serious damage.

Anne asked me if I was angry about the damage to my car, and I told her no, that it wasn't important because she was all right. But inside I knew I still had cancer. I looked around at the police, fire truck, ambulance, and twenty very odd spectators and thought, what happened to my life? It was becoming unrecognizable.

I was trying to be a spectator, but my life seemed to insist that I take a starring role. I hadn't been the star of my own life in so long the thought of taking control made me feel extremely uncomfortable, yet somehow invigorated too. I've had two secret fears that I've never told anyone—getting cancer, and being in a serious car crash. Both happened in the same week! What the hell was going on with my life?

Not used to soul searching, I didn't make time to think about my life's dramatic turns. Instead, I just kept putting one foot in front of the other. In truth, that's how I always went through life, crossing things off once they were done. That's what I was thinking about as we drove to Northwestern for my surgery—how anxious I felt being the person that all the fuss was about. I'd been invisible in so many parts of my life. Cancer was forcing me to take center stage. When we got to Northwestern, I glanced at myself in the mirror and, for all my anxiety, saw that my eyes were alive with mischief. They were asking me if I was ready for an adventure.

Luckily, my surgery was scheduled a week after my diagnosis—evidently not many people wanted surgery on June 6, 2006 (6/6/06!) I didn't care; I just wanted this "cancer" off my list. The surgery was a success, but the little tumor removed from my right breast was actually a big tumor, and it wasn't stage one it was stage three! They found cancer in my lymph nodes as well. This confirmed that I'd need chemotherapy and radiation. I am not happy as I realize that I'll lose my hair and my summer is shot. Those turned out to be the least of my worries.

### The Pity Party

A new vocabulary began to emerge about a world in which I had no desire to participate. I discovered the magnitude of this life threatening illness when doctors began the hunt for more cancer in my organs and bones. What if I died of this disease? I had never experienced that kind of raw fear in my entire life. It was the kind of fear that consumes your mind, makes your blood run cold, and locks your thoughts in a prison of worry. I was terrified; I couldn't grab hold of a rational thought. I went home and got into bed to hide under the covers.

As I lay in my world of denial, I heard *"what would you do if you knew everything was going to be ok?"* I pretended not to hear that voice in my head, but it persisted and repeated the question: *"What would you do if you knew everything was going to be ok?"* I ignored the voice again because I was convinced the cancer had spread to my brain and I was doomed. Scared and lost, I wanted to escape my life. I didn't know how to handle the situation so I reverted to the activity that had worked for me before cancer: I jumped on my mountain bike and took off.

I loved to bike and usually rode for a few hours or more in the forest preserve behind my house. It was a natural meditation. At the beginning of the ride, I'd have terrible fears and worries, but eventually my thoughts would shift to only the sound of the road. I pondered thoughts like *what would I do if I knew everything was going to be ok? What would I do if I knew this was just a bump in the road? What would I do if the doctors found cancer somewhere else in my body?*

I worked myself into a state of panic. I had trouble breathing, my eyes twitched, and fear had me in its grips, when I heard *"what would you do if you knew everything was going to be ok?"* I thought seriously about the question and, for the first time, answered it. If everything was okay, if I didn't have cancer, I'd take control of my life. I'd be grateful for every day. I'd be the best person I could be. Life would no longer pass me by!

Did I just say that out loud? Yes! I would *live!* I felt an incredible release of pressure off my mind and body. And then....

Relief, pure relief. The doctors did not find any cancer in my organs or bones. It was around the time I started chemo that I began to feel like a caterpillar morphing into the butterfly; so many changes were going on with me, physically, mentally, emotionally. I'd ask myself, *what would I do if everything was going to be ok?* This became my mantra. Saying it would instantly stop the pity-party and refocus my energy into moving forward.

The last leg of my journey was six weeks of radiation. The irony of radiation is that it takes longer to undress than it does to get zapped, yet the process is completely and totally exhausting. I laid my bald, plump, steroid-filled body down for a nap and felt so different from the woman who biked two hours a day and walked three miles every morning that I broke down and cried for the first time.

### A Seed Grows in Russia

Tears poured down my face. I didn't recognize myself, inside or out. I felt such despair and hardship. Feeling broken, I heard, *"what would you do if you knew everything was going to be ok?"* But this time the voice answered: *"You're going to Russia!"*

*What?*

As I lay there, pity party in full swing, I lifted my head and wondered, *Russia?? Where did that come from?* But it was something to think about. Though I didn't know it then, a seed had just been planted about my future.

Finally the day arrived when all my visits to the hospital ended. I returned to my life only to find that it no longer existed! I'd morphed into someone I didn't know anymore, and had no clue who the new me was. My old life gone, and not sure what to do next, I went to Russia.

I volunteered in an orphanage for two weeks in the Ukraine. Not quite Russia, but close enough. Minimal English was spoken there, so it was quite a challenge. And living in a foreign country in an apartment with no hot water was—to say the least—difficult.

Yet it was precisely these conditions that allowed me to reflect on and acknowledge that I'd gone through a life-threatening situation with courage and strength. If I'd made it through that, I could make it through anything, including living without hot water. The experience made me feel alive, deep, and spiritual. Grateful for the voice that had reached out to me, I knew I was connected to a higher source. I also felt in my heart that I'd never go through this again.

When I returned home from the Ukraine, I knew something had shifted—the old me and the new me had merged into one. At peace and not angry at cancer anymore, I was, in fact, thankful for the experience. The journey into cancer reminded me that I'm important, that I need to take the time to laugh and enjoy life's moments—all of them—good and bad. I try very hard not to take my life for granted and push myself to reach out to life with both hands.

Meanwhile, I've discovered and rediscovered my passions, which thankfully, don't allow my life to get dull or boring. I've skydived, volunteered as an extra in movies, and started playing tennis again. I've turned my one true passion—helping others—into a business.

Now the proud owner of *Cindy Giles Transformational Coaching,* I partner with women to capitalize on their cancer experience and to discover a new outlook on what matters most in life. I remember my own road while helping others. No, I don't tell them they have to travel to the Ukraine, but I do ask them: *What would you do if you knew everything was going to be ok?*

**ABOUT THE AUTHOR:** Cindy Giles is a Life and Empowerment Coach and owner of Cindy Giles Transformational Coaching. She is an author, inspirational speaker and host of a blog talk radio show.

Cindy combines her many life experiences, including being breast cancer survivor, and knowledge and skills as a coach, to inspire and transform her clients to live passionate and purposeful lives. Cindy understands that you can do anything you desire, she is known to say, "If you believe it, you can achieve it." Cindy lives in Naperville, IL with her husband of many years and together they have successfully raised three daughters. Cindy enjoys bike riding, travel and reading a good book.

Cindy Giles
Cindy Giles Transformational Coaching
www.cindygiles.com
cindy@cindygiles.com
630-219-1992

# The Journey of a "Fat Head"
## Dr. Ina Nozek

I weighed in at eight pounds and fourteen ounces at birth, and was lovingly referred to as having the chubbiest cheeks; in fact, growing up, my family teased me that eight pounds of me was my cheeks and the fourteen ounces was my body!

I went on my first diet at the age of eight. Mom was a Weight Watcher, and since I was already feeling fat, I decided to go on a diet too. Looking back, the truth is that I was a little on the chubby side but not seriously overweight. When I speak to my parents about it today, they say they never thought I needed to be concerned about my weight.

But to me, at least in my head, I was a fat little girl and I didn't like it. Miserable about myself, even at such a young age, I began to diet. I don't remember a time growing up when I wasn't either "on" or "off" a diet. I was either "good" or "bad." As I got a little older, I remember having periods of willpower. I'd create my own diets, make up my mind, and stick to it until I caved in and binged on the "bad stuff."

There were times when I'd "munch out" after dinner—ice cream, cookies, potato chips, pretzels, whatever we had in the house—and by the time I woke up for school the next day, I was so bloated from all of the salt and sugar, my jeans were too tight and I'd stay home from school feeling miserable—both physically and emotionally.

This cycle went on and on and I knew I hated feeling like a "chubby" girl, so I'd again go on crazy diets. I'd come home from school each day in my early teens, and my best friend and I would hang out at her house. Her parents were both gourmet cooks and we'd raid her refrigerator and eat all of the delicious leftovers—paella, chicken cordon bleu, stuffed mushrooms, seafood risotto, and more. Then, in disgust, we'd try to undo the damage we thought we'd done by dancing and exercising ourselves breathless in her living room.

By the time I was fifteen, I'd sneak into my mother's bathroom and take her prescription diuretics, knowing that I'd pee enough to feel somewhat better. I also began to take over the counter diet pills to kill my appetite. Between the crazy diets, starving my body of good nutrition, and taking these pills, I knew I was destroying my health, but it just didn't matter to me. I wanted to look and feel thin and I'd do anything to accomplish that!

Somewhere in my late teens I became interested in vitamins and health foods. As I became more health conscious, I decided to pursue a career involving nutrition. But the struggle went on and—still always either on or off a diet—I seesawed between knowing what was good and healthy for me, and binging on foods that were fattening and unhealthy.

When I got to college and chose nutrition as my major, I met Lisa—a fellow nutrition major—and we became best friends and roommates. We'd study together, party together, exercise together, and binge together. One night we ate what seemed like thousands of calories, and got sick and horribly angry with ourselves. We went into a bathroom in one of the college buildings that had multiple stalls and I remember hearing her throw up what we'd just eaten. I tried and tried to throw up too, but nothing would come up. I was so jealous of her! Looking back, I'm grateful I couldn't purge that way.

As I learned more about nutrition and health, it became more of a conflict for me. I knew what was right, but still found myself weak and out of control with food. Inconsistent—at times I was perfectly in control and had amazing willpower—every time I'd make headway, something would happen and I'd fall back into that same negative pattern. My weight bounced up and down as it always did, and I continued to feel badly about myself.

### Healthy Versus Thin

I met my husband in 1984. At the time I was probably my heaviest at a size nine/ten. And although he thought I was beautiful and perfect just the way I was, to me I might as well have been a size 3X! Although nine/ten is a desirable size for some women, I had a "fat head" and in my mind I felt HUGE.

Still on my journey to learn about health and wellness, I pursued becoming a chiropractor. Simultaneously, I experienced some health issues—no wonder, with all of those years of abuse to my body! After searching for the right answers, I discovered that I had Candida

Albicans, a systemic yeast overgrowth that permeates the intestinal wall, leaves microscopic holes, and causes leaky gut syndrome and food allergies, as undigested food particles and other toxins enter the body. A diet low in nutritional value and high in refined sugars and simple carbohydrates often plays a contributing role.

To combat this, I went on yeast-free diets, cleansing and fasting programs, and tons of supplements. I visited various holistic practitioners and gained greater consciousness about what was right and healthy. As I began to make healthier food choices, I realized that being thin mattered more to me then my health. And so I continued my pattern of an out of control diet.

By the time I got married at twenty-four, I was probably my thinnest, and that's what mattered to me most. Although I felt thin for one of the first times in my life, I still ate and drank my way through our honeymoon and returned feeling awful, fat, *and* sick once again.

Now a chiropractor and moving ahead toward my masters degree in nutrition, I studied to learn more so that I could help others get well. But what about me? I desired health and balance, craved more energy, and more self-control so I could choose the best nutrients for my body. In short, I wanted to feel good both inside and out!

For years I struggled, as I tried program after program, diet after diet, tons of supplements, herbal remedies, homeopathic therapy, and more. I read book after book, took course after course, attended seminars and workshops galore, and earned multiple certifications.

And then the pregnancy and nursing years went by. I recall struggling to have enough energy to play on the floor with my babies. I felt wiped out despite being extremely careful with what I ate during those years. Although my diet contained natural wholesome foods, the balance still wasn't there, and apparently it didn't make enough of a difference for me to feel truly healthy.

### The Battle of the Binge and the Bulge

Then, when I turned forty, I had the biggest awakening. I realized that I was falling short for myself by not eating balanced enough, and therefore not getting the proper nutrients into my body consistently. I knew from years of study and clinical practice how important it is to properly nourish our bodies, to keep our blood sugar stabilized by fueling our bodies with the right combination of macronutrients (protein, healthy carbohydrates, and essential healthy fats) *and* essential micronutrients (vitamins, minerals, enzymes, etc.) I also knew the importance of regular cleansing and detoxification and how toxins in our food and environment play such a key role in negatively effecting our health and body composition.

Combined with a holistic approach that included exercise, a positive mental attitude, daily gratitude, and enough fresh air and pure water, I suddenly became aware of how imperative it was for me to fuel and nourish my body properly so that I didn't use food as my enemy!

Finally—after so many years of trial and tribulation—I stumbled upon a nutritional system that was a no-brainer in terms of ease of use and its obvious benefits. Ultimately, Isagenix, the nutritional whole body cleansing and fat burning program and a state of the art revolutionary technology, is what made all the difference in my ability to gain control over my eating habits. After all those years of being out of control, I realized how I'd *never* given my body the right combination to balance both my body and my mind.

As I began to put the right nutrients into my body, my attempts at detoxification became more effective. And, as I detoxified physically, my body began to release emotional "toxins" as well. I started to feel happier, mentally clearer, and more balanced. I felt a sense of vitality I'd never experienced before. No longer hungry for foods I knew weren't going to feed me healthily, I lost my cravings for the things that made me feel bad.

My body became significantly leaner in a very short period of time and I felt myself releasing toxic fat and the emotional disgust that came along with it. As my body transformed, I felt empowered and confident about continuing along this path indefinitely because it felt so good and so right.

For the first time in my life, I truly understood how the emotional pain and disgust I'd felt towards myself from being out of control with food resulted in its aftermath: the exhaustion, depression, mental fog, and irritability I'd express for days after eating in such an unhealthy fashion. And I saw with clarity that the results of continuing down that same path weren't worth forgoing the willpower necessary to resist such temptations and experience the benefits of a healthier mindset.

My journey toward a new outlook began eight years ago, and I'm grateful because I've learned first-hand to never give up on myself. I know I possess the ability to feel great about myself inside and out because I'm nutritionally balanced. And when my biochemistry (which affects my brain chemistry, mood, and emotions) is balanced—despite periods of stress or crisis, which are unfortunately often unavoidable—it's so much easier to conquer the battle of the binge and the bulge!

I've also learned that it was a matter of becoming "health conscious" rather than "weight conscious" that made the ultimate difference for me. Never happier or healthier in my life, my struggle has blessed me with the ability to assist others. Sometimes others believe in us more than we believe in ourselves, but it's my belief that each and every one of us has the power to create a lean, healthy, and balanced body with the right nutritional program, the right mindset and—most of all—the readiness and commitment to change.

I believe that we all have the right to good health, and now know that my mission lies in helping others transform their bodies and their health in order to feel and look their absolute best. If I could do it, I believe anyone can!

**ABOUT THE AUTHOR:** Retired chiropractor/clinical nutritionist Dr. Ina Nozek's private practice specialized in stubborn weight loss for twenty-two years. In 2004 Dr. Ina discovered Isagenix International, and now provides complementary coaching for individuals who embark on this transformational nutritional cleansing and fat burning program to achieve maximum health, including weight loss. She believes that good health is every individual's birthright, and her commitment lies in her desire to guide and support individuals through the Isagenix program to transform their bodies and their health in order to feel and look their absolute best. Dr. Ina lives in New Jersey with her husband and 3 children.

Dr. Ina S. Nozek, DC, MS
Clinical Nutritionist
www.doctorina.info
www.roadmaptohealth.me
732-300-1925

# Trust the Voice Within
## Gita Pimentel

A cyst in the vocal cord! That was the final diagnosis after several months of hoarseness, being told I had a polyp, a nodule, and various others misdiagnoses. Though I drank concoctions and palliatives, they helped only for a few hours. Soon I could no longer deny reality: I'd have to undergo surgery.

I, who'd even given birth naturally with no anesthesia, had to go through a surgery? Fear ran through me, not only because—like most people—I profoundly dislike the idea of surgery, but because I was overwhelmed with concern about my voice.

A news narrator who taped voiceovers for television and radio commercials, my voice was my career! At thirty-three, I'd worked for the largest radio circuit in Venezuela for the past four years. Guilty that I'd been careless and not recognized the signs on time, I reluctantly underwent surgery.

Afterwards, I spent my time—several days per week—mainly on speech therapy and Reiki. In my despair I went to the Reiki foundation recommended by a friend long before my surgery. Reiki is a technique whereby healing energy is channeled through the hands.

My voice sounded awful—it came out very weak and scratchy. I felt a deep sadness when I heard it, because I loved to sing karaoke. I'd even come in second in a singing contest at my school! Now I blamed myself even more. *I've ruined my voice,* and *I'll never reach those high notes anymore,* I lamented in despair. From an early age I'd wanted to be a journalist and I came here to communicate!

The tormentor in me repeated over and over again *your voice will never be the same!* Heartbroken, I couldn't see a solution. Little did I know that the silencing of my outer voice signaled the start of listening to the voice within. The day I returned to work my vocal cord bled. Panicked, I realized I should have listened to that inner voice, which told me not to return to work so soon, despite the opinion of the therapist who sent me back.

But I'd feared losing my job, so I'd pushed myself to my limit. I'll never forget the words of wisdom spoken to me by my supervisor. "Jobs may come and go," she said, "but there's only one you—your health is important, take all the rest you need."

She was right! Why hadn't I seen it like that? "Give me all the sick days allowed by law," I told my therapist. "I want to feel more confident and healed before returning to the radio!"

### All the Writer Has to Do is Listen

After three months of vocal rest during which I carried a notebook with me everywhere I went in order to communicate, I discovered I loved writing! My daughter, then about six years old, was so patient and supportive as she'd make the effort to read what I wrote to her. One afternoon, tired of not being able to talk to her, I tried to do it in whispers. "No mommy, don't talk," she said with a maturity beyond her young age. "I'd rather see you heal, I'll read." Tears came to my eyes as I was so deeply moved by her understanding and love, even though I'd been unable to speak or sing to her in all that time.

I didn't care for the fact that I had to ask for help, as this demolished my sense of self-sufficiency. But during those three months, so much had happened *within* me. I began to understand that, if one has a disease or a physical challenge, there's always a reason. I also recognized that everything that happens in our chakra—or energy center—in the throat is related to communication and creativity.

Originally I loved my job. I read the news, and at the beginning I loved it, but after several years grew uninterested, bored, and unmotivated. The magic had disappeared and I no longer felt connected to that style of journalism. Then when my voice started to be sick, I continued reading anyway. At that point, I didn't know there was a relationship between my career and my health.

Eventually I realized I was communicating the wrong message, and so I was blocking not only my creativity, but my mission in life. I wasn't satisfied, and I could feel it in my work. I needed to wake up and notice! And that was the way in which, forced to be silent, I had no other choice but to look inward. I needed to be honest with myself, with my life, and acknowledge that I wasn't happy. I don't think I ever noticed that though, since I lived on autopilot, or like a weather vane, with no clear direction.

In the process of healing, I sought help in holistic therapies, and became familiar with this wonderful world that nowadays is mine! A wise and loving woman in her sixties, who led the group of healers at the foundation to which I'd taken my case, told me "I can teach you and you can heal yourself with your hands." *No,* I thought, *I can't do that, that's not for me..."*

It took me three years to believe it and desire it; that's when I started to take courses in energy healing. A year later, I even became the only instructor in Venezuela who taught a new technique that had arrived from Europe.

A couple of years after my vocal cord surgery I still worked as a journalist, but now hosted a holistic radio program called *Equilibrio y Armonia* (Balance and Harmony.) A whole array of wonderful guests inspired me to a more dramatic change in my career. I not only learned healing techniques, but also trained in the field of personal growth. I increasingly immersed myself in this world. This process not only led me to heal my physical body but to reacquaint myself with my purpose and direction in life. I also woke up to the awareness that my victim's consciousness had not helped me out my problems—on the contrary! I began to realize that it was best to take responsibility for my situation, and to work with whatever life was handing me.

I'd used my fear as the engine to drive me out of that dark time, so that I didn't stay paralyzed. I followed the therapist's medical opinion, but when my intuition told me not to listen, I didn't. I learned that medical professionals are not exempt from human error. I began to incorporate healing as a priority in my life. I realized how important it is, to surrender with faith in order to heal.

As I followed the wise inner voice that guided me to my highest good, I took up meditation—a practice my mother had taught me at the tender age of nine. I greatly appreciate her planting this spiritual seed within me! In fact, it was in a meditation that the idea of my radio show came up, which opened up to me a fascinating and previously unknown world. When interviewing my guests, I'd think *I want to do that!,* and today that is exactly what I do!

### Healing Takes Courage

I know there are many people who've been through more delicate and serious health conditions; I like to think that in my case I didn't need to be between life and death to make the changes my life required and to believe in what I share here. I also feel I needed to be healthy very quickly to start doing what I was born to do.

After the issues with my vocal cord, I have been a woman who enjoys excellent health. Meanwhile, certain episodes allowed me to test on myself every holistic technique I learned. Able to heal myself with my hands, affirmations, meditation, and visualization, I've discovered and worked with my mental and emotional discordant patterns related to each episode.

Thus I removed the glasses I'd needed to read with since I was a child. I knew my "job" was well done when I easily read the subtitles that had been a blur to me at the movies previously, and my eyes weren't teary or tired after long hours on the computer. I cured a strong urinary tract infection ("strong" is verbatim what the doctor said), without antibiotics. I healed of dengue fever and raised my platelets in a week. A van ran over my foot and what everybody around firmly confirmed was a fracture, became a simple sprain when I went to the emergency room and, in a month, was practicing yoga poses that required the use of that foot to bear my entire weight.

I heartily believe that we all have the gift to heal ourselves. In my opinion and experience, the best ways to do this are to: heed the messages our body gives us; have the firm intention to make the necessary internal change and to persevere in deep spiritual and therapeutic work that connects us to our essence—the divine within each of us that leads us to this inner change; maintain faith that there's a higher consciousness who loves us and takes care of us all the time; and trust that only good will emerge at the end of that experience.

My external changes all prove to be the manifestation of my inner transformation. This lies behind my inspiration to share and help others. I keep learning and growing every day, and look forward to the new things to come in this exciting journey that is my life. I always keep forefront in my mind that healing is possible and is in the best hands: mine and, of course, God's! I know there is nothing to worry about, though there may be much to handle—I tackle it all with enthusiasm and love and along the way make sure that I trust the voice within...

**ABOUT THE AUTHOR:** Trained by renowned professionals from the holistic and personal development fields, *Heal Your Life* and personal growth workshop leader Gita Pimentel is a master teacher of energy healing courses, a holistic healer and coach. *"I feel blessed* *to participate in healing the world one person at a time, and to provide my knowledge and skills of body-mind-emotions-soul healing for positive change and the evolution of consciousness in individuals' lives.*" Gita's personal and professional commitment to growth enhance her holistic skills, and complement her degree in Social Communication.

Gita Pimentel
Balance and Harmony with Gita
www.balanceandharmonywithgita.com
balanceandharmonywithgita@gmail.com
909-271-7804 / +58-412-0162895

# Kim Possible
## Kim Keefe Pisolkar

I was angry—*scary angry*, my husband Shailesh would say. I lay in bed, curled in the fetal position, crying harder than I'd ever cried before, because now it all started to finally make sense! The drinking, binge eating, mood swings, sadness, and depression—how I was never able to find things, never able to commit. I'd give up or become defensive when things got too tough. Everything would pile up and mock me, like a stack of unfulfilled dreams and goals.

If only I'd known then what was wrong with me, I probably would've done things a little differently—at least I wouldn't have been so angry—*scary angry*. Like the time I'd fought with my boyfriend in graduate school. Out of control and angry, the only thing I remember now is that I'd taken off my shoes and flung them across the room at him. I aimed at his head, too.

He'd had enough. "Kim, your behavior isn't normal!" he told me the next day. "I think you need help..." That was my entrée into therapy.

Much later, I knew it wasn't good when the marriage counselor asked Shailesh if he was *afraid* of me. I knew my mood swings were horrendous—I could zoom from zero to one hundred in two seconds!—but thankfully he'd told her "no." But I knew he felt he had to walk on eggshells around me because he was never sure when I'd explode next or why, and my screaming and crying on a regular basis didn't help. It was then I began to realize that my anger was out of control.

I'd always felt I had no control, though—like I was asleep at the wheel. Sometimes I thought it was because I was a rebel, or because I had an addictive personality. But really I was self medicating, trying to make the negative feelings go away.

I heard somewhere a concept that ultimately changed me forever: *You already have everything you need to be great—*you don't need to become someone or something else—you just need to be *you* and live into that greatness.

*Really?* I thought...*I already have it?* But look at all the things *wrong* with me! For years I'd heard *"you're not reaching your potential"* and *"we know there's more in you."* I vividly remember my high school teacher saying "Miss Keefe, you're lucky diamonds are made under pressure." He meant I was "lucky" I delivered such quality work because it was always done at the last possible moment.

Eventually that became my mantra, and the rationale behind why I did everything last minute. Everybody waited and expected me to be great—to offer something beyond what I'd already given. Always worried that maybe that was all I had to give, that I didn't have any more in me, I'd joke about how forgetful I was, how disorganized and messy. I never seemed able to complete the multitude of projects I'd started, and always gravitated, as one friend put it "towards the next shiny bauble." I was broken.

All my life I just wanted to know I was here for a reason; that the journey was worth it.

Diagnosed with Attention Deficit Disorder (ADD) at the age of twenty-three, the doctor put me on Ritalin and things improved drastically. Already working in corporate America at that time, I excelled even further and received a huge promotion and a raise.

A few years later, however, when I moved to New York, I found a doctor to help me work on my depression and ADD. This new doctor told me I was depressed, but didn't have ADD. That made a lot of sense to me. I never really thought I had ADD anyway. After all, I wasn't a little boy bouncing off the walls; I was a highly educated, successful professional!

### "Never Go to Bed Angry, Stay Up and Fight!" - William Congreve

Fast forward: It was a déja vu moment when I learned at the age of forty that I *really did* have ADD. Then I thought, *really God, one more thing?* Within a five year period I'd lost my job in corporate America (no wonder that without the structure of a full time job I felt like I was in free fall!), spent a year trying to get pregnant, received a diagnosis of—and endured treatment for—thyroid cancer, chose to go through fertility treatments, gave birth to a baby, experienced post-partum depression, and *now*—the ADD diagnosis!

The second time around, this diagnosis was like the perfect

storm, or my tipping point. I realized with a shock that ADD had been the undercurrent behind how I'd reacted to everything that had happened in my life. And with this realization came the point at which I cracked to pieces.

And, boy I was pissed off! I felt like years had been stolen from me. All that time I could've been "well," more functional, less angry. Now, my business was sinking, I fought frequently with my husband. Finally so out of control, I realized I had to do something.

Enter Cindy: I met Cindy, my ADD coach, at a networking event about a year before I actually called her. Yup, I kept her card on my desk for a year! One evening as I sat at my desk sobbing, I started to clear off the clutter and found Cindy's business card. Hmm, her website says she helps people with ADD get focused...I need that.

I'd never worked with a coach before but after our initial conversation I knew this was an investment I had to make. Nervously I told my husband—I was worried about the cost. He said he wanted me to be the person he used to know and urged me to try the coaching. Thus began my journey to get to the bottom of this ADD thing...

With Cindy's help I became more confident, more normal. I began to see that what I felt was understandable, that I wasn't alone, and that there were tons of resources to help me. Cindy taught me that so many of my reactions were merely self-protective.

I realized it was possible to feel in control, less angry, and that I deserved peace and happiness. She helped me create structures and routines to better manage my time and tasks. I was beginning to move away from anger and from blaming everyone and everything for all that I thought was wrong with my life.

### Don't Look Back in Anger, Or Forward in Fear, But Around in Awareness

When I think about why the ADD discovery happened when it did, I reflect on its larger purpose. What I discovered made me understand that I had deep-seated anger issues, and that I'd spent most of my life in victim mode. Much of my anger stemmed from the fact that nobody had even noticed that maybe—*just maybe*—I had a problem...

Finally, I let it all go. When I became more comfortable with myself, everything changed. I was still me, but I accepted, I forgave. As I made the conscious decision to forgive myself, and others towards whom I'd had anger, everything shifted for me. I realized that people were on their own journeys and, at the end of the day, no one was doing anything *to* me, I was the one making it *about* me. I'd excelled at the "poor me" syndrome. I always looked at women who seemed so calm and without judgment, and wondered why can't I be like that?

I see now that, had I been diagnosed twenty-five or more years ago, the potential for a negative path in the form of special classes, being labeled as different, etc., could have been a major problem. Now I know that everything happens for a reason, and I feel so lucky because it was the journey I was *supposed* to take. I got to live most of my life—especially my formative years, without a label that could have held me back.

Also, I know now that I was meant to have those experiences so I could be who I am today, and help others on a similar journey. During the past year especially, I've not only let go of anger, I've stopped blaming others and being a victim of circumstances; carrying all that anger left me so focused on myself that I couldn't be the wife, mother, or friend others needed me to be. When I stopped trying to control everything and everyone, life began to feel lighter and freer. When I finally loosened the reins, I was even able to shed the forty extra pounds to which I'd been attached!

Along the way, I let Shailesh be who he is, with no more anger or resentment towards him.

When I accepted and owned the fact that ADD is *part* of me, but not the sum *total* of me, many aspects of my life became unstuck. Prior to that, it was like a secret that held me back and kept me playing small. Letting go of all of that provided me with major release and clarity, and I stopped allowing circumstances and other people define how I responded to the world.

Now, on any given day, I choose how I show up to the world. Yes, some things may make me a little quirky or whatever, but it's a choice. I may never have the most organized house on the block, paper continues to be my nemesis, and I may drive people crazy getting things done at the last minute. So what if it takes me a little extra time to find my keys or I lock myself out of the house?

"Why don't you become a coach?" people had asked me for years. *Yeah, right—if they only knew how screwed up my life was, they'd never make that suggestion!* I used to think. But little by little, I began to see that it wasn't impossible, my life wasn't really screwed up—just a little off-kilter. My work with Cindy, and a few other magnificent coaches, instilled in me the value of coaching and ultimately led me to become one.

I work with business owners and professionals to help them get "unstuck." Together, we concentrate on unearthing their potential so they can own their own power and connect in a more authentic way to themselves and others. Today, I love me. I love who I am—my quirkiness, dry humor, reflection, and yes—even my indecisiveness! No longer *impossible,* I now know the sky's the limit because I am *Kim Possible!*

**ABOUT THE AUTHOR:** Bring your "A" game to every facet of your life with the assistance of certified professional coach and human resources consultant Kim Keefe Pisolkar. Kim specializes in helping you connect your purpose and passion to everyday life, so you can better focus your time, energy, and financial resources on the things that matter most. She partners with both individuals and groups to clarify goals and create paths that empower and motivate. What matters most to Kim is her family, and showing clients how to achieve their goals *and* find time to enjoy their journeys along the way.

Kim Keefe Pisolkar, SPHR, CPC
Achieve It Inc. Coaching & Consulting
KimPisolkar.com
Kim@KimPisolkar.com
973-868-2061

# Awake, Aware, On Purpose
## Michelle Pitot

My only thought that sunny October afternoon was how to beat the traffic and get home quickly. My last meeting ran late, an email demanded attention, and my computer decided at the last minute to install updates. On a normal day just one of those things could double my drive time home and I left the office, annoyed.

I watch the construction crew begin to leave the building site across the street and know it will be a long slog home. As I turn right onto Broadway, the green light in my favor, I glance left and see a police car with lights flashing speed through the intersection. Forced to yield and even more annoyed now—*You could at least use your siren so I'd know you were coming!*—I pull around the corner and follow, childishly minimizing the space between our cars.

An aging juvenile delinquent, a.k.a. *"juvie,"* my reaction to cops is not always positive. Lucky enough to get help as a kid, I quit a brief but serious drinking career, became a social worker, and have had far more positive interactions with law enforcement than negative. Yet I still go back to that angry and rebellious teenager—usually when I'm scared or I've broken a rule. Personally, I believe a true *juvie* never really grows out of it. We may live a miserable life or spend time in prison, or turn things around as I did, but that rebellious seed of "just tell me what I *can't* do and I'll show you!" never really dies.

The cop in front of me turns right abruptly and stops, leaving half his cruiser in my lane. I pull over to pass him, exasperated—*cops think they rule the world! They're clueless about how they get in people's way!*—when I'm unexpectedly forced to jam on my brakes.

Ten feet in front of me I see a man waving a gun, running straight at my car. As he sprints towards me, I swear he's aiming his pistol right at my face. Without thinking or looking over my shoulder, I throw my car into reverse, back up across three lanes, and stop only when my tires hit the curb on the other side. And the whole time the gun-wielding man stares directly into my eyes. To this day I can still see his eyes—hard points of brown light—as they laser into my head.

Then he abruptly turns away from me, changes direction and runs back toward the cop car. I watch as he jumps into the driver's seat and races away. The officer who forgot his keys in the ignition didn't forget the rest of his training. He drops to one knee, pulls his gun, and begins to shoot at the departing police car. Later I find out he's a good shot, and the guy with the gun dies that night at University Hospital.

My Prius and I are now frozen, parked halfway across Broadway, when another police officer appears out of nowhere, waving his arms to tell me to move along. "We have to keep this area clear!" he yells, and silences even my *juvie* rant as I obediently follow his order.

The street was empty when I'd backed across it in a panic, but now the light at the corner has turned green and I pull blindly into three lanes of traffic, all filled with drivers who only want to get home—just like me a minute ago.

I grab my cell phone from the passenger seat, speed-dial my boss back at the office, and burst into tears when he picks up. We don't always see eye to eye but at that moment he becomes the most understanding, supportive person in the world. I stumble through telling him to warn people in our building that the guy with the gun is out there somewhere. He keeps asking if I'm ok, do I need him to come get me, drive me home, escort me—anything? By then I've pulled into a Safeway parking lot and think I've regained a measure of composure. I thank him but refuse more help.

I get out of my car, lock it carefully, and pocket my keys—*no way anyone's driving off in my car!*—walk into that grocery store, straight to the liquor aisle like it's something I do every day, and buy a liter of Smirnoff Citrus. I walk back to my car, pop open that bottle, still in its brown paper bag, and take three long swallows—*just like a homeless person or a nut case,* juvie pipes up. I call my boyfriend who agrees to pick up my son at school, go home and climb into bed. I don't go back to my office the next day or the next.

### Trauma Redux

A few days later I board a plane with my boyfriend for a long-awaited three week trip to New Zealand. This geographic cure extinguishes the nightmares that began after the shooting incident, but I was already drinking myself into oblivion every night. After twenty-eight years without a sip, I'd returned practically overnight to the misery of active alcoholism.

When we got home from our trip it was clear I needed to get back on the right path. I got down to basics and returned to the self-help meetings that saved my life when I was a kid and would surely do so again now.

Clean and sober again a few months later, my boyfriend and I were in the parking lot of Best Buy where we'd just bought a new electronic toy we didn't need. It was January eighth, and I received a frantic call from a girlfriend who told me that Arizona Congresswoman Gabrielle Giffords and many of her staff and bystanders had just been shot in a Safeway parking lot two miles from my house. They were on their way, she said, to that same University Hospital where they had taken my guy with the gun.

I panicked as a vision of the gun-wielder's eyes lasered into my head again, and insisted we go home immediately. The following Wednesday I left work at noon to pick up my son at school so we could wait in line all afternoon to attend the big event in honor of the people who'd died in that shooting. My fourth grade son is crazy about Barack Obama and, not grasping the bigger picture of the tragedy, couldn't wait to see him in person.

On the way to his school that day I stopped at another Safeway, picked up some Smirnoff, poured it into a plastic water bottle, and all afternoon broke my core value of never drinking around my ten year old. The afternoon ended with me in the hospital, only scattered memories of how I got there. Later a friend told me the details of how my son, who'd never seen his mother drink before, watched as they carried me off on a stretcher into an ambulance. I checked myself into an alcohol treatment center the next day.

### Everything to Lose

During the next two weeks of hard internal work, I wanted to blame my situation on the trauma of the shooting downtown and being retriggered by the events of January eighth. Yet while my trauma was real, I was forced to admit that those incidents were only the final straws on the back of a very weary and overloaded camel.

Yes, I had gone through a terrifying event, and sure, I still had some healing to do. And yes, it only takes an instant to change someone's life forever. Gabrielle Giffords, her staff, all of us, would never be the same because of a guy with a gun. But for years I'd made a myriad of choices: security over joy; predictability over risk; safety over trust in the unknown. It was the sum total of all those choices that left me vulnerable to taking self-destructive actions in response to my own ordeal.

It is our reaction to circumstances that makes each of us who we are today. Regardless of genetics, parenting, growing up with privilege or without, good health or bad, I believe that who we are today is not merely the result of these factors. Each of us is the product of choices we make in response to whatever hand we've been dealt.

After all that had happened, nothing in my life was sacred anymore and everything received close examination. Friendships, family relationships, significant other, parenting role, job, even hobbies, fell under the microscope. Last month I quit my corporate job of fifteen years. Many friends are no longer in my life. My primary relationship still stands, but on much shakier ground.

Only my relationship with my son is still strong—even stronger. When I woke up in the hospital and realized what I'd done, I knew I was in danger of losing the most precious gift in my life. And that was unacceptable.

My actions of the past year can't be erased, and the lessons that came out of those actions can also never be unlearned. Yet it's crystal clear to me that I couldn't be where I am today without every single event in my life so far. Did I throw out twenty-eight years of recovery after picking up the bottle again? No.

Did I screw up? Yes. Every day I regret the torment my family went through last year because of me. And while I don't recommend my path to anyone else, I'm grateful as hell for where it has taken me. The absolute conviction that I had *everything* to lose is what finally allowed me to walk away from so much of what previously stood for security in my life.

Am I terrified to venture out into my own business during today's shaky economy? Truthfully, not as much as people tell me I should be. No matter what happens now, I believe in the power to choose life over self-destruction, happiness over misery, and growth over safety.

We each have the ability to make choices in response to our reality and we can't control the outcome of those choices. We can only live knowing that our lives are the result of our own actions, and that's where our power lies. It's our truly and uniquely human gift to choose that allows us to live our lives awake, aware, and on purpose.

**ABOUT THE AUTHOR:** Teacher, coach, and consultant Michelle Pitot recently started *ProMojo Coaching and Consulting* to inspire others to find and express their voices and lead conscious, purposeful lives. Michelle works with women in mid-life who are in transition in their lives to motivate and empower them to "Find your Mojo—Live on purpose!" She also helps companies and non-profit agencies that are seeking to grow leadership skills, increase team cohesion, and reconnect with their purpose, no matter their clientele or industry. Michelle lives in the desert of Tucson, Arizona, with her fantastic fifth grade son Ben and the pugs, Bandit and Chico.

Michelle Pitot
ProMojo Coaching
www.promojocoaching.com
michelle@promojocoaching.com
520-344-4288

# The Shocker
## Suzanne Toepperwein

Overcome with weakness, I leaned on the counter at Taco Bell, where my family had stopped for a quick bite. I asked my husband Randall for the keys to the truck so I could wait for our food there. Later he told me that I'd asked for a glass of water and he then escorted me to a bench where I sat down, took a sip, and collapsed onto the floor.

A call was placed to 911, and a gentleman from behind the counter and an off duty EMT who heard the call while eating next door at Jack in the Box, ran over and began CPR. Able to pick up a faint pulse, they sustained life until the ambulance arrived and the medical team took over.

The hospital was informed that I was being transported in cardiac arrest. The clinical term, "torsades de pointes" is French and means "twisting of the points" or "state of confusion," a lethal form of ventricular tachycardia. My heart beat at an extremely rapid rate, and the doctors were unaware at that point what had caused a seemingly healthy young individual to go into cardiac arrest.

My heart beat so out of control that it restricted the blood flow to the brain, causing seizure after seizure. There are four chambers of the heart. My upper chambers beat normally while my lower chambers pulsed at a rate of two hundred beats per minute. This caused a back flow of blood, essentially regurgitating it.

When I arrived at the hospital, medics performed a serum drug screen and accused me of trying to commit suicide by overdose, as the symptoms were identical. Anoxia, a total decrease in the level of oxygen, triggered status epilepticus—a life threatening condition where the brain is in a state of persistent seizure and the patient does not regain consciousness.

When I awoke I was being resuscitated in the hospital emergency room. There'd been no prior warning before my episode of cardiac arrest. I flat lined three times, was clinically dead, and shocked fifty-six times to be brought back. I am noted in medical journals as *The Shocker*. Highest count ever recorded was seventeen.

During this process I encountered the most peaceful calm I'd *never* experienced in a living state, the interruption of which by doctors—on August 12, 1992, at the young age of twenty-six—caused much resentment towards those who'd interfered with Mother Nature. The ordeal leading up to that wonderful state of calmness was anything but...

### *Now is Not Your Time!*

However, I did regain consciousness and awoke to some extremely cruel treatment. Met with hostile attitudes—they took it as an insult to have to help save the life of someone who didn't care enough to save herself and who lacked appreciation for life, while so many battle disease and illness and wish for nothing more than good health. Understandable...

They rushed me into the cardiac intensive care unit where for the next six hours they performed fifty-six external shocks (defibrillation) to bring me out of cardiac arrest. In and out of consciousness, the pain was excruciating, like no other pain I'd ever endured, and a thousand times worse than childbirth. I flashed on being hung up in a torture camp, and in a Chuck Norris movie where he's strapped up, hanging from the rafters, and shocked over and over and over again.

They wouldn't release me from the restraints or stop the electrocution. Nor could they risk administering any more meds including pain medication or sedation, due to the toxicity built up in my system. I could no longer withstand the pain. I balled up and fought the medical staff and shouted to them to leave me alone.

Completely surrounded by bodies shoulder to shoulder that forcefully stretched my arms and legs apart while they strapped each extremity of my body to the cold metal hospital bed, I shouted *Get your hands off of me!* and *Who do you think you are? Do you think you're above God? I've got a directive from my physician and you won't get away with this!*

Nothing I said would stop them. All the while I couldn't believe this was happening. I thought, *I'm an American, I have rights, yet I'm powerless to do anything to stop this cruel inhumane treatment!* No matter how hard I fought they wouldn't stop.

Well, there was an older RN, very brave I must say. Her name was Jean. Jean got in my face and pointed that finger like it was the barrel of a gun right between the middle of my eyes and yelled back "YOUNG LADY, STRAIGHTEN UP! You're too young to die!" For some reason that struck a nerve, maybe because my normal character is respectful, especially to elders.

I stopped fighting and tried to grin and bear it, as Jean talked me through the process. Shock after miserable shock, fifty-six times, machine turned to one hundred joules—as high as it would go—burning through multi-layers of skin with the repeated application of paddles atop the very same spots over and over, as that was the only thing that proved successful in pulling me back time and time again.

With her stern voice of reassurance Jean continued to coach me through those six torturous hours that seemed like forever. "You've got two beautiful kids out there waiting for you—now is not your time!"

Luckily Randall returned home to retrieve my medications and brought them to the emergency room. He assured hospital staff that in no way had I taken any medication that was not prescribed. He explained that one medication treated my psoriasis (due to a rash on my neck and elbow), and the other sinusitis, which I didn't even know I had until going in for the rash treatment.

I encountered a near death experience after being prescribed two drugs that shouldn't have been taken in combination. One slowed the function of the liver, whereas the other had to be processed through a normal functioning liver. After nine days of taking the dangerous combination it built up such toxicity that it poisoned my system and caused me to go into cardiac arrest.

Upon a change in shifts Dr. Frank came onto the scene. It was by the grace of God almighty that this humanly angel was sent to my aid. Within a prior two week timeframe he'd attended a conference in Chicago which identified this very condition. He immediately recognized the symptoms and administered a drug that instantaneously stopped the torsades de pointes. Unbelievable!

### *"Not to Use Life—That Alone is Death" - George Sand*

Later I learned that "Dear Doctor" notes had been sent to European physicians alerting them of the reaction to this particular drug combination. The U.S. Food and Drug Administration (FDA) had not proven it as fact, therefore no official notice had been released to American physicians. Of all reported occurrences in Europe, the oldest victim was nine years old. I instantly became not only the oldest but the first reported American to experience this particular interaction.

The most significant result of this entire episode is that my case spawned the development of a computerized database to track ALL medications. Now it electronically alerts a pharmacist if there is ever a combination of prescribed medications that could prove harmful. For that I am thankful.

From that episode, I was diagnosed with Prolonged QT and Sudden Arrhythmic Death Syndrome (SADS) and given two years to live. In order to combat these conditions I was a prime candidate for an Automatic Implantable Cardiac Defibrillator (AICD) with pacemaker, which I received in November 1993. I have since been in for four replacements at the end of each battery life.

My heart itself is very healthy—it's the electrical system of the heart that needs assistance. The device is basically my life insurance. An electrically charged device, implanted in the lower abdomen with four leads threaded into the right atrium and right ventricle, is positioned to deliver a shock inside the heart. Should the heart start beating erratically it will deliver a life saving shock to sync the heart back into rhythm.

Initially given two years to live, my priorities changed quickly and I became a happiness seeker. I wanted to make the most out of the life I had left. It's amazing what positivity can do. I'm still here— I have an implantable cardiac defibrillator with a pace maker and live with SADS, and prolonged QT, so as they say, I'm in mighty fine shape for the shape I'm in—and to much whom is given, much is expected!

By 2002 my resentfulness had worn off and gratitude set in. In pursuit of understanding and purpose I came up with this phrased acronym as a way to seek insight from my higher force. *Please give me SPECK and direct me in that which thou finds most purposeful for all as long as I am graced with this life,* I said to myself. Translation: Please grant me the strength, patience, endurance, courage, and knowledge to excel in the path you have chosen, and to do what is meant for the greater good...XLR82GR8 (accelerate to great.)

Several unique and unexplainable incidents have occurred throughout my life that drove me to seek a greater purpose and changed my entire point of view. Materialism lessened and I've been on a personal passage, drawn to seek the deeper meaning of life for years now.

There have been numerous awakening moments in my life. I continuously look for a means to be part of something bigger than myself, to spread the message of hope and encouragement, lead by example, and help others dig deep to reach their greater good as well. I believe in divine connection, am drawn to special people, as His plan will bring the right people into my life.

I've learned I must stay in faith to bring my dreams to pass. The biggest key is—I just gotta believe—it's all in divine order! My emotional journey of perseverance includes never giving up.

It's easy to get beaten down by disappointments. Negative emotions weaken cells and negatively impact the immune system. It's so important to keep a cheerful mind as a cheerful, positive mind works healing. Having survived near death and all, I realize that life is about choices and absolutely too precious to spend being miserable. When I was given two years to live, happiness became my ultimate desire. I once said life is too short to live miserably; twenty years later, I say life is too long... happiness is the key and the most fruitful ingredient to life!

*"Henceforth I shall accept what I am and what I am not. With my limitations and my gifts, I shall go on using life as long as I am in this World and afterwards. Not to use life—that alone is death."* - George Sand

**ABOUT THE AUTHOR:** Suzanne joined the leadership team of Municipal Golf Association in 2007, at which time MGA partnered with the city of San Antonio to manage seven golf facilities and the Texas Golf Hall of Fame. Prior to joining MGA, Suzanne spent 18 years with a national insurance carrier as State Compliance Auditor and owned an independent insurance agency, maintaining active licensing and professional designation. Suzanne went to state in golf in high school and currently heads up the Women's Golf Program in collaboration with PGA's 2.0 Grow Golf America initiative, and enjoys networking & empowering women through the game of golf.

Suzanne Toepperwein, Business Manager
Alamo City Golf Trail
www.alamocitygolftrail.com
suzanne@satxgolf.com
210-602-8840

# Secrets, Fibs and Skirting My Truth

## Sue Urda

I sat on the edge of my bed and wiped the sleep from my eyes when suddenly I realized my mother was standing before me. *What's she holding in her hand?* I wondered.

Her words rang in my head as an enormous surge of adrenalin rushed through my tired mind and my whole body went into high alert. "Code Red" as the government would say.

"No, mom, I know what you saw but it doesn't mean what you think it does!"

"Sue, it's not normal," she told me. "But don't worry. It's okay. We can get you some help. We can go to the priest at church and they'll be able to help you."

She held up the book in her hands and I saw it was the Bible. The Holy Bible. *Oh shit, this is serious!*

I know the thoughts cascaded through my head only for a few seconds, but it seemed like hours. *She thinks I need help. She thinks something is wrong with me. She thinks I'm not normal.* Fear gripped my belly as her words and the fire in her frightened eyes ripped through me.

I felt the heat rise up into my cheeks and my immediate response was to defend myself. Defend myself against my own mother. The thought was so foreign to me. And although I knew in my heart she loved me deeply and was doing what she thought she should to protect me, I could feel myself slipping away.

I looked at my mother and recognized how incredibly vulnerable and afraid she must have felt. She didn't really know what to do or think and she wanted us to seek answers and comfort from the source she'd relied upon for years–her faith in God and the Catholic Church.

"Sue, answer me."

I remember looking directly into her eyes but I didn't recognize her as my mother. Instead, what I saw before me was a woman who was afraid and grasping at straws. I felt as if she was incredibly angry, and I remember experiencing her pain and fear as she looked at me. She looked like a woman who didn't know what to do. Perhaps for the first time in my twenty-one years, I saw my mother simply as a human being.

Wasn't my mother supposed to love me unconditionally; support me and protect me and have my back? Now who would I turn to for help in sorting through this confusion?

"Mom, you're wrong. It's not what you think. It was just a kiss to say goodbye."

"You leaned into her car three times," my mother replied. "I can see once or even twice, but not three times."

"Mom, I'm telling you you're wrong. We're just friends."

### And So the Lies Began

I tried to convince myself that lying was the only way to protect myself. I mean, if a mother can't accept her daughter for who she is, then what about the rest of the world? How was I going to live? The truth was that I didn't even understand it myself.

Years of conditioning had etched into me that I would go to college, get a job, get married, and have babies and grandbabies; yet, hard as I tried, I simply couldn't see myself living this life. These newfound feelings had come forth to help me discover the truth of who I was. And as good as I felt when I was around "people like me" I felt a hundred times worse trying to be someone I wasn't around everyone else.

My world had become an unfamiliar landscape and, hard as it was to distance myself from my family and hide some of the best parts of my life–my loving relationships, my friends, what I did, and where I went—somehow I knew I had to live my own life.

I treaded water for years and presented myself to the world as a career-driven woman because this took some of the obvious questions off the table: "No time for a relationship, Sue?" and "What's a beautiful girl like you doing without a boyfriend?" All the while I was making my way and doing my best to accept the real me, but the lies continued.

## Old Habits Die Hard

The truth is that the habit of lying had started much earlier in my life. I always wanted to be a "good girl" and have my parents' approval so I often hid things. My earliest memories include sneaking food into my room because I didn't want to be yelled at for eating too much. I was a butterball of a little girl, and it didn't help that I had a very skinny sister only fifteen months older than me.

My mother enjoyed dressing us alike and, while my sister wore slim size clothes, mom had to take me to the "chubby girls" department. I felt what I thought was her embarrassment and disappointment if we couldn't find my size in the dresses she wanted me to wear, and I often ended up wearing ones that cut into me just so we could dress alike. Add to this the fact that often as kids one of our reward systems was snacks like candy, ice cream, and soda; I felt easily confused by the mixed messages.

Shame and hunger haunted me at the same time. What I recognize now is that I wasn't necessarily hungry for food, but for love. I wanted to fit in, make it easy for my mom, and look pretty and skinny like my sister, but I couldn't help stuffing food into my mouth. Looking back at some of my old photos, I see that I wasn't actually fat, just pleasantly plump—too bad I didn't feel that way.

I remember a specific question that still echoes in my head today, and probably even more profoundly at a subconscious level—*"what will people think?"* This question comes to me as the voice of my mother and grandmother often around the issue of my weight, but also about attending church, achieving good grades, behaving obediently, dressing properly, and being clean and well-kept. I can't help but wonder if that's how they lived their whole lives too...worried about what others would think. So much pressure. So much wasted energy. Will the voice ever go away?

## It Only Hurts When I Move

A feeble laugh escaped my lips, followed by a mild groan. The pain ripped through my shoulders and neck, down my spine and arms, and even, it seemed, right down to my toes. Even laughter made my whole body hurt. In the past weeks, the pain had increased from annoying and sporadic to throbbing and ever-present...but only when I moved. It sounded like a bad joke, but it was the truth.

This pain had popped in and out of my life for thirteen years. Some months passed with little or no discomfort, and then *wham!* I'd become incapacitated, weak, and itchy. The doctors had no idea what was going on and numerous inconclusive tests left them baffled. Various drugs masked or relieved the symptoms for a while, and then it—whatever *it* was—would rear its ugly head and I'd find myself unable to tackle even the simplest tasks. The eruptions on my skin made me feel like a leper, and I felt lucky to at least be able to hide them with clothing or to simply work from home.

I kept my condition a secret largely because I didn't want to appear weak or incapable of taking care of myself. Lucky for me, my amazing partner of nearly twenty years, Kathy, loved and cared for me through it all and understood my need for secrecy.

### Here We Go Again...Or Not

It was 2011 and my symptoms had exacerbated to the point that I could no longer stand the intense pain, massive inflammation, and unnatural discoloration of my skin. I decided this autoimmune disease—finally diagnosed—was not going to have its way with me any longer!

I explored alternative therapies and finally, after many months and a few sessions with a shaman who reminded me "drugs are not a failure, they are an assist," I resorted to steroids to help me function normally again. It was miraculous and immediate, and I wished I hadn't waited so long. Perhaps the lie I'd been telling myself lately was the biggest one of all—that I could *control* everything myself.

During the year I looked deeply into this disease that wracked my body. What I learned is that an autoimmune disease is one where the immune system malfunctions from its natural state and the body attacks itself. As I looked closely at my patterns of thought over the years and how I had been living my life, it became very clear to me that my body was mimicking my constant barrage of punishing thoughts about being fat, gay, and broke. I attacked myself—literally! And always I worried "what will people think?"

All those years I'd been so unkind to myself! I'd looked in the mirror with disgust at my weight, which ranged from 5-50 lbs. heavier at any given time. I looked at my short hair and clothes, and bashed myself for not looking feminine enough. I looked at my bank account and the abundance I so desired that wasn't flowing to me. I was most struck during this self-exploration by the stark realization that I was completely out of alignment with my own priorities and values—and ultimately, the truth of who I was.

In this defining moment I realized the pattern I had lived my whole life: worrying what others would think. The time had come to stop! My mother had been a wonderful loving teacher and I would not be the woman I am today without her bravery, encouragement, and willingness to grow alongside me. And now the time had come for me to live my truth.

Although I knew in my heart that my purpose was to empower and encourage women to wholeness and authentic ways of being, I also knew I was not living this way myself. I could easily speak to others and help them become more powerful in their lives, and in a flash of insight I recognized that my public persona was disconnected from my private one. I appeared to be strong, connected, loving, and powerful on the outside, but deep down I felt like a fraud because I felt none of these things for myself. I had stuffed the real me into something so small that I was almost non-existent.

As I sit here in this moment, I know I must stop the secrets. Stop the fibs. Stop skirting my truth. I have made what may be the biggest, most empowering decision of my whole life—I have decided to live my life as me.

*"And the day came when the risk to remain tight in the bud was more painful than the risk it took to blossom." - Anais Nin*

**ABOUT THE AUTHOR:** Sue Urda is known as 'The Connections Expert'. She is an Author, Speaker, Inspirer and Co-Founder of Powerful You! Women's Network and Powerful You! Publishing. Sue is a two-time honoree on INC Magazine's list of the 500 Fastest-Growing Private Companies. Her award-winning book, *Powerful Intentions Everyday Gratitude* is designed to inspire women tap the inner wisdom of their hearts, to feel their personal power, and to live each day through deliberate creation and intent. Sue loves assisting women in their own pursuit of success, joyful living & freedom. Her mission is to connect women to each other, their visions & themselves.

Sue Urda
Powerful You! Inc.
www.powerfulyou.com
www.sueurda.com
973-248-1262

# PART TWO

# Conscious Relationships

*"Each friend represents a world in us,
a world possibly not born until they arrive, and it is only
by this meeting that a new world is born."*
*~ Anais Nin*

# There's No Place Like Home
## Debbie Arrigo

"How do you like this color?" I remember I'd asked Joe. It'd taken us all night to agree on a living room paint color. Good thing we'd started seven months before our wedding!

Now, as glistening daylight flowed through the half open blind, it revealed shadows of outlines where photographs once hung. As we peered into empty corners, only the echo of our shoes and the faint smell of early morning coffee lingered.

"You're getting all melancholy on me" Joe said, breaking my thoughts. Huge nickel wooden beams clung to the ceiling, accented by thick finger-splattered plaster and speckled paint that we'd painstakingly created together. "How about I reach up and take one of these infamous beams down and you can keep it as a souvenir?" We both laughed since we knew all too well what a nightmare they'd been to put up!

"Did you check the closets?" Joe called as he headed toward the front door. "I'll get the car started—I'll be outside..." His voice faded as the outer door closed behind him. Just hours before, all our treasured belongings had been right here; now they were jam-packed into a moving trailer on its way to Roanoke, Virginia. And tomorrow at this time we'd be right behind.

The familiar door slammed and I heard the lock turn. I leaned my head heavily against the door and thought to myself, *this is the very last time I'll be leaving this apartment—our first special place.* As I walked toward the front door, the light flickered on, reminding me how I'd asked the landlord for an automatic outside light for late night arrivals home. He told us we reminded him of his kids and was kind enough to put one in, and he never raised our rent.

I folded the keys neatly inside an envelope and pushed them through the mail slot outside for him to retrieve. He and his wife had been very sweet, always dropping off homemade cookies or fresh chicken soup on cold nights...

Then there was the not so big kitchen with the not so big counter where we'd squished together and scrambled eggs, stirred pots of sauce, and rolled dough for cookies. And our wonderful doorbell that sang out the arrival of our beautiful neighbors and friends who dropped in for visits.

How can I forget the sweet smell of the rose garden outside our window, and Mr. Snooze, the ever-sleeping lazy cat on the doorstep always waiting for a pat or two and a bowl of warm milk? If walls could talk, they'd reveal the laughter and tears of our first year here together as a married couple. So many feet had happily tapped, danced, drank, and slept on the thick shag carpet that now it virtually cried out to be replaced. Lots of good times!

"Ready?" Joe asked, his voice tinged with excitement. One chapter of our life was closing and another was about to begin.

### Post Traumatic Move Syndrome

I remember people saying how much I'd love southern warmth and hospitality—the generosity, open doors, and welcoming ways. How people in the south were laid back and enjoyed "the good life." Once we arrived in Roanoke, Virginia, I waited expectantly for the doorbell to ring and anticipated my delight when, opening the door, I'd find a friendly neighbor holding a hot apple pie to welcome me into the neighborhood.

Almost forty years have gone by since then, and I'm still waiting for that doorbell to ring! Later I discovered that southern hospitality was frowned upon there unless your visit was announced ahead of time, you brought a casserole-covered dish and, last but not least, *always* brought your own bottle!

Our few connections there were those who'd also braved the move from New York, and the handful of people with whom Joe now worked. One fellow was Floyd; he was the first African American in the company, hired by my husband. Extremely grateful for the opportunity, Floyd was available the day we moved in, and gladly lent us a hand. He held open the door and helped me direct the movers where to place our furniture and other items in different parts of the house.

From the start I found myself alone. Within three days of our arrival, Joe had to return to New York for another whole month. After his departure, I saw the vacuum cleaner in the middle of room, and thought to myself I must be careful not to trip over it.

Shortly after, I tripped over it, broke my toe, and had to drive myself to the emergency room!

Another day, as I painted the bedrooms upstairs, the windows wouldn't stay up. Eventually a window fell on my fingers and I ended up with a swollen hand. But the worst was the electric stove. In New York we had gas, but our new home was electric. I didn't notice the rag lying so close to the still hot electric coils, and as I picked it up to move a pot off the stove, I was halfway to the sink before I realized my hand was on fire!

All by myself, I cried on the steps. Every day Joe called from New York and asked "well, did you meet any neighbors?" and I'd say "no!" After a year of wondering where all of these friendly southerners were hiding, and why they'd never shown up, apple pies in hand, the lady across the street informed me that she and the other neighbors had dismissed me when they'd seen Floyd—who they'd mistaken for my husband!—holding the door for the movers as they'd peeked through their curtains on the day we moved in! "Well dear, we assumed a mixed marriage had moved in to the neighborhood," she told me. That was my welcoming wagon down there. Not something I'd anticipated!

When Joe returned his time was limited because of work. He didn't realize how serious my post traumatic move syndrome was. While my family drove down as often as possible—and brought with them half of Brooklyn's Italian bread, pepperoni, supersod (a.k.a., sopressata, or Italian salami), bagels, pastries, and an array of other goodies we missed—I remained lonely and hungry for my family, friends, and the familiar places we used to go.

Sometimes after speaking with my mom and sister Joe would give me a pep talk and make me laugh. My family—my parents and Allison, my younger sister by ten years—maintained a special closeness and warmth. It was a bond of love few are lucky enough to have, and leaving it behind had been so difficult. I wanted so badly to be there for Allison, who at fourteen was just beginning to become interested in boys—we'd have endless conversations by phone, but I felt cheated that I wasn't there for many of her "first" experiences.

Then I found out I had cancer of the cervix and advanced endometriosis. The surgeries were successful, and the cancer eliminated, but the lining of my uterus had deteriorated and they said it might take me years to conceive due to so much scar tissue. However, within six months I did get pregnant!

When Vanessa, our first bundle of joy was born, Joe and I

cherished the moment with family—by phone. When I found myself pregnant again only three months later, we were ecstatic but giving birth to one after the other proved to be taxing. Every other day Joe would arrive home to find me on the couch crying hysterically for no apparent reason, the two babies on either side of me. Frustrated, with a lonely heart, a new family, and no one close, my responsibilities were endless, and caring for two babies under two was overwhelming for me.

Thankfully my old friends called as often as their time allowed, which warmed my heart and kept me in the loop. All my dear friends kept in touch and came to visit. I had more fun with those friends when they visited than with the people I'd met here, except for the other transplanted New Yorkers.

### *Home, Sweet Home!*

"Wake up, sleepy head! The girls are hungry!" I lifted my head and opened my eyes. The first thing I saw out of the car window was water gushing from a nearby fire hydrant and a bunch of boys squatting to play skully, a street game played with bottle caps. Next I saw the park, filled with stickball players, and then—down the block—I spotted the best scene of all...mom's front staircase, decorated with white taffeta and the biggest "Welcome Home!" sign I'd ever seen!

Sun glared through the trees on our block as dad hosed the front concrete. Mom and Alison jumped up and down on the front porch with delight waving us out of the car. "How was the trip?" Dad asked, as mom pushed forward to get to the girls. "Where's my little sweethearts? Ooh, come here!" she swooped down to cover Vanessa and Krista with hugs and kisses.

"I have a pot of coffee on–want a cup?" Dad asked. "Of course!" Joe and I answered in unison. When we entered the house it felt as if the entire neighborhood was there! Overwhelmed, the tears welled up in my eyes. There were good friends and my "adopted" grandparents, sitting and having coffee—so many well-wishers awaiting our arrival home.

In a flash I was reminded of all the times we'd gathered with friends and family—how we'd joked, laughed, cried, and kept each other's secrets close. Saturday shopping, dinner at mom's on Thursday nights, sauce and meatballs on Sunday while the wash tumbled and the guys watched football and yelled like morons! The smell of Grandma's bread baking, my sister forever taking something but never returning it, and her infamous weekend sleepovers, music blasting, lights on for hours...

The next morning, the smell of Dad's coffee permeated the air and rose all the way up to the second floor and, as I dressed, I could hear the familiar sounds of pots and pans brushing against each other. Dad was making one of his famous morning breakfasts! I hoped there'd be his great pancakes and, ooh bacon too! My favorites!

"Rise and shine everyone! Breakfast is about to be served in Al's kitchen!" Dad shouted up. Always a kidder, he'd do anything to get us all out of bed as early as him! But his breakfast always made it worth it! We all sat around the table passing the coffee and talking as if it were any other Saturday morning.

Joe and I looked at each other and smiled. It was like we'd never been away, and I knew instantly we were thinking the same thing: *there's no place like home!*


**ABOUT THE AUTHOR:** A high-energy, goal-driven individual, Debbie holds an M.A. in Special Education/Psychology, an M.A. in Administration & Supervision, and is a teacher, educational consultant, author, associate real estate sales broker, and a personal mentor. The recipient of numerous gold awards for real estate sales, Debbie continues to forge ahead with new endeavors. Her relentless optimism and gift for connecting people has helped Debbie establish successful relationships within her community and work environment. An elementary teacher, Debbie prides herself on her passion for teaching children, is actively involved with the Autism Society and the American Cancer Society, and enjoys writing children's literature.

Deborah Rae Arrigo
debbiearrigo.com
debbiearrigo@yahoo.com
ziadeedee@aol.com
646-235-4086

# The Phoenix
## Miriam Belov

Shirley stands frozen on the bustling train platform, a small suitcase in hand. Her husband is nearby with his. Her little brother is at a distance, empty handed. She knows better than to draw attention to herself. As the train approaches, she turns to face him and, then with a barely discernible wave, turns away and abruptly boards the train. Her husband follows quickly behind her.

She loves this young boy so very much and doesn't know if she'll ever see him again. Sadly, she never did. Her small gesture goodbye was all she could do in order not to be discovered, as she and her husband flee towards what they hope will be a safer life.

The year was 1918; the place Tolnoya, a small town outside of Kiev, then in Russia. As the Russian Revolution engulfed her family, Shirley realized she needed to go. Nineteen and scared, she exiled herself from the only life she had ever known.

Shirley grew up well educated in a loving, affluent household with her two sisters and two brothers. Her enterprising father was prosperous and her mother, Miriam, a beauty. Their house was the first to have electricity. The girls had a teacher who came to their home to give them dance lessons and in the cold, snow-filled winter Shirley would go on long sleigh rides, bundled up and warm. The family donated regularly to charity. She dreamed of studying at the university in Moscow.

During the early years of the twentieth century, Shirley had the courage to leave it all. Dressed as a man, she and her husband traded their gold wedding rings to a border guard for safe passage out of Russia and into Romania. In the country for four years, she gave birth to a daughter in Bucharest, the capital city. Shortly afterwards, they traveled to Istanbul, Paris, and back to Istanbul, all the while trying to find a way out of Europe and into America.

Finally, they boarded the ship the USS Canada and landed in Rhode Island in 1922 with a six month old infant—my mother.

And here I am now, part of that unknown future for Shirley is my maternal grandmother, a woman whose memory I cherish. Indeed, her memory is a blessing.

When her husband passed, she moved in with my parents. Then an only child, I loved having her so close. We shared a room for a few years from when I was four. She calmed me when we saw "The Wizard of Oz" at the movies and the wicked witch appeared on the big screen. It was a special and safe time for me.

Everything I did with her resonated with a life that spanned decades and continents. Listening to her stories always instilled in me a longing for my own great adventure into the unknown...into freedom...

She left her whole family so that her descendants could be free. It was Shirley who gave me the inner commitment to further expand my horizons. Her brave departure on that train inspired me to continue the journey to which she'd opened the door.

### *Living Consciously*

The longing for my own great adventure into freedom also included a conscious journey inward. Compelled by my passion to learn various ways of wellness and healing and to better understand this precious planet's cultures, I developed a burning desire to travel beyond my Ivy League Master Degrees from Brown University. I craved to experience a more direct knowledge of numerous climes and locales and to truly honor our great mother earth.

I put aside my hesitation of leaving the familiar and allowed my convictions to lead me forward into the unknown. Back and forth I went—across America and then to England, Morocco, France, and Israel—exploring cities and countrysides as I internalized new healing perspectives, always feeling a deep connection with the land. Each of these places called to me but India mesmerized me.

Unencumbered by personal responsibilities to a husband or child, and having accumulated funds from my wellness work, off I went to a corner of south India brimming with the future. Auroville, the experiment in international living recognized by UNESCO, draws people from around the world who pioneer this unique township.

They plant trees, build ecological dwellings, schools, and cultural pavilions, and create sustainable ways of living, all the while experiencing the evolutionary impulse that permeates the atmosphere. There is a palpable intensity in the air to express one's psychic being through sincerely living an integral life.

As the lotus grows in the mud and breaks through the water's surface to bloom in the sunlight, so it matches my aspiration to yoke all into a flowering of enlightened and true consciousness. The tropical heat burns everything else away. I nestle in it for as long as possible.

Fast forward to 2011: Soaring over the bay in Key Largo a thousand feet up, the warm air cushions me. I feel like a bird as I gaze out to the sea. The water is crystal clear, a turquoise shade of blue, and the late afternoon sun shines brightly. The whole view is serene and spectacular.

I am parasailing with my daughter. It is her idea—one I had resisted for weeks. Scared, I worried if it would strain my body. It looked dangerous. Would I hurt myself physically? I summoned all my daring and finally agreed.

As we uplift, I laugh and shout for joy. My long hair blows back, but once at full altitude calmness descends over me as I look out in awe at the land and sea. I am silent. The balloon catches the wind allowing me to hover, and my body relaxes.

I am living consciously in the now. All my seeking has brought me to this very moment, the culmination of so much searching. Filled with exhilaration, my spirit flies free in this most physical of experiences. Is this how the mythical phoenix must feel?! With a great sense of empowering gratitude, I have moved through my fear and taken this upward leap.

I wonder if my courage is in some small way at all similar to what Shirley felt so many years ago on that train platform.

### The Matriarch

During the especially cold winter of 1982 Shirley began her final passage out of this life. She had lived with her daughter and son-in-law for almost half a century since losing her own husband and she had helped raise me and my two younger siblings. Our special name for her was Mama, beloved Mama. She had led a good life, filled with family and friends, and was an honored wise woman.

Mama often had dream visions of her parents and husband who had gone on before her. She shared them and other psychic precognitions with me. The warmth of her presence infused the ethereal planes of intuitive knowledge with a natural familiarity for me. During her whole life the mysticism of her youth brought strength to Shirley. It was just there in all she did, which allowed me to accept my own precious gifts inherited from her.

The winter leached her life force. Shirley grew weak. Pain filled her belly. Her strength was leaving her now. I would drive out from New York City to the familial home as often as possible, frequently staying days and long nights. Finally in the hospital, it was just too much for her. Gently, on March 7th, Shirley voyaged into the light.

She dropped her physical body and passed over into the great love. I believe it was an easy release for her but those of us she left behind mourned and coped—each in our own way. Although we nurtured one another, we could not fill the void left by Mama's departure.

Two years after her death, I make another trip around the world. I return to the heat of Auroville to stay a few weeks. While there I have preparatory talks about the Nakashima Sacred Peace Table which in two years is sent from New Hope and dedicated. Then it is on to Cairo and its pyramids. Finally I fly up to Jerusalem. Having previously visited Israel from America with my family, it was fascinating to experience travelling to it from India in the east. Yes, indeed, the region is the Middle East—merging traditions from both parts of the globe and vibrating with a myriad of prayers. May they all arise in a unity of peace.

I had been to Bethlehem and Safed but this time I visit Haifa to see some of Shirley's relatives. It is early spring. Cyclamens are on the window sills. These flowers remind me of a delicate bird's head with feathers. I have tea everywhere with people, each of whom has a fascinating story.

While visiting yet another household, I walk into the parlor and unexpectedly behold a treasure—a picture of the great matriarch Miriam, Shirley's mother. After all these many years, I finally see her! She takes my breath away. I gaze upon her beautiful face for a long time. Refined, with an intelligence and sensitivity to which I can easily relate, I look upon her for whom I am named. Amazed by coming full circle, I am overwhelmed and infused with a deep sense of astonishment and fulfillment.

Shirley taught me to have the courage to explore the world and to push the limits of experience as far as they could possibly go. Now, standing in front of her mother's portrait, it is as if I were led here by Shirley herself. For she is the one who instilled in me the conviction to follow my heart and live consciously in all I do—be it using my gifts as I channel a Reiki energy session, soar through the air, or gaze at a picture.

The following poem was written by me. I read it at Shirley's funeral.

## The Phoenix

City streets send up pulses with rhythms of life,
Iridescent vibrations of heat.
Wave hands like clouds and sink into the root.
Sun glows into

Yellow moon floating like a ripe peach in the evening sky.
A velvet whisper caresses my limbs.
Glowing so deeply, I move through lush waves of air
On the scents of dreams in the balmy nights.

Green hills pushing towards the sky,
Clusters of flowers with their faces turned up to the sun,
These stretches of earth refresh:
Cool, quiet movements.

Wings of the angels brush us gently
As the wind moves through metropolis and dale.
It is all the same—each expression an act of supplication.
Life speaks in a cabal, carefully opening the gates
If we only know how to know.

On her soul the aspiration ascends.

**ABOUT THE AUTHOR:** Compelled by her passion, Miriam Belov, MAT, RMT made several global excursions and then founded The Wellness Agenda. For over 35 years she has been involved in mind body spirit work, creating programs for countless individuals and institutions - including The Metropolitan Museum of Art and The United Nations. With a Master of Arts from Brown University, Miriam teaches via all media, corporately and civically. She is a certified Reiki Master Teacher and a public speaker who often leads meditations. Miriam hosted her own radio talk show and created the DVD and download "Relax...Feel Great! Stay Young" to help and inspire other women.

Miriam Belov, MAT, RMT
The Wellness Agenda LLC
www.wellnessagenda.com
Miriam@wellnessagenda.com

# Connecting the Dots

### Karen Bummele

Life is constantly changing and moving like the waves of the ocean. We have to be ready to adjust our sails, see the gift in the moment, release, and go with the flow. That's when serendipity, the act of finding something valuable when you're not looking for it, occurs...

I remember the day as if it was yesterday—a beautiful crystal blue sky Saturday afternoon in May. On my way home from the Hirshhorn museum I decided to grab a cup of coffee and impulsively hopped off the bus one stop early.

I walked toward the entrance of Starbucks and found myself in line behind a tall man with dark brown, wavy hair. I caught a glimpse of his face whenever he periodically looked back, and I wondered what he was looking at. As we waited patiently on the long line, I heard several barks and whimpers from a golden retriever by the door. Instinctively, I asked him "is that your dog? I think he might be trying to get your attention."

He replied in a thick accent that the dog was his friend's and, as we began a casual conversation, the long line suddenly didn't seem so long anymore. Soon we'd made our way to the front, where he ordered his coffee and headed towards the condiment bar. What a nice conversation, I thought to myself, and ordered my decaffeinated coffee.

"I'm sorry, ma'am, it'll take about five minutes to brew the decaffeinated pot. Is that okay—do you mind waiting?"

I could have waited five minutes, but something told me not to and I ordered a regular coffee instead. I headed toward the counter where he stood grabbing several napkins to clean the waterfall of coffee that had spilled everywhere. I chuckled to myself quietly, thinking this could easily be me.

With little coffee left in his cup, I suggested he ask for a refill. Strangely, he said no and, as we headed towards the front door, unleashed his friend's dog and asked me to join him outside. I didn't even know his name yet, but I accepted without thinking twice.

For the next two hours, we had a refreshing and lighthearted conversation about travel, life, and his experiences in the United States. I found myself not realizing how much time had passed until I felt the coolness of the breeze. I thought I should get going, but before I could say anything he asked me "what are you doing tonight? Do you have any plans?"

Opportunities come and go everyday and it's about being in the present, paying attention to the clues, listening to our hearts, and trusting that everything will unfold as it should–perfectly. A part of me wondered, who is this guy? He is a complete stranger from Germany and I should be careful, and yet something within told me I had nothing to lose. The randomness of this afternoon had me curious and I chose to say yes to our first date together that very same night.

Over the next few months we went on many dates and I introduced him to my friends. Many of them were intrigued by how quickly we had developed a strong connection, including myself. Our quiet walks and long conversations, where we shared our very different upbringings were some of the small moments that meant the most to me.

The protective cocoon in which I'd surrounded myself for so many years slowly softened as I let go of worry, doubt, fear, and uncertainty from the inside out. I found myself shedding old beliefs and layers that kept me safe. The Chinese concept of "saving face," ingrained in me from childhood, seemed to carry less weight. I became less consumed with fear or judgment from family and friends.

I did what I felt like in the moment, not bound by dating "rules," worries, family obligations, and what if's. I relied less on friends' advice, learning to trust myself more. I would take the initiative to call or ask him to do things together, and not get caught up in the "chase" or the "right" thing to do. Sometimes things got lost in translation, but in many ways our cultural and language differences helped us to be more patient, honest, inquisitive, and less judgmental. He wasn't afraid to express his feelings and, in turn, provided me a safe space in which I could open up and express myself more fully.

I watched myself transform into a new way of being—fearless and courageous, as the quiet voice within strengthened, renewed, and guided me with a newfound wisdom that I didn't recognize. I was not held back by the past or the future, but rather open to the possibility of something that I couldn't explain, define, or describe in words at the time. I had no idea where this was going, but I was in for the ride.

### Finding Purpose in the Unexpected

On 9/11 our ride together took a dramatic turn, and our relationship was tested in ways that we never could have imagined. He was traveling in Canada with his friend, and wasn't reachable by phone. I was consumed with fear, worry, and panic about him and loved ones in New York. When we finally connected, he told me he had to return to Germany.

Disappointment, anger, confusion and emptiness flowed through my tears as I felt that life was cheating me, life was unfair. How could this happen to me? Had it all been too good to be true? Despite his reassuring words that nothing had changed between us, everything felt like it was spinning out of control.

He returned to his small village in Germany, and we talked for several weeks, trying to figure out how we could stay together. He invited me to visit him, but my mind swam with negative thoughts. How would this work in the long run? How would we stay together an ocean apart? It's too complicated—maybe we should walk away from each other and move on.

As my head and heart waged battle, I weighed the pros and cons of my next step. I found the answer within and the courage to listen to it. I couldn't wait, walk away, or give up. I told myself *if you don't dare yourself to make a move, you'll never know what would've happened.* There were no guarantees—I might get hurt, but was willing to take that risk. The consequence of not going outweighed my fears. I booked my ticket to Munich. I never felt more uncertain in my life, yet so certain that this was something I needed to do.

My visit to southern Germany opened me up to his small world. Unable to speak a drop of German, he did everything he could to make me feel welcome and comfortable. He introduced me to family and friends, translated for me, and showed me his most special and memorable places. I watched him interact with others and saw him even more clearly as a humble, caring, patient, and giving man. He made me laugh with his wonderful sense of humor. We focused on each day; awakened to each moment as a gift, even though we both knew I'd be leaving soon.

As the visit came to a close, we chose to stay committed to each other and not give up, despite the uncertainty of our future and its exact path. We didn't have the answers immediately in front of us, but we accepted our situation and trusted that somehow we'd find our way if it was meant to be. On the day we drove to Munich airport, I had a sinking hole in my stomach. I didn't know when I'd see him next. I wanted to hold on to him and not let go.

When I returned home and we spoke again, he told me he'd gone to an outlook point by the airport to watch my plane take off. I smiled because somehow I'd known he was watching my take-off from below. In my heart, I knew he was home for me, and it didn't matter how far apart we were.

### Serendipity to Synchronicity

It's been almost eleven years since the day we met. Happily married and still on our evolving journey together, I sometimes wonder what would've happened if I'd been in front of him on line instead of behind. Would we have spoken? There were so many small decisions that could have altered our meeting, yet the precise timing of everything that unfolded that day—and since—have led me to believe that this was more than serendipity. This was synchronicity.

Paulo Coehlo once said, "Love is not to be found in someone else, but in ourselves; we simply awaken to it. But in order to do that, we need the other person." We were both happy and content from within when we met, and not searching for love. Yet, in finding each other, we realized our own capacity and worth to love and to be loved.

I look back at our past and see how all the challenges and struggles we've endured served a purpose—they tested, guided, and showed us the mystery of love and life.

We thrived through many ups and downs, twists and turns, highs and rock bottom lows by letting go of the outcome and always coming back to the question "what am I doing this for?" We held onto the vision of what we wanted and never lost sight of the direction. Each small choice, intention, decision, and action was a conscious act of trusting our intuition, accepting and having faith in something much larger. I wouldn't change any of our story today, even the difficult parts.

When things don't always make sense or I feel overwhelmed by circumstances or situations, I reflect on one of my favorite quotes by the visionary Steve Jobs. "You can't connect the dots looking forward; you can only connect them looking backwards. So you have to trust that the dots will somehow connect in your future. You have to trust in something—your gut, destiny, life, karma, whatever. This approach has never let me down, and it has made all the difference in my life."

Reminding myself that change is constant and everything is impermanent allows me to be open to the depth and wholeness of life. Everything that comes our way is meant to be a part of our journey and if we are open and aware to noticing the abundance and opportunity in all situations, we discover how everything connects.

My trust in my husband, and in my own heart, allows me now to look back and recognize the connected dots of my future's past. When I look at them all together, they form the pattern of my own beautiful constellation as it glows brightly against the nighttime sky.

**ABOUT THE AUTHOR:** Certified Professional Coach and founder of Your Conscious Footprint℠ LLC, Karen Bummele inspires socially conscious businesses, individuals, and organizations to live their values and vision, awaken to their true potential, and lead more consciously and authentically. Karen explores how culture impacts energy, relationships, intentions/actions, and works with those whose mission is to create sustainable and impactful change in the world. Her over ten years experience in culture, diversity and inclusion, combined with her core energy coaching, visualization, yoga, and holistic processes empower clients to incorporate mindfulness in action, balanced living and the engagement of head, heart, and spirit into all they do.

Karen Bummele
Your Conscious Footprint℠ LLC
www.yourconsciousfootprint.com
karen@yourconsciousfootprint.com

# The Soul Mate Within
## Angelika Christie

I close the door to the bathroom, and lock it quickly, but softly, so as not to be heard. I need to be alone. After ten years, I still recognize the large mirror, but my reflection has changed. My body looks thinner, and my eyes reflect back the angst and pain of loss, separation, and grave disappointment.

My body feels raw and heavy. I turn on the bathtub faucet and the strong, loud stream of rushing water muffles the moans that begin to escape my tightly closed mouth. I want to scream, but do not want to be discovered right now.

I sit bent over on the toilet seat, and sway slightly as I cover my mouth with my left hand, and with my right clutch the area of my heart that feels as if it wants to be released from my body. How can I take this pain? I must hold back what starts to feel like an emotional runaway train.

I gaze into the quiet flame of a rose scented candle that flickers slightly as it sits in its elaborate crystal container—a gift from one of my loving Reiki practitioners for initiating her to the master degree. I rarely use this candle, but today its pure scent of roses and lavender, mixed with the vapor rising from the large bathtub, begin to soothe my pain just enough. I close my eyes and, like a film racing backward, see parts of my life in a flashback.

Behind my closed eyelids I see the gentle blue eyes of my father, whom I adored. As they transform into the beautiful amber eyes of Benno, the man for whom I left Germany and my first family, again I feel the strong attraction, not just from my body, but from my soul. I knew I was destined to be with him from the depth of my entire being. I knew I'd found my soul mate, and we became husband and wife. I loved him so much, I promised to start a family, and gave life to two beautiful children—one after the other.

The years flashed past, and I started to feel a void. At first my new life in the Bahamas had stimulated and excited me, but soon I felt isolated and powerless. This sun-filled foreign land and culture became more like a prison that afforded only limited access to the things I used to enjoy back in Germany.

My days were long and filled with family life, while the wee hours of the nights belonged to me alone. I studied health, healing modalities, and metaphysics; I was like a dry sponge soaking up knowledge. Meanwhile, Benno's deep passion was to create our financial security, and so he worked long hours and found relaxation on weekends in a sport in which I had no interest. My spiritual search intensified and seemed to create a deeper rift between us.

I wanted him—my soul mate—to pay more attention to me, to be with me, spend time, share, and grow together spiritually. The flashback stopped here, and for a brief moment I felt just a calm sadness.

In the distance I heard the running water's softer flow as it slowly filled the large bathtub. I opened my eyes slightly to check the level—it was only half full—I still had a few minutes. I closed my eyes again, trying to relax.

I was immediately catapulted back into my past, and saw the very moment that changed my life forever. Kneeling at my altar, where images of Jesus and other ascended masters, framed and in small statues, seemed to look straight at me, I cried out to God. I felt such soul pain and disappointment about my marriage, that I offered it back to God, and begged Him to release me from my vows, pleading as if I had a right to renege on such a sacred contract.

Next I began a dialogue in my head about what I expected from my husband, my life partner. I even compared him to my father who, I thought, was the most wonderful soul partner to my mother. In love forever, they lived for each other more than for anything else. *This is what I wanted too!* Mustering all of my passion and power, I called out to God: *I deserve no less, and therefore I, Angelika, call to me my true soul mate, one who understands the delicate fabric of my soul and emotions!* I practically demanded it from the Universe.

### Soul Mate: The Person Who's Love Motivates You to Find Your Soul

Only months later, my knight in shining armor arrived with all the attributes I desired. My soul recognized them the moment he lay on my Reiki table. My whole body vibrated, as did his; we knew instantly. My chakras, from my heart up to above the top of my head, took me for a magic ride. A feeling of limitless freedom tingled through my body. I was flying! *This must be a sign of spiritual approval,* I thought.

Emmanuel reminded me so much of my beloved father who left the earth plane so unexpectedly, and for me, in the cruelest way. My father loved the Bahamas. He loved nature, but mostly he loved the ocean. Visiting with my family at Christmas, my parents surprised me with a promise to "semi-retire" and spend autumn to spring with us on our island in the sun. This was the greatest gift, because I'd suffered so from the separation between the Bahamas and Europe.

But he never made it back home. He died from an aneurism in a hospital in Florida shortly after arriving to spend a few months with me. Angry with God for a long time, only through my growing spirituality did I slowly begin to understand that pain often triggers growth. Eventually my mother shared with me that she, too, found a new and bigger purpose in life when she began to paint again. This was her gift and she loved it, but had little time and inspiration for it while living so intimately with her husband, her soul mate.

But I still saw my father as the perfect man with all the attributes my heart so desired. I missed him terribly, and for a very long time...But now, I found him again, sort of, in a much younger man—much younger even than me. I was so sure that Emmanuel's arrival was no coincidence, I had to follow him. After all, wasn't he God's gift to me? Had he not been sent for the development of my soul, my bliss, my happiness forever?

I tried to make the separation as easy as possible for my husband and my children. Only our youngest would still be with me for a short while before boarding school in a different country would keep her away for most of the year. Benno and I had decided to give our children the best education, even before they were born. The Bahamas would not be sufficient to bring up well-rounded cosmopolitan young adults. They left at age twelve for a much colder country. I am happy to say that it was a good decision for the children...my internal movie stops again.

I open my eyes. My bath is ready. Slowly I slip into the scented warm water and close my eyes again to fully enjoy the sensation of my body's weightlessness fully emerged. Time seems to stand still as my body starts to relax. It's all good, I'm back with Benno. I never really stopped loving him anyway.

Oh, how I've grown in the ten years since I left. After all I put him through I'm more than grateful he took me back. Ten years is a very long time to see me in the arms of another. How he must have suffered!

But I suffered too, and arrows of pain again dart through my heart. I'd left Emmanuel in part because he was such a dreamer. I'd lost everything with him, but I'd grown so much spiritually. I now saw both the illusion and the reality, and understood that sometimes we choose to bring someone into our lives to experience growth. With Emmanuel, I wasn't controlled, the world was open, we traveled a lot, and I had the freedom to explore my spirituality.

I can't stop the streams of tears and uncontrollable sobbing. How can the pain of loss be so intense that it burns like fire through my body? I can't live with this conflict...I won't live with this!

So, for the second time in my life I cried out to God to remove this pain and heal this wound in my heart, or let me come home...and I meant it with the powerful intent and stubbornness for which I am known in my family. I was ready to leave my body right there in the bathtub.

Then something extraordinary happened—through my tears and intense anguish, I saw the rose candle's flame triple in size and intensity with a swooshing noise, only to return quickly again to a silent calm flicker. All feeling in my body stopped. No pain, no agony, no sadness. Nothing. I stopped breathing in anticipation of what would happen next. But there was only silence.

Suddenly I felt a stirring within my heart and soul, and a freshness and reverence filled my bathroom. I'm not sure whether I actually heard a voice, or had an out-of-body experience, but something within me whispered: *You are my beloved, I have sent you parts of your soul that you still have not recognized as whole. Everything you looked for in another you already have within yourself. You are perfect. Recognize it within you, and you will not feel any lack...*

I'll never forget the certainty and calmness I experienced at that moment. It took the pain right out of me, and I wanted to stay in that moment forever. When Benno knocked gently on the bathroom door, and asked if everything was alright, I answered with certainty: *"Yes, my love, everything is just perfect."*

Our life started anew with a deeper understanding for each other. Both of us grew through pain and forgiveness. The moment I recognized my perfect self, I could also recognize the perfection in him. Now I don't expect to receive what I *think* I should, rather I create my own joy and share my truth without fear of rejection or ridicule. Today we are stronger as a unit, as well as alone.

As soon as I stopped looking for approval, or completion, through another, a *soul mate*, I became free to step into my true power. My soul is now free to experience its own magnificence. When I recognized the beloved within, my loneliness vanished. Only then could I call to myself my true soul mate, the one who can assist me in the advancement and understanding of my true nature and purpose: *the soul mate within...*

**ABOUT THE AUTHOR:** Angelika is a native German who moved to the Bahamas in 1979, and still lives in Freeport, Bahamas with her husband. She is a mother of 5 grown children and 8 grand children. There, her spiritual journey began through personal inquiry, and a deep connection with Nature. She is a Naturopath, Hypnotherapist, Reiki Master Teacher, Yoga and Meditation Teacher, Writer, Speaker, and Life-Transformation Coach. Angelika is an Expert in Evolutionary Spiritual Transformation. She is the Author of the book: "Your Intelligent Cell" Intrinsic Relationship with your Body, and co-authored two other books. "WIN" Winning Strategies from Today's Leading Entrepreneurs, and "The Thought that changed my Life".

Angelika Christie ND
info@angelikachristie.com
www.angelikachristie.com
Freeport, Grand Bahama Island
242-352-1010

# The Love of My Life

## Bice Del Galdo

I arrived home feeling good after delivering a speech at one of my women's groups. I'd successfully conquered my fear of public speaking, and now I could concentrate on the upcoming Christmas holiday. Over the next few days, I began to wrap presents, decorate the house, and prepare our favorite holiday foods.

I usually prepare dinner for Christmas Day, while my daughter handles Christmas Eve. My husband Roger and I returned home from our daughter's house on Christmas Eve and were shocked to find our Christmas tree lying on the floor! In all the years we've put up a Christmas tree, nothing like this had ever happened.

We quickly picked up the tree and looked over what was broken. The damage didn't seem severe, and we reassembled the decorations until the tree looked almost as good as before. "This should be the worst thing that happens to us," I sighed with relief, and we went to bed.

Christmas day was wonderful, but left me exhausted. Normally Roger is a great help, but this time he sat at the table and hardly got up. I noted this mentally but kept silent. Just prior to Thanksgiving he'd gone for a full medical check-up and gotten a clean bill of health.

Two days after Christmas Roger told me he was going to the doctor for his usual B12 shot, and I quickly responded "I'll go with you." I joined him in the examination room, and asked, "Doctor P. how does he look to you?"

Roger's doctor is a man of few words. He started to feel Roger's stomach, poking and pressing around the lower and upper parts. It was clear Roger felt some discomfort in the upper part of his stomach. Doctor P. suggested he go for an MRI. Immediately, I scheduled an appointment for the following day—I wanted to get to the bottom of this as soon as possible.

Worried, my mind bombarded me with thoughts. *Oh my God what could this be—not the C word? Stay positive and don't look alarmed!* After all, just a month ago Roger's lab reports were normal. Something serious doesn't just develop overnight, does it? I pretended to be as normal as possible for Roger, but fear and anguish overtook over my body to the point where I almost felt the need to step outside of it. Roger appeared calm, but I hardly slept that night. Looking back, I wonder if he'd been pretending, like me.

Outwardly quiet, on our way to Roger's MRI, my internal chatter seemed non-stop. The procedure didn't take long, and although we were told  Doctor P. would have the results within twenty-four hours, we got the call less than eight hours later. Old enough to know that no news is good news, sure enough, the MRI showed a shadow in the pancreas, and Roger needed a CAT scan to determine exactly what that meant.

My worst fears confirmed, I sank to my knees upon hearing the words of the doctor through the telephone: Roger had a pancreatic tumor. I began to panic, still holding the phone, but something inside of me knew better. I knew I had to be strong—that Roger would count on me to help him get through this. I knew I'd do anything—go to any lengths—to help him beat this.

### You and I Against the World...

The man I've loved for twenty-seven years—the moment we met I knew Roger was the man for me!—still makes my heart sing and evokes the same emotional joy as when we were introduced on that blind date in June 1984. So taken was I by his gentle demeanor, assured ways, and good looks, the more I got to know him the more I liked him, and felt excited to just be in his company. My emotions surprised me as I fell deeply in love with this man...

We had such synergy—whatever we did, we always had a good time together. Supportive and comfortable, we soon knew we wanted to spend the rest of our lives together. How could it be that we were together for twenty-five years and still I'd feel emotional excitement whenever I saw his face?

Our relationship was so rare, how do two people live together for twenty-five years and never have an argument? We had differences of opinion, of course—Roger was the more traditional one, conventional in his approach, while I'm more of a risk taker, open to explore alternatives. Even so, he respected my point of view and, on occasion, agreed to disagree. He's my best friend, lover, biggest fan, and confidante. Able to read me like no one else, able to anticipate what I want before I'd even ask, he knew my deepest desires and dreams, understood my tiniest nuances, related to my fears, and stood solidly behind me to support me and cheer me on.

Glued to the internet, I feverishly researched pancreatic cancer. The statistics for survival beyond eighteen months were pessimistically depressing. I kept this information to myself, and hoped for a miracle as we began the endless trips to doctors and hospitals.

Roger's situation was considered fortunate because the tumor hadn't spread to other organs and could be removed. Only one out of every five diagnoses of pancreatic cancer is suitable for surgery. The procedure—one of the most dangerous—is referred to as "whipple."

Roger's surgery proved successful, and after seven days he came home from the hospital. A month later he felt strong enough to travel to our Florida home for three weeks before starting chemotherapy. He looked happy, and seemed the same Roger I so deeply loved. I almost forgot how sick he'd been just a month ago.

Back to New Jersey for the first cycle of chemo, by the second week of treatment his hair started falling out and his mouth filled with sores. Barely able to eat anything by the third week, Roger decided to stop the chemo. He informed the oncologist of his decision and asked "what's the probability of the cancer coming back?"

"I can't guarantee that it won't come back even if you continue with the chemo, but I *can* guarantee it will come back if you stop," the doctor replied. His words pierced my heart like a sharp knife—I can't imagine what they must have felt like to Roger. He looked at me.

"It's your life, only you can decide," I said lovingly. He paused, then asked "are there any other options?"

"Not really, but I can reduce the dosage to see if you do not have such an adverse reaction," responded the oncologist. Roger paused. "Okay, let's try it," he agreed.

His reaction wasn't as severe as before, but Roger's body began to look frail. He dropped weight and had zero energy. I'd look at him—he was slowly vanishing right in front of my eyes!—and hold back my tears. "You're almost finished, you'll get better once the chemo is completed," I kept saying.

Finally, the last chemo infusion! His tumor markers came back very low, and the overall lab results looked good. We happily booked our flights to Florida for three weeks—*let's get some sun, feel stronger, and prepare for the next phase of radiation,* I thought. I had hope again that miracles *do* happen, and nobody deserved a miracle more than Roger.

In Florida no more than ten days, Roger began to feel some pain. As it worsened, we flew home and went directly to his oncologist, who referred us to a gastroenterologist. "I'm sorry, but your husband's stomach is totally blocked by a mass—whatever he's eating or drinking isn't being absorbed by the body, and sits above the stomach, similar to when a sink is clogged," this doctor informed me.

"What are our options?" I asked, frightened.

"I can make a hole in his stomach and insert a peg to drain all the stuff sitting in there and give him some relief," he explained. Realizing my confusion, he added "your husband can no longer eat food."

Still confused, I nevertheless understood the severity of it. I began to feel numb, like I was standing outside my body. Calm outside, inwardly my mind raced fearfully. By now, Roger was not only dealing with severe pain from the cancer and diabetes, he couldn't eat or drink!

I lost all hope as he became more and more frail. After four days at the hospital, they released him to come home. I learned how to administer all his medications, and became his nurse night and day.

### The Beginning of the End

From that moment on, every night before falling asleep, I'd pray to God to give me strength to get through the day and be able to comfort Roger. To watch this wonderful man, the love of my life, slowly disintegrate right in front of my eyes filled me with heavy grief and sadness.

"We are in this world, but not of this world" is a quote that kept repeating itself over and over again in my mind. Somehow I found comfort in it. How can I prepare for what I saw was inevitable? *Be present, focus on the moment,* my inner self whispered. What happened to the woman who, when faced with adverse circumstances, would think *let's see—what can I learn from this?*

I was angry, but that didn't make me feel better. Thinking about the wonderful relationship we shared, our twenty-seven year-long love affair, made me feel better. How lucky to have had such an experience! Some people go their whole lives and never experience such a supportive and loving relationship. I simply had to be thankful.

He was in so much pain my heart was breaking. I don't know what's worse, watching him suffer or letting go the love of my life. He gently squeezed my hand and whispered "I love you." Those turned out to be his last words to me as, one day later, Roger peacefully took his last breath at home surrounded by loving family.

Although he's gone, Roger is still the light of my life and the comfort of my soul. I'm starting a new journey in search of my authentic self, listening to the woman within who's lived through many lives.

How can lessons learned, and happy memories, help me now as I embark into widowhood? I'm emotionally fragile, but I can feel Roger cheering me on to be all I can be while I'm still in "this world."

All I need to do now is see myself through his eyes—see the strength and confidence he saw in me, and allow his love and my intuition to guide me. Roger might not be with me physically, but he is with me every step of the way and continues to be the wind under my wings and the love of my life!

**ABOUT THE AUTHOR:** Life coach, consultant, author, and speaker, Bice *(a.k.a. "B.J.")* helps individuals and groups to identify what they want out of life, and teaches them how to change self-limiting beliefs in order to gain deep personal satisfaction and fulfillment. Bice's career in human development spans more than twenty-five years in various leadership positions responsible for global human resources programs and initiatives in the United States, India, and Europe. A certified Senior Human Resource Professional (SPHR) and a certified Health Coach, Bice holds a B.S. and M.A. in counseling from Montclair State University, and an M.B.A. from Fairleigh Dickinson University.

Bice Del Galdo
Joy2Life Organization
www.joy2life.org
bice@joy2life.org
973-503-0351

# Knocked Into Consciousness

## Elayna Fernandez

The carpet felt fuzzy and warm, and I derived strange comfort from it as I lay there, unable to move, unwilling to try. I licked my lips and tasted my own blood, then closed my eyes. I disconnected from reality as I finally gave up my unsuccessful attempts to stop replaying his hurtful voice inside my head.

"You're worthless!" Adam said with disgust as he kicked me with all his strength and mercilessly walked away. Before he'd pushed me fiercely to the ground, he'd hurled abuse at me by criticizing virtually every part of my body, tearing me apart with brutal words. I felt unclean as filthy rags. I felt ugly, undeserving.

He's probably right, I thought. I felt worthless not because I wasn't worth anything, but because I'd lost all sense of worth. "Destitute of worth, having no value, virtue, excellence, dignity, or the like," is how Webster's dictionary defined me.

As I thought about Eleanor Roosevelt's quote "no one can make you feel inferior without your consent," I realized I had given him consent—numerous times. After years in this unhealthy, painful dynamic, dysfunctional submission had become my norm. I'd justify his behavior as related to his childhood issues or his stressful days at work. I told myself I could fix this, and that my love would inspire him to be better. Yet the more he became a king, the more I deteriorated into a slave.

He interrupted my thoughts by shaking my body with his foot. I sobbed with pain and opened my eyes as he remorselessly called me a "faker." Although thick black curtains in his apartment darkened the room, no amount of light, self-help books, or three-day seminars could give me more clarity than this moment. I'd literally been "knocked conscious." This was my first moment of awakening.

## *"To Be Awake Is To Be Alive" - Henry David Thoreau*

This wake-up call was just the start of a long, long journey; a quest, if you will. Someone once said that the quality of your questions determines the quality of your life. And so I asked myself *what had kept me stuck in a miserable, unfulfilled, abusive relationship?*

Very early in our relationship I'd recognized some red flags. Adam was controlling, condescending, verbally abusive, and began to try to isolate me. It started out quite subtly—he'd tell me that he wanted me just to be with him and not go out with my friends. He'd manipulate me by saying "that friend, she doesn't like you," so he could keep me in his sights. He'd tell me he needed me to take care of him, and made me feel guilty if I did anything that kept me away from him.

In the beginning it centered on verbal negativity. He was incredibly, obsessively attracted to me, but his verbal abuse was ongoing and became confusing. He'd brag about how beautiful I was, want to touch me, sleep with me, and say he loved everything about me. Then he'd say horrible things. Now I realize it was his attempt to relegate me to a level where I didn't like myself.

When I asked myself why I stayed, and why I'd put up with his behavior and allowed it to eventually deteriorate into physical abuse, I saw the truth. In my naiveté, I thought that if he recognized my love for him it would actually inspire him to be a better person. It didn't help that he told me I was the only person he'd ever loved, said I taught him what love was and to be a man, and that I did make him a better person. When he promised me over and over again that he'd change, I believed him and gave him another chance. Now I see how Adam took advantage of that part of me that wanted to be a mother figure for him.

Ironically, it was also my strong belief in my faith that allowed me to stay so long. Taught to be unconditionally loving, I assumed self-sacrifice was a positive attribute. What I didn't realize at the time was that I'd missed the real meaning of the second part of the equation about unconditional love—that I can be godly, loving, giving, self-sacrificing, and unconditional, but also deserve to receive these things as well; to be with someone who loves me back.

The physical abuse started in little manifestations a few months before I was knocked into consciousness. At first he'd give me a little push here or there, a light slap in the face, and he'd apologize and say it had gotten out of hand and that he felt badly about it.

And I'd justify it, thinking he'd just had a bad day.

But that day woke me up. At that point his apologies didn't matter anymore. *If you don't feel that way, then you don't talk to me that way,* I silently reasoned. None of the novels I'd read, the romantic movies I'd watched, or the real-life love stories that touched my soul ever included emotional, physical, or sexual abuse. The loving relationship I desired involved commitment, affection, appreciation, support, freedom of expression, and mutual care.

I did not enjoy the pain, the heartache, or the humiliation; however, I'm thankful for the man who knocked me into consciousness. Ultimately, he was instrumental in my ability to break the cycle. He reinforced for me the importance of my faith, making intentional choices, and clarified for me that I am as entitled to receive as I am to provide unconditional love.

### "What the Daughter Does, the Mother Did" - Jewish Proverb

The moment I decided to take responsibility for my life, stop giving away my power, set healthy boundaries, and design the relationship I'd always longed for, was one of those defining moments of my life. It changed the way I live, the way I love, the way I show up, and the way I parent.

I had two young daughters, and even though my daughters were away on vacation when his real abuse took place, I realized they would model my behavior eventually. It took a little while, but just knowing that God had a better plan for me made all the difference. When it dawned on me that I am a daughter of God and that nobody should treat me that way, I thought *if God is my father, what would he say?*

Suddenly it hit me—I was a lesson for my daughters! Armed with this knowledge, I solidified my determination to find within those deeply buried golden nuggets of personal wisdom, excavate them, and use them to become the best role model for my daughters.

This truth fueled me into heavy research and a deep commitment to learn everything about "relationship bliss." I became an avid fan of lists—lists with hundreds of answers to quality questions around the intelligent design of the relationship I longed to attract. Regardless of how a relationship starts, develops, or ends, I began to recognize that everyone is "here" to teach me something. Every relationship I experience is just that, an experience, and each experience equips me with a mirror that reflects my weaknesses, strengths, core values, and deepest desires. There is no such thing as failure!

A single parent, I had decided to endeavor in the creation of a network that would connect mothers worldwide. I wanted to share the story of how I used the principles of vision, faith, preparation, diligence, and discipline, to turn my life around.

I began to speak and write about parenting, and noticed that my words inspired and impacted the lives of many. Single moms resonated to my message about how letting go of an unfulfilling past can launch us into a future about which we've always dreamed. Because so many single moms may have a failed marriage or relationship it's even more important for us to model a healthy relationship to our children. In order to have, do, or be what we desire, we must relinquish that which we're holding on to now and live deliberately and with purpose. Only in this way can we achieve our most cherished goals.

### Positive Role Model

I knew how much I loved being an instrument of change in connection with helping others learn to love themselves. Thus was born my non-profit organization, The Positive Mom Foundation. My foundation teaches parents how to impart values and moral character to their kids. It does so by reinforcing to others that partners are a gift to one another; different, but complementary in their goal to create an "intentional partnership." When a couple works together as a team towards a common purpose, it's a win-win for both them and their families.

I pass the same messages on to my daughters, as I explain to them the importance of deciding the desired attributes of their ideal partner beforehand, and share with them the negative consequences of my involvement with a partner who didn't understand, support, or respect my core values and beliefs. They have seen me vulnerable, they have seen me cry.

Deepak Chopra was recently asked what steps he believes individuals can take to shift human consciousness. "No social transformation happens in the absence of personal transformation," he replied. "Therefore, without worrying about other people, the questions to ask yourself are these: can I be the change I want to see in the world? What kind of world do I want to live in and how can I become an agent in that world for myself?"

When we transform our lives and operate from a higher level of awareness, we become a blessing to the people who mean the most to us. We are also more energized when carrying out the activities that fulfill one or more of our own needs. We put the mask on first and then assist others who may need help.

I've now learned that the art of receiving is a beautiful one. Previously I'd believed it was almost wrong to be treated like a queen, I'd think oh my gosh, I'm being selfish! But now I see the beauty of how it makes others truly happy to see me happy. It's genuine and not manipulative anymore.

I'm confident that, even at eight and nine years old, my daughters will each choose a good man. My consciousness about partnership affects them, even at this age. Right now I engage in a relationship with a man who is giving and loving—he gives and I give, he receives and I receive—it's the healthiest way for me to be who I am, and to offer all the love that being knocked into consciousness now allows me both to share and to receive.

**ABOUT THE AUTHOR:** Elayna Fernandez is a proud mom, Author, Speaker and founder of *The Positive Mom Foundation*, a non-profit organization with the purpose of strengthening families and communities worldwide through principles of Character Education. An award-winning Digital Branding and Marketing Trainer and Strategist, Elayna is considered one of the leading international online visibility experts, trusted by some of the World's most successful leaders. Elayna is best known for creating powerful brands and marketing strategies to facilitate business growth. Elayna's philosophy is "Be Positive and You'll be Powerful."

Elayna Fernandez
The Positive Mom Foundation
www.ElaynaFernandez.com
Elayna@PositiveMom.org
239-465-7868

# My Moon/Pluto Baby

## Sheri Horn Hasan

"Put your hands down and let me pass!" I told my thirteen year-old son Zacharia, who stood glaring at me as—arms outstretched from wall to wall—he blocked my way in our hallway.

"I want *all* of my money!" he persisted.

"No! You can't have it," I replied, trying to remain calm.

"Yes I can! It's *my* money and I want it *now!*"

"I told you that I'd give you what you need when you need it," I said, becoming agitated. "You don't need to have it all now."

Zach was now my full height—five foot two inches, and as he leaned forward in an intimidating fashion, arms still outstretched, he repeated, "I want my money now, *or else!*"

That was it. I lost it. "You need to put down your arms and get out of my face!" I told him. "I don't know what's gotten into you—if you got up on the wrong side of the bed today or something—but you're not getting *all* of your money!"

We were now eyeball to eyeball and I was shaking with anger. As we stood glaring at each other, I hoped he'd back down so we could quickly de-escalate this whole ugly incident.

"Give me my money!"

There was a split second during which we both hesitated. He stood there in his menacing position, defiant. Suddenly the dam broke. "Get out of my house!" I screamed. "Get out and don't come back—I don't want you in this house! Don't you threaten me! You can live somewhere else if you're going to act like that! *Get out!*" With that he turned and ran out of the house, slamming the door behind him.

The money in question was birthday money he'd received two months before, and which I'd doled out to him little by little. In truth, I might have honored his request for the remainder of the money—somewhere around one hundred dollars—but his combative stance was one I couldn't abide.

Shaken, I was glad he left and in truth at that moment didn't care where he went. I was tired of his defiance, rebelliousness, tired of him...I knew his father would be happy to take him in. Divorced for nearly five years, his father always said he wanted more time with Zach, but he was a workaholic, and often ended up not being home. *Well, now that will have to change, I suppose,* I thought.

### Wanted: Dictator of a Small Country

Zach's due date had been May 6, and I'd fully expected a sweet, calm, serene Taurus baby, kind of like, well—*me*....Far from being born a snuggly Taurus baby who'd absolutely want to cause little fuss, arrive on schedule, and immediately sleep through the night and nap regularly, Zach is in fact an Aries child. He thrust himself upon us three weeks to the day early from his estimated due-date, and it was clear he'd *chosen* to be born under the archetypal sign of the ram: the warrior, the athlete, the competitor, the *winner*. It surprises me to this day how differently he turned out to be from what I'd originally planned.

As an infant, he'd never lie down in his stroller, always had to see what was going on and, still pre-verbal, would scream, cry, and throw tantrums well before he hit the stereotypical "terrible two's" era. At only fourteen months, alert and ever-conscious, he'd refuse to sleep until he was an exhausted screaming mess.

He seemed to have the uncanny ability to know the difference between brands of orange juice, distinguish one bottle nipple from another, and understand that he'd been given the "fake" keys to play with instead of the real ones. He'd have none of that, and vociferously make his displeasure known to anyone and everyone within his vicinity! Exasperated, I'd finally separate the rest of the keychain from my car key, and hand it to him. Then, and only then, would he contentedly play with it and spare mommy one of his screaming and crying fits—complete with attempts to eject himself from his car seat—for the entire forty-five minute trip to grandma's.

I was *never* awake before him, no matter how late he'd gone to sleep the night before, and always woke to him screaming from his bedroom down the hall. Other miraculously well-rested mothers would tell me their toddlers went to bed, woke up, and napped like clockwork, and I'd think *wow, why isn't that my kid?*

I realized how different he was from other toddlers when I'd speak to various moms at the park, at mommy and me classes,

Gymboree, you name it. They'd give me advice, tell me to try this or that, and always I'd say "thanks, been there, done that, didn't work..." I felt like an outsider, a foreigner in the world of mommies. *Why was my child so different* I wondered. *Why do the other babies and kids seem so compliant, but Zach so difficult?*

Impatient, persistent, energetic, and willful—in short, exhausting—Zach ran *this* mother ragged. I used to joke that if there was ever an advertisement for a position as the "dictator of a small island nation" Zach would be virtually tailor-made for the job!

### One Size Does Not Fit All!

Constantly exhausted, I sought help and advice from a social worker who led me to several eye-opening books. Simultaneously, I took up the study of astrology, something in which I'd been interested since I was fourteen, but too busy to ever really pursue.

I read *How to Raise Your Spirited Child*: *A Guide for Parents Whose Child is More Intense, Sensitive, Perceptive, Persistent, Energetic,* by Mary Sheedy Kurcinka, and it was a life-saver! In its pages I found Zach—intense, energetic, and most of all, persistent. It always amazed me how many times I'd say "no" to him, only to hear him continue to ask again and again for whatever it was that he wanted.

Meanwhile, as I began to study astrology, I dug deeply into Zach's natal chart looking for answers. What I discovered surprised me, explained a lot, and validated for me so much of what I'd thought initially was abnormal behavior. I began to see it was just who he was, and that as a child, he possessed many seemingly unpleasant traits that would actually serve him well as an adult.

I knew his was an Aries Sun. An Aries—ruled by the planet Mars—acts first and learns from the reactions of the world around them. They place huge emphasis on their ability to freely express their personal will. In astrology, the Sun represents one's ego identity. In Zach's case, his Aries Sun/ego takes on the flavor of Scorpio because it resides in Scorpio's natural house in his chart.

Turns out Zach is also a "Moon/Pluto" individual. The Moon represents one's emotions—what one needs to feel secure in this world—and it was easy to see early on that Zach's emotional nature was that of a Scorpio: intense, volatile, passionate, and control-oriented. Since the Moon was in the sign of Scorpio as it approached Scorpio's ruler Pluto in the sky at the time of his birth, the emphasis on his natural emotional Scorpio nature is further compounded.

Let's put it this way: the combination of these energies—Mars/Aries and Pluto/Scorpio (Zach's Sun and Moon/ego and emotions)—when negatively manifested translate into a power-hungry, competitive, manipulator who brooks *no* interference and who wants to rule the world! An Aries-Scorpio on steroids!

In short, Aries individuals learn by being free and unrestrained, and Scorpios are not happy unless they can probe deeply into life and focus their laser-like attention on getting to the bottom of whatever interests them. Scorpio individuals want to know—*really know*—what makes people and things tick; the deeper essence of the meaning of life.

An astrological chart analysis shows the energies inherent in a person at birth. A snapshot of where all the planets were in the sky at the precise moment and location of one's birth, it's like a blueprint for the soul. What's fascinating about astrology is that an individual can consciously *choose* how he or she wants to manifest these "birth" energies.

So, I learned that Zach could *choose* to be a secretive, competitive, power-seeking, dictator, or that I could guild him to learn to manifest the high side of these same energies. This would allow him to express himself both emotionally and physically in a powerfully competitive, potentially positive transformative way.

By the time Zach was a little older, I began to see how his intensity translated into useful, productive—even *artistic* endeavors, as he became intensely interested in performing magic tricks, and took up the Japanese-based art of origami, or folding paper into intricate shapes representing animals, flowers, etc. At nine years old, he'd craft intricate figures out of paper that would amaze me and other adults. He'd spend hours perfecting a sleight of hand magic trick. I encouraged him in these and other endeavors, and recognized them as positive uses of his innate energies, even though he sometimes drove me crazy!

I watched as he took up sports and recognized his *need* to be physically free. As he progressed through school, it became clear that his way of looking at things was different from his friends. He often provided that alternative viewpoint and had the guts to express it. In short, I became proud of his persistence to get to the bottom of things, and recognized that once he was free to move, he was less liable to act frustrated, impatient, and controlling.

*Epilogue*

Zach returned home that summer after spending a full month with his father, instead of going back and forth between us weekly, as usual. It was a well-needed break for us both. We'd gone to the therapist and Zach now understood that his behavior had been threatening. He knew I feared that one day he'd be bigger than me and if he didn't control his anger and impatience, I couldn't allow him to live under my roof.

Upon his return, I sat him down, told him I loved him, and that we needed to work together and trust one another. I told him that as long as he communicated calmly with me I'd do everything in my power to support his desires. He apologized and told me he loved me.

Zach has brought many gifts into my life, among them the awareness that we are not all the same. Though I've struggled to understand his differences, I now accept him for who he is, appreciate our similarities, and applaud him for his individuality. As I cheer him on into adulthood, he knows I'm his biggest fan. We still have a ways to go, but one thing I know for sure: no matter how old he is, he'll always be my Moon/Pluto baby!


ABOUT THE AUTHOR:

Writing coach, editor, and professional astrologer, Sheri enables her clients to give voice to their vision and inspire their audience through the clarity, conciseness, and beauty of the written word. Editor of Powerful You!'s Women Living Consciously anthology series, Sheri continues her mission to bring authors' individual stories to fruition through her writing/publishing business. Separately, Sheri seeks to inspire, transform, and empower through astrological insight clients who utilize astrology as a tool for greater consciousness and soul growth. She brings astrology and other holistic modalities "down to earth" for the layman through her writing. Have an idea for a book? Contact Sheri today!

Sheri Horn Hasan
www.SheriGetsTheWordOut.com
Sheri@SheriGetsTheWordOut.com
www.KarmicEvolution.com
732-547-0852

# My Own True North
## Caren M. Kolerski

There were no goodbyes, only the sound of the ambulance siren as it rushed my mother to the hospital that hot sunny day in August 1976. She did not recover from the cerebral aneurysm and died early the following morning, just two weeks before my nineteenth birthday.

Forty years old, she and my father had celebrated their twentieth wedding anniversary only six weeks before. In shock, the weeks, months, and years that followed were overshadowed by grief and sadness, as my three younger sisters, widowed father, and I reeled from this tragedy. Often I felt lost, like a little lamb looking for its mother. It was as if my compass had vanished into thin air and took with her the wisdom I needed to guide me from a young woman into adulthood.

I returned to college ten years later as an adult student to complete my bachelor's degree, determined to find my own place in the world. Knowing that I was looking for work, a fellow student connected me to an elderly person in need of a companion. It turned out to be the perfect job—the hours were flexible and accommodated my class schedule, and it proved to be a relaxed environment with good compensation. I found myself continuing to work as a companion to seniors and enjoying it after my graduation with a degree in social work in 1989. Each client became a teacher of life for me in one way or another.

And then there was Ethel. I'd received a referral call for a position as a companion to her—a widow for more than a decade who needed help due to an increasing loss of mobility. From the first moment we met, we "clicked."

What started out as a temporary position evolved into a friendship for well over a decade. *How did I get so lucky?* I wondered at times. But this was not luck; it was destiny. I was convinced that we were two human beings meant to meet by divine assignment! As Ethel often said, "It was meant!" It didn't take long to realize that I'd attracted Ethel into my life for many reasons.

### The Song of the Trees

Ethel leaned toward me as we sat on the porch one breezy summer afternoon, her eyes bright and mischievous. One finger against her lips, she lowered her eyes and said "shhhhhhh...listen carefully. Do you hear it?"

"Hear what, Ethel? What are you talking about? Are you okay?"

"The *song*," she replied. "Listen!"

I strained my ears, trying to make out music in the distance, but heard none. When I looked at her quizzically, she smiled an impish smile, and said brightly "it's the *Song of the Trees!* Listen as the wind rustles through them...if you close your eyes, you'd almost think you were listening to the sound of the waves at the beach..."

And sure enough, she was right. When I closed my eyes, it was as if I was indeed listening to the waves as they hit the shore. It was all part of Ethel's philosophy of life—simple and stress-free living! This resonated strongly with my spirit and quickly became my cup of tea.

We often enjoyed listening to *The Song of the Trees,* accompanied by a cup and some wonderful, stimulating conversation. Nature was always one of my favorite reflecting spots, and I became an avid bird watcher as Ethel introduced me to chickadees, slate-bottom junkos, woodpeckers, blue jays, cardinals, sparrows, mourning doves, and other visitors, along with all their songs, calls, habits, and mating patterns. We read poetry aloud at the kitchen table from some of her favorite texts. As I listened to the words of some of the authors I'd been forced to read in high school literature class, I developed a newfound enthusiasm for the creative expression of thoughts to which I could not then relate.

Critical and perfectionist residue from my mother melted away as Ethel encouraged me to "just try it and see what happens!" There was never any formal instruction to do it like she did; rather enthusiastic urging just to be free to find my own methods of expression. A simple card table set up in the kitchen became our art studio where I experimented with water colors and charcoals. I even learned how to do crossword puzzles, something I once thought unattainable.

I'm convinced that having fun was also part of Ethel's

philosophy. And oh, did we! We took car trips just to get out and feel the sun on our heads through the sunroof! We enjoyed "outings" to the waterfront, grocery stores (even if we did bump into some displays here and there!), mystery rides from which we'd view the pallet of autumn's colors, summer's outdoor markets for fresh fruits and veggies, art galleries in town as well as out of town, *and* what would any successful outing be without *lunch?*

I learned so much about gardening and, through Ethel, became an annual fan of perennials. I never ceased to be amazed at how many butterflies would be attracted to rest on this gentle spirit when we visited the Butterfly Museum. We colored Easter eggs, played Scrabble, and celebrated Ethel's birthday for weeks! All sprinkled with our frequent doses of laughter as we poked fun at each other about daily life and the season of aging.

We chatted about what it might be like to move through menopause; Ethel always said she was too invested in living to notice night sweats or mood swings! Often late in the fall we'd eat supper by candlelight; the moon was our frequent dinner guest.

Conversations about the magnificence of the Universe were more filling than dessert. Filled with awe and wonder at the perfect order of it all and our place in it, working for Ethel *never* felt like work! Always easy to love and care for, Ethel had a very gentle presence and only kind words and unconditional love; she was never critical and always supportive. Always interested in what I was up to when not caring for her, she saw me through several business adventures. Never once did she dissuade me from reaching for my goals for fear of losing me—she always knew I needed to fly! Her unselfish enthusiasm often helped to buoy my growing desire to continue to follow my passion.

### An Angel Dressed as Ethel

It occurred to me that—over nearly thirteen years—Ethel fulfilled many roles that were indeed missing from my life for a very long time. She was a mother filled with the unconditional love, gentleness, and support I needed to heal from a somewhat rocky start.

I experienced with Ethel what I so longed to experience with my own mother—friendship as adult women. Hanging out on the couch enjoying one of our famous picnic suppers and a movie, you'd have never noticed that Ethel was nearly twice my age!

Reminded of one of my last special memories when my mom let me stay up at night with her to watch a movie while having a snack as a young teen, Ethel sometimes also filled the role of an older sister, and other times that of a wise Grandmother.

She became, over the years, the compass I needed to show me that nothing was missing. She mirrored to me everything for which I'd been searching. Gradually, I discovered it had all resided within me the whole time. I came into the world through my mother, and it was an angel dressed as Ethel who helped me become the woman I am today.

This wise woman, now a centenarian, began to make life changes of her own during the past few years. As she spent more time sleeping and began to need more assistance with daily life, our relationship shifted. Most of our lessons complete, one final exam remained: that of *being* and preparing for transition.

A fractured left fibula due to an accident left me unable to return to care for Ethel for nearly three months. In a cast and on crutches, I was challenged on a number of levels. Suddenly, I felt as though I was being asked to let go of someone I'd grown to love deeply— someone from whom I was not yet prepared to separate. Or was it that I wasn't yet convinced that I could successfully navigate my own life, including developing my business as a life coach and retreat leader?

A card given to me recently began to make sense. Prophetically, it read: "Surrender to whatever opportunity presents itself, instead of what you think *should* happen. Disengage from the current and float."

Ethel had always taught me not to push against the river, but rather to flow *with it*. As I witnessed her rhythmic ebb and flow of aging and transitioning, I learned that it was time for me to really let go of the controls and *allow* life to carry me. During this wintering time I not only rested deeply to allow my body to heal, I also studied, meditated, and wrote.

My creativity really began to soar as I developed and planned retreats for women and caregivers. Inspired by Ethel to name my retreat space *Tree Song Sanctuary,* women began to respond with enthusiasm. I saw the opportunity presenting itself as a gift! Indeed, the mantra I declared so many times in the months prior to the injury—"I need a break!"—was exactly what I got. A woman in transition—my dream and passion were alive and well!

I realized now that I had to let go of being with Ethel full-time and allow other caregivers to take my place. I learned to trust that if I were meant to be part of the rest of her journey, then it would happen in the most perfect time. I tried to stay focused much more in the present moment, and to move forward one step at a time—as my crutches taught me!—knowing that I'd be guided and supported every step of the way.

As I move through this transition, often the story of the much-adored extraterrestrial character, E.T., and his friend Elliott, come to mind. Just before E.T. returned "home" both he and Elliott were in a deep resting state, not unlike Ethel and I. Elliott awoke to return to life on earth with his family, while E.T. prepared to meet his family in another dimension. Ethel's spirit will move on when it is the perfect time and I will always be grateful to have received such a gift, and to pay it forward as I live and teach others!

E.T.'s parting words echo in my mind as he touches his finger to Elliott's heart and says "I'll be right here!" These words bring great comfort as I realize I've found my own true north...right where it'd been since I came to Earth...in my heart!

**ABOUT THE AUTHOR:** Caren M Kolerski, Buffalo-Niagara native, an inspired speaker and author, makes a world of difference in people's lives so they can make a difference in their world! As a Retreat Leader, Licensed Heal Your Life ® Coach/Workshop Leader, and Certified Laughter Leader, Caren's rich experience supports her clients' expansion and growth; champions them toward success. Her powerful, intuitive presence holds the space as clients access their Inner Wisdom and return to their True Nature: happy, healthy, peaceful and prosperous! Caren, your Go-To-Coach for every Season of your Life, specializes in women's, caregiver, Seasons of Change® and custom-designed retreats.

Caren M. Kolerski
Pathway to Presence Retreats and Life Coaching Services
www.Pathway2Presence.com
coachcaren@gmail.com
716-983-7714

# Living in the Now
## Lily J. Lee

I watched as my phone dropped onto the floor and shattered—much like my heart—into a million pieces. Overwhelmed and shocked, my mind raced with thoughts I couldn't comprehend. I ran into the bedroom, slammed the door, threw myself onto the floor, and curled into a fetal position. Stricken by grief and despair, I sobbed uncontrollably. I'd always known this day would come, but I never knew it would affect me this way. I heard my dad's death sentence—only three months to live—and every night and day since, I've panicked thinking *"he's the only person who loves me unconditionally—what will I do without him?"*

Angry and inconsolable, this news struck me like a bolt of lightning. No words can describe the incredible grief and emptiness of losing a loved one. It is life-altering. Cancer is such a horrible disease. If I could trade places to transfer the pain associated with this illness, I'd do it in a heartbeat. So much grief and suffering from this illness makes it really difficult to stay positive, but I will—*I have to*—for his sake. Life without my father seems unfathomable. My inspiration, dad has always been a tremendous presence and support my entire life, no matter what.

Every memory I have is of my father's sense of humor, generosity, and thoughtfulness—he's always gone out of his way to do things for people. Wise in so many ways, he emigrated from China, married my mom, and didn't have a lot of opportunities, because of his limited English. Yet he still managed to provide for his family. Education was paramount. My father studied at Pace College in New York, and worked hard because he had a vision. He held many jobs to make ends meet as a waiter, and a captain. Eventually dad was offered a position as a sales trainee by a customer who felt he went beyond his call of duty. He'd often refer to this pivotal moment as a turning point in his life, and an illustration of the importance of a person's character.

Always a part of my life, to him I was the princess, and I could do no wrong—he'd never reprimand me for anything. My brother's older by a year, but my dad spoiled me rotten. It definitely shaped who I am. I'm very confident, especially when it comes to knowing my self-worth, particularly in a relationship. My dad showed me through his unconditional love, support, and nurturing, that I deserved nothing but the best, and he protected me my whole entire life. This allowed me to push the envelope—I knew I could because he was always there to catch me.

Growing up, I knew my mother loved me too. Well-intended, but often emotionally unavailable, she was very blunt and distant, and rarely offered kind words of encouragement or hugs. She found herself thrust into an arranged marriage that she really didn't want, and became bitter and resentful. Looking back now, I can understand why I felt disconnected from her. I've since realized that my mother gave me as much love as she possibly could, based on her situation, and over the years we've established a better relationship.

On the other hand, my father was always enthusiastic and encouraging. He's the sweetest man and I am the luckiest daughter to have him as my dad. If you asked him what is the most important thing in life, he'd say *family*. He practically had to work two jobs initially just to support us, but did it because he wanted to provide us with all the things that he never had. He's the most generous person who often provided his time and attention, even after an exhausting day at work. I recall sitting on his lap for hours and listening to him talk about the funniest stories.

### What Doesn't Kill Me Makes Me Stronger

"Daddy, how do I know who I am?" I remember asking him one sunny afternoon at the age of nine. I was a precocious child, to say the least.

"Lily, honey, it's not the difficult challenges we face everyday—it's how we react to them," he replied wisely. "Life is about choices, and it's our choice to act or not. And how we react during tough times is in direct proportion to who we really are." Well, that was an eye opener for a girl of only nine, so needless to say, I tucked it away in the back of my mind.

As I grew and matured, many times my dad's words of wisdom became the foundation for decisions that led me to who I truly am today. During my life's most adverse challenges, his words proved a great source of strength. It also became a constant reminder that my most difficult challenges represented catalytic moments that propelled me toward self-discovery and transformational growth.

Throughout my life, I experienced other traumatic events—news of a tragic accident, death of a loved one, loss of a job, and failure with a business endeavor after years of committed service. The shocking discovery of an unexpected breakup, combined with the revelation of a cheating partner—these experiences were a significant part of my personal journey and led to conscious intentions of introspection for a deeper meaning of who I am.

When I lost my job after ten years of loyal service at a prestigious law firm, I seized the opportunity to re-invent myself by starting my own business. When faced with the reality of a cheating partner, I proactively secured myself emotionally by seeking counsel to deal with trust issues.

I remained positive and embraced the endless possibilities. Rather than feel self-pity or sadness, I pushed past my feelings of helplessness and sadness and adopted the adage that "what doesn't kill me, makes me stronger." I emerged triumphant as I worked through a lot of my issues, and remembered my father's message about the importance of action versus non-action, and how that shapes the person I am destined to become.

### The Light at the End of the Tunnel

I'd never taken time to consciously think about who I am until after I became a mom. After all, who had time to ponder the meaning of life's existence when spending countless hours caring for everyone else? I was too busy changing diapers! But if I had no clue about who I was, what could I pass onto my children? What would be my legacy? This revelation that I didn't know was frightening.

Carving out extra time for me to work on personal enrichment was difficult to achieve without feeling guilty. However, I realized quickly that if I really wanted to make a difference, my outlook had to change. To figure out my purpose became my mission. But first I needed to uncover my true passion. Through introspective research, and the willingness to be open-minded—even vulnerable—I dug deep. As afraid as I was, I knew that the hardest part was getting started.

During my journey toward finding a purposeful and meaningful life, I realized I had to be brutally honest with myself and get out of my comfort zone. I had to be realistic when assessing situations no matter how painful they were. The painful feelings were simply an indication that I was moving in the right direction toward personal growth. By making this conscious shift, the understanding of my true purpose became clearer.

I became so fascinated with the subject that I went back to school determined to learn more. I worked during the day and attended school at night to earn my masters degree in organizational leadership. I learned so much—I had an insatiable appetite for knowledge—but soon realized there was so much more that I didn't know. The discovery that I lacked so much knowledge about who I am from a deeper sense of consciousness was a humbling experience.

One thing I learned was that it's not about the titles or roles, but the essence deep within that truly matters. For instance, knowing who I am, what I stand for, and my life purpose and vision, are the keys to my self-preservation. My many roles—wife, mother, daughter, sister—and professional titles—entrepreneur, founder, realtor, coach, and humanitarian—do not describe the essence of who I really am, nor define me on a deeper level.

In other words, titles or roles don't make me who I am as a person. It's my internal core values that define who I truly am—another breakthrough! As a dynamic visionary and a resourceful go-getter, with a never quit and unstoppable attitude, what truly matters most to me is to empower others to achieve their greatest potential.

I never gave up hope and, after years of trials and tribulations, my relentless pursuits paid off. My strong beliefs guided me on a path toward deep authentic introspection. It became a gut-wrenching process filled with disappointments, regrets, and mistakes that led me to make the commitment to never quit. I'd remind myself that there was a light at the end of the tunnel.

### Epilogue

Since the news about my father's dramatic condition, I view life differently. He'd taught me years ago that we have choices and that our decisions define us. I choose not to feel sorry, but instead to spend as much quality time with him as possible. I plan to continue finding the best solutions and to act quickly. I've learned first-hand that it's important to focus on the present, be proactive, and remain positive. Adverse moments, such as this, forced me to face the truth, accept and embrace what I cannot change, and focus on what I can do to overcome my challenges.

My father is my greatest mentor, truly an amazingly inspirational, humorous, and generous soul. I am blessed everyday that my dad is with us. He is definitely a fighter. It hasn't been easy, but his courage, strength, and will to survive, amaze and inspire me—even from his hospital bed as at one point he receives oxygen to breathe, and continues to endure constant painful probing. His dignity and his humor intact, he leans closely, smiles gently, and says: "It's better to do something, than not to do anything." Always an optimist, he tries to make everyone happy—even now.

To date, we've celebrated a birthday we weren't sure he'd make, and it's been almost two years since the dire news that he had only three months remaining. My family is fortunate to have the most amazing doctors who've made critical split-second decisions to prolong dad's life. As I pray and remain hopeful, I know he will one day leave us. But his memory and indelible legacy will live on in our hearts forever. I picked him up from the hospital today—thankful that his time with us has been extended indefinitely, and extremely grateful to cherish every moment of living in the now. God bless.

**ABOUT THE AUTHOR:** Lily is a dynamic visionary, resourceful go-getter with a never quit and unstoppable attitude. She is an entrepreneur and the founder & CEO of Optimum Coach, LLC, specializing in business success and leadership coaching. Lily's passion is to teach, motivate, and empower her clients to pursue an authentic and meaningful purpose in alignment with their personal and professional vision. She holds a M.S. degree in Organizational Leadership, and has an extensive background in legal research, real estate, sales, marketing, business development and management. She has also helped entrepreneurs and businesses increase sales and profits through customized strategies towards achieving successful results.

Lily J. Lee
Optimum Coach, LLC
www.optimumcoach.com
info@optimumcoach.com
800-288-7673

# A Mom, a Dad, and a Bobbi
## Bobbi Paine

"Your wife is pregnant!" the doctor had reportedly told my dad. My father reacted with shock, but not quite the kind of shock experienced by many new parents-to-be. No, he wasn't just shocked at learning my mother was pregnant, he was stunned because—only moments before—this very same doctor had attempted to perform a tubal ligation on my mom in order to ensure that she'd never become pregnant again.

My parents, happily married, already had their ideal family and were told they couldn't conceive again. They never worried about birth control, until ten years later, when they found themselves pregnant with my brother.

Eight months after his birth, not wanting to repeat this situation, they took every precaution until mom was able to have her tubes tied. The day arrived and when they wheeled her into the operating room, mom was content knowing that there would be no more little ones added to her everyday life.

That day God smiled, maybe even laughed. Mom didn't. As the doctor started to perform the tubal ligation, she noticed mom was pregnant, stopped what she was doing, stitched mom back up, and went to notify my dad. I can only imagine the surprise in my dad's voice as he reacted to the doctor's news. "*You* have to tell her, *I'm* not!" Right from the beginning I was destined to make an impression! I was chosen.

Many years later I found myself once again making an impression—this time with an energetic blond-haired, brown-eyed little eight year old guy named Geoffrey. The moment we met there was a connection. I'd fallen in love with his handsome, brown-eyed dad Rick, and before long there'd be two gentlemen greeting me at the door when I came to visit—one six-foot three, and the other much shorter.

Early on, Geoffrey and his older sister, Andrea, appreciated the love I had for their dad. They always laughed at his jokes and enjoyed his quirky personality, and I truly felt they were pleasantly surprised that I did too. When I married Rick, I knew my role was to help him when we had the kids, not to take the place of their mother.

It wasn't an arrangement they were born into, but Andrea and Geoffrey chose me to be one of their parents, and I gladly accepted the role. We chose each other. They had a mom who loved them, a dad who was crazy about them, and a Bobbi!

How special were these two kids? I never imagined this choice would have such an impact on my life until one day when our lives changed forever. That little eight year old guy I'd connected with so many years before embarked on the greatest challenge of his life.

### All I Want For Christmas...

In December, one month shy of his seventeenth birthday, Geoffrey was diagnosed with a brain tumor. We strapped ourselves in for the wildest rollercoaster ride ever imagined, and I held my breath.

Geoffrey walked into Children's Hospital straight out of the very normal life of a high school student. An honor student with a wonderful voice, he'd been selected to tour Europe the following summer with a choir from our state. He held aspirations of becoming a pilot, and had already logged hours towards getting his license. He'd learned to drive, held a part time job—and he'd accomplished all this—with a large brain tumor pressing against his brain stem.

The blood drained from each doctor's face, one after another, when they looked at scans of Geoffrey's brain and then saw a walking, talking, functioning sixteen year-old with an appetite for life. It didn't match up. It was one for the medical books.

*This rollercoaster ride shouldn't be too bad,* I thought. Our plan of action was in place: The neurosurgeon told us she'd remove the tumor, and that Geoffrey would be in the intensive care unit for a day or so. Then they'd transfer him to the neurology floor of the hospital, where he'd stay for about a week. Optimistic, Geoffrey made up his own song *All I Want for Christmas is My Tumor Out,* and sang it cheerfully.

The night before his surgery, I chose to stay with him until he fell asleep. Standing at the foot of his hospital bed I drew strength as I remembered the days he'd slick back his hair and apply cologne in anticipation of my visit. I recalled the time he accidently ran into the garage with his car, bravely confessed what had happened, and paid for the repairs. I chuckled softly inside when—just days before, when he'd learned about his brain tumor, he looked at his dad and asked for the money back. I was so proud, and amazed at his strength, his courage. He showed no signs of fear. These memories allowed me to get through that night.

The next morning the family gathered and stayed with Geoffrey until they rolled him into surgery. "What's the square root of two hundred and fifty six?" his father called to him as they wheeled him out the door. "I expect an answer from you when we see you in the recovery room!" he continued as he accompanied Geoffrey's gurney as far as he could go, and then watched through the window of the surgical hallway until he lost sight of his son.

I was confident. They'd told us he should be ok. Sadly, this was not the case. Instead, Geoffrey never regained consciousness. The one night we prepared for him to be in the ICU turned into weeks. Christmas and New Year's came and went. Nothing changed.

My trust and belief in the medical staff flickered like a light bulb ready to burn out. Doctors performed additional surgeries to no avail; Geoffrey was non-responsive. Where's my strength now? I couldn't draw it from his voice, his smile, his laugh; I couldn't gain it from any doctor, nurse, or social worker. I tried to tap into the deepest part of my soul. Some days I was successful, others not.

After months in the dark, a neurologist finally shed some light on what had happened. Geoffrey suffered a brain stem stroke some time after the initial surgery, he reported. Now our son had a one percent chance of ever recovering past a persistent vegetative state, and was discharged to a nursing home. We were encouraged to place him on a "Do Not Resuscitate" and let "nature" take its course.

Immediately we knew this was not an option! No medical staff was going to determine Geoffrey's outcome! They'd proven themselves wrong and lost our trust. Let him heal, albeit in a comatose state, and let him rest...

### The Square Root of Two Hundred and Fifty-Six

Rest he did. Months passed at the nursing home, and one afternoon we decided to drop in to visit Geoffrey just as he'd gotten out of the bath. As the nurse left to get his clothes, we noticed his toes started wiggling. For a moment we just sat there and stared at his feet—we couldn't believe it!

"Geoffrey, can you hear me?" Rick asked quickly, "if you can, wiggle your toes!" As Geoffrey responded positively, he continued to answer his father's questions, including communicating the square root of two hundred and fifty-six! His toe wiggling eventually led him to move his extremities, blink his eyes, communicate with an alphabet board, eat, and live—though in a much different way. But the stroke still confined him to a wheelchair, partially paralyzed his vocal cords, and blurred his vision.

The long process took years, but Geoffrey made more than a conscious effort to live. He pushed through so many barriers that doctors no longer made predictions. He beat the odds. He was alive, he could communicate with us, he once again had hopes and dreams—he even graduated from high school! I was ecstatic, I could breathe!

But the celebration, the hope, the miracle, came with a price. Geoffrey's health was compromised even though he'd made supreme strides. He needed continued surgeries, numerous medications, and to live in a group home, as he required care twenty-four hours a day. Day to day life was a production. His once five-foot-ten frame grew to six-foot-four and he relied on assistance for every run-of-the-mill task we take for granted. Patience became the operative word to describe his life.

A brown cloud lingered over us, though we tried to live a normal life. The phone would ring and my heart would skip a beat every time I saw the familiar number on caller ID. My adrenaline kicked into overdrive, I'd run to grab my shoes, purse, and car keys. In the car, Rick and I would look at each other and ask "what hospital are we going to this time?"

We lost count of how many times Geoffrey was rushed to the hospital. Prepare to say your final goodbyes, we were told on numerous occasions. Yet Geoffrey always rallied. Endearingly, we called him the Energizer Bunny, though each time I could see the spark in his beautiful brown eyes grow a little dimmer, his speech become a bit more labored, and his broken body seem weaker.

Ten years passed. One night we received one of the dreaded phone calls telling us that Geoffrey was being transported to the hospital. My initial thought was "here we go again." I expected it to be like all the other times—doctor's would stabilize Geoffrey and send him on his way. Not this time. Something was very different, very wrong. Upon arrival, we learned that Geoffrey was dead.

At twenty-seven, my little blond-haired, brown eyed guy was gone! In shock, they escorted us down the hallway to see him. I wanted to cry, scream, or sit down in the middle of the hallway and will the whole thing away like a stubborn child. Not until his death did I realize that after all the years of heartache and sadness, I was the one parent who had an option. I could have gotten off the rollercoaster ride at any given time. There was no obligation as with birth. I chose Geoffrey as my son, as he chose me to be one of his parents so many years ago.

### Epilogue

In Geoffrey's life and death I learned to live. Instead of lying on the floor in a fetal position, I chose to pick myself up and give a helping hand to anyone that needed it. I forced myself out of my comfort zone and found a passion for people like I have never known, particularly those with physical challenges. I deeply love and respect my family, and would go on a million rollercoaster rides to be by their sides in times of need. After all, I survived the odds, even when my parents were told that first memorable day I would not be carried to full term. I was chosen.

**ABOUT THE AUTHOR:** More than twenty years of customer service, training, and sales experience makes Bobbi Paine a high-quality trainer and speaker with a vibrant, interactive style who specializes in customer service training and workshops through her company, Miner-Paine Solutions. At a young age, Bobbi's passion for customer service blossomed, and her dream of training the philosophy was born. She's always found tremendous satisfaction in treating everyone with great pride and respect. On many occasions she has lectured on a number of topics, and Bobbi will soon be expanding her speaking engagements to include this wonderful tribute to her son, Geoffrey.

Bobbi Paine
Miner-Paine Solutions
www.minerpainesolutions.com
info@minerpainesolutions.com
719-488-2827

# Journey to Feminine Power
## Laura Rubinstein, CHt

My fiancé walked into our bedroom one evening and sat me down on the side of the bed, took both my hands in his, looked me straight in the eye, and said "Laura, I love you, but I'm just not in love with you, and I'm sorry, so, so, sorry...I don't want to hurt you, but..." His voice trailed off, leaving me in a void...

If that wasn't shocking enough, earlier that very same day my boss called me into his office, said he no longer wanted me as a manager in his department, and offered me a position as a software tester. Horrified to be relegated to such a boring job, I didn't last long, and I soon found myself unemployed.

That night, after my fiancé left, I collapsed into bed in a fit of tears. How could this be happening to me? What had I done to deserve this? Seven and a half years together, and for what? To be told, thank you very much, but I think I'll move along now with absolutely no comprehensible reason?

Alone now, newly single, broken-hearted, and in shock, my resilience amazed me. Looking back, I'm astounded that, despite the depth of my emotional turmoil, I still functioned! I now know that my saving grace was the revelation that I was actually partly to blame for our breakup. Although sad and nursing my wounds, slowly I realized that I'd been a deeply unhappy person who didn't like herself very much. And, without a man to project my dissatisfaction onto and a job to try and fit into, I eventually came to see that these losses had been inevitable because of my *own* limiting beliefs, feelings, and behavior.

In the process of putting my life together again, I made some important decisions. First and foremost, I wanted to uncover how/why I'd created a life of such dissatisfaction, and then learn how to create both a richly rewarding relationship *and* career.

Furthermore, I deeply desired to learn how to create a soul-connected joy-filled relationship with my divine life partner.

This became my mission, and a most amazing journey ensued...but my journey wasn't a simple one. It involved lots of trial and error. Initially, I didn't understand that my optimal learning style is experiential. Fortunately, when I gave myself permission to try various ventures and jobs for a specific period of time, it allowed me to honor myself like never before. I began my transformation simply by going with my authentic tendencies.

Throughout the years I acquired a belief that something must be wrong with me if I felt uncomfortable. I soon learned that feelings are wisdom communications from my soul, and that when I chose to use these emotions against myself or simply "fix" myself, I only became more uncomfortable. I needed to understand the language of my soul and the wisdom being communicated, in order to be better guided by it. Wow was that powerful!

### *"Know Thyself"* - Socrates

I immersed myself in self-exploration and research. Determined to learn how to be happy, I chose to seek counseling, enroll in personal development programs, explore my spirituality, read books, find new girlfriends, seek mentors, write a journal, and begin to "practice date."

Once my long-term relationship ended, I knew that simply finding another man wouldn't make me truly happy. I'd been with a really nice guy who treated me well, but all I'd wanted to do was change *him*. When I was able to acknowledge my role in creating my unhappy relationships a whole new world opened up.

I began to explore how I influenced results in my life. I focused my thoughts and feelings in new directions. First, I recognized the feelings I had in the moment. Whether it was disappointment in myself, sadness, excitement, fear, love, anger, joy, pessimism—you name it—I learned to identify it and be with it. My automatic, unconscious reaction had always been to criticize myself or others. Instead I challenged myself to get very clear on my desired outcomes and to take responsibility for achieving them.

Second, I began to practice how I wanted to feel and interact in relationship. I practiced being grateful, loving, romantic, generous, and graceful with everyone in my life, and praised myself and others. It wasn't easy, but eventually I was able to transform my patterns of avoidance, which I realized only caused unhappiness, and embrace the wonderful parts of me. Over time, I learned to generate joy, and watched my life turn into a magical unfolding of love and heart-connected relationships.

I wanted to "do" relationship differently, and awareness of my actions, beliefs, and feelings, became of paramount importance. I spent time with couples in love because I wanted their loving energy to positively influence my life. When I'd see happy couples, I chose to perceive them as an affirmation of the inevitable: that I, too, could find a deeply rewarding, soul-connected relationship. I knew in my bones if they had it, I'd be having it too!

One day at a networking event, a savvy therapist got up to give her thirty-second elevator speech, and said "I hold gatherings for succulent wild women where we explore feminine power!" Immediately, I wanted to know more, and felt she could help me grow. Eventually she became one of my trusted mentors and facilitated my greater understanding of feminine power and how I could achieve clarity in my future work.

We had many conversations about what feminine power means, and how women are far more powerful then we realize when we live from our feminine essence. She described *feminine* as something completely different than I'd previously believed. I hadn't perceived myself as feminine at all because growing up I didn't like dolls, was very logical, and didn't enjoy wearing frilly things. I realized my knowledge of the feminine had been rather limited.

I came to see there was a whole side of me that I'd unconsciously discounted and that remained unexplored. In the process I awakened a dormant, beautiful part of myself that I hadn't known existed. Soft, nurturing, playful, intuitive, loving, and joy-filled, I had to coax this part of me out. Shy and afraid to emerge, this uniquely feminine part of me, that could adore and interact lovingly with others, had been in a box tucked away in my soul.

I noticed that when I allowed myself to feel and honor the language of my soul, people appeared to help me, and I experienced more positive outcomes. I *allowed* everyone—and myself—to be "ok" just the way they are (or aren't). For example, from a heart-centered, playful, curious state, I remember saying to myself *I wonder how I can go to the Olympics that just started this week?* Two days later, a friend called me up out of the blue, asked if I wanted to go with him, and told me he'd pay for it. We had a great time!

Men started showing up, asking me out, and falling in love with me. I fell in love with a couple of them along the way too. Discerning about who I'd spend time with, if something didn't feel right, I honored that. Often I only had two or three dates with a man. I'm deeply grateful for every one of them; they taught me how to honor myself and them at the same time.

### When Transformation Beckons, Go With It!

I also practiced being more grateful, and expressed my gratitude, either to another person or in my gratitude journal. As a result, my life overflowed with wonderful opportunities. The change in my perspective was key. As a single woman trying to identify and establish a successful career, the power of attraction made everything easier.

Another mentor appeared when I attended a local Chamber of Commerce luncheon and listened to a dynamic speaker's talk on being fearless. Immediately inspired, I asked her if she needed any help. She hired me to book speaking engagements for her, and trained me about the speaking and coaching business. Experienced in management and coaching from the corporate arena, I'd enjoyed helping staff members chart a course for their careers and overcome obstacles in the past. Now, friends began to approach me to ask me to "coach" them.

Next, a teacher whom I very much respected offered me the opportunity to train in hypnotherapy. When I asked her why she thought I should take her course, she said "because you'd be good at it!" As I learned the powerful ways in which hypnosis helps people—pain management, stress reduction, weight loss, overcoming phobias, and more—my soul responded with a "yes" from deep within. I practiced on friends and family over the course of the next year, and received 99.9% positive feedback!

Low and behold I married the two concepts of hypnosis and coaching, and was one of the first people to combine the two modalities back in 1998.

Soon I'd gone from burned out to blossoming, and my coaching career was in full swing. By learning the language of my feelings, I discovered the driving force behind them, and could accept responsibility. Understanding my feelings allowed me to make more aligned decisions.

Today the process continues. When I decided to create full-time income from my new path, I envisioned a great work-from-home coaching career. The very next day I received a phone call from someone who referred me to the perfect coaching position—work-from-home with excellent pay. Perfect!

My career evolved from life coach, to business development coach, to marketing consultant, to social media and marketing consulting. I still maintain a small hypnotherapy practice and remain open to continued evolution, especially as the market changes.

Much better now at attracting quality men, still "the one" with whom I desired to have that soul-connected joy-filled relationship had not yet shown up. I practiced more inner personal work from an open and loving state, and realized I was still afraid. Deeper levels of trust in myself and my life was necessary.

Finally ready—I liked myself a lot, had great friends, didn't *need* a guy in my life, and was happy on my own—I put it out there. "Bring me the man who's for my highest good and I'll do my very best to receive him," I said aloud to the universe. Shortly thereafter I met my now husband. In awe of him and our relationship every day, he adores me and is a conscious co-creator. Neither he nor I are perfect, but we use our imperfections to draw each other closer and to support each other in our own processes.

I now know the heart has greater wisdom than the head. My journey to feminine power took me from my head to my heart and into my true soul, from which I have created a much more fulfilled life.

**ABOUT THE AUTHOR:** Laura Rubinstein is a Certified Hypnotherapist, Author, and Social Media and Relationship Marketing Strategist for women. Coach Laura helps people create a brand, buzz, and profitable and fulfilling relationships. With her 20+ years of marketing experience and focus on relationship building, Laura's creative, innovative, and elegant strategies make her a highly sought after trainer and speaker. She is President of the Social Buzz Club, LLC and author of the *Transform Your Body in the Mental Gym*™ program and the *Feminine Power Cards* which offer practical tools that allow people to make profound shifts in their relationships and businesses.

Laura Rubinstein, CHt
Social Media and Relationship Marketing Strategist
www.TransformToday.com
Coach@TransformToday.com
619-940-6569

# The Road Without Fear
## Nancy Shults

We pulled into the gas station a couple miles from our house on our way back to town, and I watched from the back seat as the store owner came out and asked the girl driving our car to get out. He spoke briefly with her, and immediately she started to cry. Afraid that something bad had happened to her dad, a truck driver, I watched as others got out of our car and upon hearing what he'd said they too, began to cry.

The back door of the car opened, and one of the ladies who'd been with us at the beach spoke to me, as another escorted my brother Bill into the store. "Your dad, mom, and sister were in a car accident this morning," the woman informed me with tears in her eyes. "Your mom and sister are in the hospital and, I'm so sorry, but your daddy isn't with us anymore."

I looked at her, and tried to understand what she was talking about. My dad was always there, he never got sick, and was the one that righted all the wrongs in my world. I sat down on the hot ground, looked up into the clear blue Carolina sky, and wondered how it could be that the sun was still shining.

My dad, a United Methodist Minister of two small country churches about ten miles apart, preached at nine-thirty a.m. at one and traveled to the other to preach there at eleven a.m. The following week they would switch times. That morning, as he drove from one service to the other, somebody ran a stop sign and my dad was killed instantly. We lost everything that day—our home, our car, everything. The outpouring of generosity from our church family, friends, and the community overwhelmed us. They raised thousands of dollars and helped us buy a house and get back on our feet.

The night before I'd left to spend the last weekend of the summer at the beach with our church youth group, I'd argued with my dad about something trivial. "I hate you, I wish you would die," I'd muttered under my breath. By the next morning, I'd forgotten all about our little argument. Fourteen and about to start ninth grade, I was like every other teenage girl.

When my dad dropped off my brother and me and I got into the other car to travel to the beach, he came over to say goodbye. "Have a good time, I love you!" he told me. We hugged and kissed and, as he started to leave, I leaned out the car window and said "I love you daddy, be careful, don't have a wreck and don't break your neck!" We both laughed as he turned and walked down the driveway into the darkness of that early morning.

On our way home from that trip three days later on August 20, 1978, I was excited to be going into the ninth grade because I knew that from that point on everything I did counted and would prepare me for college and my future. As I sat in the back of the station wagon contemplating these things all the way home, I wondered where I'd be next year this time, and five years from now, and ten and fifteen years down the line. What about twenty years from now? I was ready to begin the rest of my life...

### The Freedom of Forgiveness

According to the accident report the estimated speed of both cars was fifty miles per hour. It was a near head on collision. Everybody was thrown from both vehicles. Eyewitnesses told me my dad was found lying in the middle of the road, on his back. It was like someone picked him up and placed him back down. He died instantly of a broken neck.

My sister was eighteen. She'd planned to travel back for her sophomore year of college that day after church. She injured one of her knees, broke an arm, and cut her head open. After surgeries to repair these, and missing one semester of school, she returned to college, graduated with honors, and went on to attend graduate school.

We almost lost my mom. She'd sustained multiple injuries, required several surgeries, and was in a body cast for several months. Her body eventually healed for the most part, but she suffered from bipolar disorder before the accident. I took care of her, committed her to the state hospital over twenty times before getting her into a rest home where she lived a mostly happy life until she died at eighty years old. She often told me that I was her "someone special." I developed the strength to do the things I had to do over the years because I knew my daddy had done them too. She was mine, and it was an honor and privilege to step into my daddy's shoes.

I often think back to that day when I was fourteen. I haven't lived the life I imagined that day on the way home from the beach. As a teenager, I was angry and felt guilty for my silly mutterings about hating my daddy and wishing he would die that last night I had with him. How could my last words spoken to him have come true? I'm sure he knew how much I loved him. I knew that he loved me. We had no unfinished business.

Over the years as I grew up I matured into the understanding that I wasn't significant or powerful enough to speak something like that and make it happen. I also knew that I had to forgive myself, and to choose to forgive others because I refused to be a prisoner to anger and regret.

### The Best Holiday Gift Ever

In December 2011 my best friend and her husband were out Christmas caroling and riding in a car with another couple from their church. They passed through the  intersection where my dad had been killed and the man driving started talking about my dad's wreck thirty-three years before. My friend told him about my dad. It turned out the man was the retired state patrolman who'd been first on the scene of the accident that day.

As they talked, he told my friend that what he remembered most about that day was  how remorseful and heartbroken the seventeen year-old boy who was driving the other car had been when he woke up and realized what had happened. After I got this information, I knew I needed to find this person.

On Christmas day I went to my brother Bill's and told him all of this. He got up, walked into his office, and handed me a copy of the accident report. When I got home that night, I googled and found him. I picked up the phone and called him. "Is this Jerry?" I asked the voice that answered.

"Yes," responded the voice. "Were you in a car accident in nineteen seventy-eight?" I proceeded to ask him. "Yes I was," he replied. I then explained who I was, and told him that—for thirty-three years—I had been thinking of, and praying for, him. I explained that I'd never had any hard feelings toward him personally, and told him I knew he was just as much a victim as everybody else.

He responded by telling me how sorry he was, that he wished I'd called him twenty years earlier, and said this was the best Christmas present ever! We talked for a long time and, much to my surprise, he told me that he'd never been back to the scene of the accident because he had no idea where it was. I offered to go with him if he wanted.

A few days later I met Jerry, got in his truck, and took him back to the scene of the accident. On the way, we passed the church where my dad and mom are buried, and Jerry asked if we could stop. He took a flower from behind the seat and said "I brought this to put at the accident scene, but would it be okay if I leave it at the grave?" As we stood there I couldn't imagine how this man had lived all those years without answers or any closure. We stood there for a while; we both had tears in our eyes.

After a bit we left the cemetery and proceeded to the scene of the accident. I took him the exact way he'd traveled the day it happened. As we came closer and closer I told him that we were approaching the curve. The "stop ahead" sign is now twice as far back from the intersection than it was the day of our accident. He rounded the curve and we were there. We got out and, as we stood at the side of that busy road, he understood why he never remembered the stop sign and how it all happened. If my dad had been a few seconds earlier and if Jerry had been a few seconds later, it never would have happened. But it did and I believe the miracle that day was that nobody else had died.

Jerry broke his C2 vertebra which is referred to as "hangman's break." This is the break of the neck that kills people who are hung—the snap that instantly paralyzes them and cuts off their breathing. After months of healing, Jerry made a full recovery. His passenger, a seventeen year-old junior in high school, sustained head injuries and a severed index finger, cut off at the tip. He spent several weeks in ICU but amazingly also made a complete recovery.

Jerry and I are now in contact regularly. He visits my parents' graves and leaves beautiful flowers that he photographs and sends to me. He rides motorcycles with his wife and has become a great friend. "I have often wondered over the years what happened to the

Briggs Family after 8/20/78," he wrote to me after we'd visited the accident scene. "I always thought through the years that the wreck was on Hwy 27. Every time I saw that sign it gave me cold chills and I remembered it as a bad road. I am so sorry for my actions that day. It was like a bad dream and I had no way of knowing. It was like I was guided. I was on a road I had never been on before. Then I met you, and I went down that road again without fear."

**ABOUT THE AUTHOR:** Nancy Shults is an inspiring, dynamic communicator. Her zealous attitude makes her a great teacher and leader. She inspires hope and gives encouragement as she shares her life lessons with others. At 14 she began caring for her mentally ill mother after the death of her father. She survived by seeing challenges faced as opportunities for growth. Nancy has spent a lifetime dedicated to making a positive difference in the lives of others. Nancy lives in Charlotte NC near her 2 children, enjoying 5 grandchildren. Her heart's desire is to live her life in truth and speak the truth in love.

Nancy Shults
nancyshults@nsmail.com
www.nancyshults.com
704-201-0763

# The Magic of Nina

## Net Stewart

I lay on the massage table as the familiar sense of powerful emotion rose up from within. It was early November, the second day of my Reiki Master training and, as my fellow practitioners channeled universal life-force energy through their hands into my body, the emotion kept building, like a huge unstoppable wave. I began to cry.

Overcome by Reiki's transforming energy, I broke down completely. I sobbed uncontrollably as Marina, an older woman at my head, protectively hovered over me and instinctively placed her hands on my chest. I sensed her motherly love and my emotional pain intensified.

Wracked with deep unanswered need, I felt totally helpless, like an infant. I noticed the presence of my spirit guides next to me and suddenly I understood the experience: I knew with complete certainty what it felt like to be a child dreaded by her mother, an unwanted child—not a love child, but a *hate* child.

Our Reiki Master led me from the table to the floor, where I laid down, utterly lost to this feeling, and hugged the teddy bear she placed in my arms. I wept as I struggled to understand if these emotions were mine or Nina's—the thirteen year-old daughter I had not wanted—at home, deeply depressed, and slowly slipping away.

### The Early Years

Two years into my marriage I knew something was terribly wrong. A stay-at-home mom, I adored my toddler Hannah, but struggled with my husband who was increasingly anxious, angry, and highly critical. He seemed unable to connect with us emotionally. I'd known him only seven months before I married him, maybe not such a wise decision.

Our completely different responses to a miscarriage three years into our marriage made it obvious we were seriously at odds with each other, practically enemies. I became depressed, and he harassed me about getting pregnant again. I slept less and less and told him I wasn't even sure I wanted another child. "You'd better find out!" he demanded, with the ring of an ultimatum.

After six months of therapy I decided I did not want another child. Absolutely devoted to my magical Hannah, then almost three, I came home from my therapy session ready to tell Haroon my decision, when I realized I was pregnant. He rejoiced. I walked around the house crying. I feared this baby's demands would destroy the loving bond I'd established with my first-born.

### Beautiful and Difficult

The moment the nurse handed her to me I was overwhelmed by Nina's beauty. From her father's Pakistani side she'd inherited those hauntingly beautiful eyes, like the famous National Geographic cover of the girl from Afghanistan. I had the immediate sense that I would lose her—a premonition of sorts, though I didn't know it then.

Nina was a difficult baby. Nothing that had worked with Hannah worked for Nina. A lousy nurser, she wouldn't take a bottle either. She didn't want to be cuddled, sung to, rocked, or held. At my family's reunion in New Mexico when she was only six weeks old, my sisters tried to help soothe her, while everyone else looked at me like, "You're the Mom! Can't you fix this kid?" Finally I put her in her car seat in the middle of the dining room table, alone. It worked! I was bewildered by this beautiful child.

In preschool, Nina's teacher told me our town's conservative, college preparatory schools would be a poor match for her—she was bright and creative, but didn't fit in socially. I suggested to Haroon that we find a private school for Nina. Adamantly against it, he said: "We're paying a fortune in property taxes and we moved here for the schools. The problem is not the school, it's Nina!" Intimidated, I dropped it.

As Nina's struggle grew, so did my depression. This went on for years. Sadly, my husband and I were more willing to fight with each other than to advocate for our daughter. He believed the answer to our marital problems was to find the right medication to treat my depression. I tried at least a dozen different pharmaceuticals over ten years. Nothing really helped. Heavily medicated, I became a shell of a person.

Nina muddled through elementary school, but middle school was much harder, socially and academically. In sixth grade she came to us and said, "Something is wrong with me. I have ADHD or something. Please, can we find out what's wrong with me?" We brought her to a neuropsychologist but the test results were inconclusive. The doctor thought he saw early signs of depression, so we started her on antidepressants.

Around this time, my "medicine man"–the doctor who prescribed for me–passed away unexpectedly at the age of fifty-six. Devastated, I suddenly realized my health was my own responsibility. I sought alternatives to traditional medicine and pharmaceuticals. Homeopathy and Reiki helped me begin to feel alive again. As I reconnected to my spirituality, I was on the mend. But Nina was crashing.

Eighth grade was brutal for her–nearly all her friends dropped her. She had only one girlfriend, and they weren't really very close. She struggled with homework and her grades began to fall. Teachers' complaints filled her progress reports. When I met with these same teachers, they reported a Nina withdrawn from her peers. One of them noticed that she hung around her locker after school until the other kids left before she headed for home.

By the time I went away for my Reiki Master training, Nina was home sick often. When she did attend school, she'd go to the nurse's office to sleep. Upon my return, I found she'd pretty much given up. When she described herself as sitting at the bottom of a wet, muddy, dark hole too deep to climb out of, it hit me: "You need a ladder, Neen!" It was time to rescue my Nina. I'd believed all along this school was torture for her. I'd find a way to get Haroon to agree to move her.

### The Whole Truth

It's the end of January, and I'm in my hotel room on the phone with my older sister, Jude. I'd flown from New Jersey to Utah with my precious, fragile daughter the previous day to bring her to a psychiatric hospital for observation, assessment, diagnosis, and treatment. Though terrified for her unknown future, I console myself that Nina is finally safe, and a huge weight lifts from my heart.

"And how was Haroon through all of it?" Jude asks. As I recount the events leading up to our arrival in Utah, something strange happens. I slowly leave my body and it's as if my spirit is floating up in the corner of the room. I watch myself talk to my sister, and as part of me observes, I witness myself deftly and automatically cover for my husband as I put a positive spin on the truth of how hostile and combative he was nearly every step of the way.

I don't tell her the *whole* truth—how we'd screamed at each other, night after night, as I tried desperately to get him to agree to do something for Nina, only to listen to him repeatedly insist that only medication would change her to the point where she'd fit in and function like the other kids, that the school didn't matter. How when I went to her as she brushed her teeth she said to me, "What's the point of me going away to get help if I'm just going to return to this?" I leaned over and whispered in her ear, "I don't know what you will return to, Neens, but I promise you, it will not be this." I fought like a mama grizzly, teeth bared and claws out, to get him on board to finally help her.

And, from up in the corner of the room, I finally recognized how I'd played the victim all along. I realized I sounded like an abused woman, justifying her abusive husband's behavior, minimizing his brutality, highlighting all the ways in which I probably contributed to his frustration and anger. And suddenly, the thought I'd repeated to myself like a mantra, over and over again in the weeks leading up to this trip, became a call to action: *I will get Nina safe, and I will divorce this man.* I was halfway there.

### Peace at Last

Nina has been in treatment for nearly two years now. Diagnosed with Asperger's Syndrome, anxiety and depression, she has grown so much. We all have. Through Nina's diagnosis, we eventually realized that Haroon also has Asperger's. That explained a lot about our difficulties with communication, and why we weren't able to connect emotionally. We are now divorced and, amazingly, we get along better than ever.

I love being alone and treasure this time as I get to know myself and become whole for the first time in my life. My little house on a lake brings tremendous peace and serenity, and when I look back, I now understand Haroon did his best all those years. A loyal husband and father, he worked hard to provide his family with the best money could buy. Without his tremendous success we'd never have been able to afford Nina's high level of care.

My experience on the Reiki table that day was a mystical, life-altering event. I'd tried to bury my feelings about not wanting Nina not only because I was afraid she'd feel badly about herself, but because I feared it meant I was a terrible mother who didn't really love her child. That day I understood that Nina must have known what I'd felt all along; surely a mother cannot carry a child for nine months and dread her arrival, without that child knowing the truth. If she already knew, then I no longer needed to hide.

When I went home, I found my voice and, as I fought with my husband, I came face to face with my overwhelming love for Nina. In the heat of the battle I realized my fears about being a bad mother weren't justified. It wasn't that I hadn't wanted Nina; I was simply terrified I wouldn't have enough love inside me for another child. And, as I fully engaged in the present and became the ladder that Nina so desperately needed, I began to appreciate what a devoted, loving mom I truly am. I began to admire myself.

The magic of Nina, the girl I didn't think I wanted, is that in my courageous fight for her, I ended up fighting my own battle too. I didn't want her to come because I was so sure I would fall short. The truth is, because she came, I learned to soar beyond all limitation. When I finally, actively gave her what she so desperately needed—all the love I have for her—she showed me how to love myself.


**ABOUT THE AUTHOR:** Net Stewart is thrilled to be a contributing author to Women Living Consciously. Net rose from the ashes of lifelong, debilitating depression by feeding the flame of her spiritual connection and learning to trust her own inner wisdom. This led to the end of a soul killing, twenty year marriage. Net found a powerful voice within and negotiated a fair and just divorce settlement for herself. A writer, artist, musician, Reiki Master, mother, and trusted friend, Net is an uplifting and truly inspired being. She seeks to ignite a spark in women to take charge of their lives and live joyously!

Net Stewart
Netska2000@yahoo.com

# Eyes Wide Open
## Sheila Turner

Seven weeks of "normal" life was all we'd had. Seven weeks to laugh, love, nag, fight, stress, and do all the things that every day married couples do. Just seven weeks to take each other for granted and just seven weeks to believe that we were going to last forever. Did I mention that seven weeks is a mere forty-nine days?

The doctors discovered an inoperable tumor in my husband Jeff's brain in 1995, after seven weeks of marriage. Little did we know that on day forty-nine the remaining 5,289 days of our marriage would consist of attempting to live some type of happy, normal existence dominated by cancer, pills, radiation, surgeries, chemotherapies, clinical trials, depression, and resentment.

Jeff's diagnosis came out of nowhere on the eve of his brother's wedding in rural Pennsylvania. We wrapped up a fun rehearsal night with our friends and family, jumped in our car, and started down the dark road back to the hotel.

"Jeff...Jeff, what's wrong? Do you smell something?" I asked when he suddenly leaned forward towards the steering wheel, sniffing the air. No response. He reached for the volume on the radio and turned the music off.

"Jeff, is there something wrong with the car?" No response. He turned to look at me and without warning, his body tightened up and his face contorted. I'd never seen anything like it. I reached for the steering wheel and pulled the emergency brake as he began convulsing violently. I have no idea how I kept us on the road, and how we didn't go into a ditch or on-coming traffic, all I know is that we came to a screeching halt. The convulsions seemed to last forever.

"Jeff! Jeff!" I screamed. His body collapsed and I couldn't hear him breathing. Complete silence replaced the violent convulsions for what seemed an eternity. I didn't know where we were, didn't have a cell phone, and had no clue about the location of the nearest house. Only twenty-two years old, I was on a dark, deserted, unfamiliar road, with no idea if my husband was dead or alive.

I jumped out of the car and ran up the street screaming at the top of my lungs. I just screamed and screamed and screamed "help, please help!" I was shaking, crying, and screaming, hoping that someone would hear me and stop to help.

And that was how we grew up in a matter of minutes. Gone were our carefree, hopeful lives. I held Jeff's hand as he lay in that hospital bed and we tried to digest all that had happened.

"Sheila, your husband has a brain tumor," the doctor said. "Unfortunately it's in a very critical area of the brain, which makes it impossible to remove without causing significant deficits. We're going to refer you to doctors in Philadelphia for further evaluation and treatment."

## Days 51 – 5,289

As the shock wore off and our lives took a major detour, anger and resentment set in. This wasn't fair. This wasn't our plan, our future. Cancer took center stage along with seizures, pills, radiation, and chemotherapy. We had plans, we had goals, we had a life to live—and cancer was in the way!

Forced to make a new "life" with our unwelcome guest, and although we tried not to focus on it too much, this ugly tumor was clearly the reason behind every decision, every goal, every breakdown, every argument, and every plan. Jeff's dream of owning his own gym was replaced with staying in his current job for the medical benefits, and my plan to work for a marketing firm and travel the country was traded for "flexible and local" careers so I could drive him to treatments and take care of him.

So first comes love, then comes marriage, then comes babies...oh wait, scratch that. Then comes the biopsy, the diagnosis, and the once easy, now suddenly impossible decision to start a family. Hard enough to wrap my mind around this diagnosis and what it meant for our future, now we had to think seriously about bringing children into the picture. Pre-diagnosis, we both thought we'd have at least two, maybe three kids. Post-diagnosis, my anxiety level shot through the roof at the mention of getting pregnant.

Jeff wanted to be a dad, and I think he wanted it even more as the days and months turned into years. I, on the other hand, became more and more hesitant. Although a very optimistic person by nature, reality wouldn't let go, and I couldn't shake my doubts.

What if we have kids and Jeff's condition worsens? How can we afford to have kids when we're already struggling? How will we tell our kids that Jeff has cancer? What if he dies? What would I say? How would I get them through that? Can I raise them on my own? What if this is genetic? The optimists of the world will tell you "don't get too far ahead of yourself." But when you're faced with the decision to bring children into what realistically is an unstable environment, I'll bet money that those same optimists would think twice, just as I did.

I finally put my fears aside, took the leap of faith, and in May of 1999, welcomed our son Kyle into the world. He brought much-needed joy to our lives and put the focus on something other than cancer. Kyle was Jeff's legacy, and at the time, the only one to carry on the Turner name. Jeff's purpose in life was restored. He was a dad.

There were many times I would look at Kyle and think *what's going to happen if Jeff dies? If he does, it'll just be the two of us and that's not fair to Kyle.* I knew I put off having another child because I feared not being able to handle it myself. But Kyle deserved to have a sibling, and I realized I was being selfish.

So, three and a half years later, we welcomed Eve to our family. There was no doubt my leap of faith was worth it—Jeff fell instantly in love with his princess, and she completed our family picture...dysfunctional maybe, we nevertheless had a "perfect" family: mom, dad, boy, girl...and oh yeah, that inoperable brain tumor...

On the surface, we lived the "American Dream"—in fact, we did it so well that we became indistinguishable from our friends and other families. People forgot what we were going through, and sometimes didn't even know about Jeff's brain tumor. They'd "vent" to us about their problems, and so many times I'd listen to my friends, and even strangers, talk about their lives and think *what would it be like to have a 'normal' marriage? What would it be like to talk about future goals? What would it feel like to know that if you broke down and lost it for a while, your partner would be there to pick up the pieces and carry you through? What does it feel like to just be husband and wife? How do couples fight a really good fight, say what they really want to say, make up, and move on?"*

I thought *and how can you say you're saving up to go to Disney next year? Don't you ever stop to think that maybe you won't be here next year? Don't you have to live your life in between MRI scans?*

Eventually I realized my bitterness was taking a major toll. Not really sure how or when, I decided to do something positive to off-set all that negative. Probably somewhere around day 2,734—I just knew I was sick and tired, Jeff was sick and tired, and our lives were being swallowed up by this ugly disease.

"We've got to figure something out here or neither one of us is going to make it," I told him. "We've got to at least show our kids that there's a lot of life to live out there. We can't just look at everyone else's lives and wish we had them. It's our job to *show* them that, no matter what we're faced with, we're going to at least try to make the best of it."

Jeff, knowing that something had to give, agreed and we put our plan in motion. No more helpless victim. Cancer would ultimately take Jeff's life but between now and then we'd do all we could to raise money and awareness for new cancer research and support. Our mission became showing ourselves, our kids, and the world that *doing* something about cancer was a hell of a lot better than crying about it.

## The Gift

The church was packed that overcast February morning when I buried my husband at the age of thirty-seven and watched my two beautiful babies say goodbye to their father.

My roommate from college had just finished singing Jeff's favorite hymn when I turned to my kids and said "Ok, it's time for me to go up there." It was one of those moments I'd always known would arrive eventually. Although I'd rehearsed it a million times in my head, I could never quite wrap my heart around what it would actually feel like. Kyle tapped me on the elbow. "Mom, can we come up with you?" he whispered.

I looked at Eve and Kyle, just six and ten years old, and thought *can they handle this? Is this going to be really awkward?* It's not every day a spouse delivers the eulogy—never mind a spouse and two young children.

"Are you sure you want to stand up there with me?" They nodded convincingly so I grabbed their hands, took a deep breath and said "Ok, let's go." As I spoke about their father, told stories, and called on every person in that church to do his part in the fight against cancer, I noticed that the three of us were smiling from ear to ear.

Nothing like what I'd envisioned, this was so much more perfect than that. Kyle and Eve belonged up there with me, and they stood proud and tall by my side as I eulogized their father. For all the pain and suffering we'd endured, it was worth every minute as we *showed* the congregation what was really important in life. I will always cherish those moments together at the pulpit, and they remain my proudest.

That day, we taught a church full of people that good things *do* exist even when bad things happen. Our strength that day and in the days since comes from knowing what it feels like to live in a very uncertain world. May our lives, much more stable now and filled with so much joy, continue to benefit from the lessons learned and compassion gained as we now move forward with our eyes wide open.

**ABOUT THE AUTHOR:** Sheila Turner is a business owner, Realtor, and avid supporter of cancer and grief support organizations. Her involvement in grief and support stems from the loss of her husband in 2010 to brain cancer. Sheila was faced with raising her 2 young children and quickly became an advocate for cancer and bereavement programs. She has spoken on behalf of The Moyer Foundation, appeared on "The Anderson Cooper Show", and writes an online forum for grieving parents. Sheila has been published by Penn Wissahickon Hospice, The Philadelphia Tribune, WHYY Radio and the Leukemia & Lymphoma Society.

Sheila Turner
www.sheilaturner.com
info@sheilaturner.com
610-613-0322

# PART THREE

# Conscious Career

*"To succeed you have to believe in something
with such a passion that it becomes a reality."*
*~ Anita Roddick*

# Faith: The Key to Transformation

### Betsy Cerulo

The phone rang, and it was Cheryl, one of my dearest friends calling from her hospital bed. What was supposed to be a short hospital stay after feeling faint turned out to be acute myeloid leukemia. My world stopped as I and a core group of friends and siblings became Cheryl's caretakers. She passed away two months later. Though the summer of 2007 was a blur, I'd do it all again to see my dear friend once more.

That summer also marked the prelude to the testing of my resolve for the next four years. As I re-entered the pace of work as the CEO/owner of AdNet, a successful professional staffing company, the economy was in early stages of a downward shift. Emotionally worn out, and grieving, I began to notice breakdown everywhere. First, the internal infrastructure of the company started to weaken, then a key employee left. Clients started to pull back their level of hiring, and the new team wasn't jelling. Everyday presented an implosion!

When 2008 was in full swing, I headed back to the recruiting desk and juggled the business development needs, putting on hold my passion for integrative healing for which I received a Masters Degree in 2005. The team was burnt out and complacent so every day felt worse than the one before. Money began flying out the door faster than it was coming in. I knew something had to shift—and quickly!—or the company I started in 1990 on my credit cards and determination would be a statistic of the recession soon. Small businesses were closing left and right, and large ones downsized now at break neck speed—nobody would have been surprised if we'd gone under.

I'm not sure how I got out of bed each morning. Something had to change, and since it clearly wasn't going to be the economy, it would have to be the only thing over which I had control—me! So began my painful enlightening journey...I started to journal every day, wrote mantras, repeated to myself where I wanted to see the company in revenue, prayed constantly, and leaned on family and friends for support.

When it occurred to me that the only entity hiring during the recession was the federal government, that's where I headed. I declared we were going to be a government contractor and figure it out as we went along.

I read books, joined a group called The Alternative Board, and surrounded myself with successful CEO's who owned government contractor firms. This group pushed me to stretch myself and—being very competitive—I wasn't going to show up at each meeting with anything less than a completed "to-do" list. I soaked up their guidance like a sponge and was inspired. I dissected my company's structure and business strategies, and recreated the company and myself with their support.

Opportunities began to surface in the form of pages of government mumbo jumbo. At night, I read over proposals, took notes and, in the morning I walked in and said to the staff "let's go for it!" We forged ahead knowing nothing about how to write proposals. Our first government contract hit with the National Institutes of Health—we were in! It was a beginning.

### Transformation Continues

After Thanksgiving dinner in 2008 I sat with my oldest brother, Jack. As I laid out the facts—potential looming salary cuts and lay-offs—and my worst fears, he said "you know what to do and these are the right steps to take. You'll be fine and stronger on the other side of the recession."

I headed to work the following Monday to impose salary cuts at the onset of the Christmas season. Things couldn't get much worse, or so I thought. Then our bank, who'd once named us their poster child for success, called in our line of credit because we'd had a big loss. Some bankers showed no compassion for the small business owner.

I found another bank who listened and lent us $350,000.00—a *very* uncommon move during a recession, especially when our previous year showed a loss! They'd recognized our long term good track record. Someone opened the door for funding, we ran through! Visibility in the business community made a difference.

By the fall of 2008 we were awarded a significant contract. This life-line was the assurance necessary that shifting our business sails amidst the storm had been a wise move. It would take about twelve months before we'd see the contract in full swing. We had to keep going. Another change in employees left us with the cream of the crop who tirelessly worked forty-plus hours per week to help rebuild a much-loved company.

When I discovered an inaccuracy on reports and started to dig backwards, I found that someone was taking more than they were authorized. I took a firm stand for what was right and kept clear audit trails. The legal system ruled in our favor. I should have let that person go in 2006 when a similar issue was discovered! Lesson learned—a leopard doesn't change its spots.

AdNet was now faced with downsizing office space to cut more expenses. Thank God for good friends and my other big brother Tommy! We cleaned out and moved into a smaller suite. Looking back it was the best thing we ever did.

We headed into 2010 with our large contract about to start, but our bank suddenly changed its mind about how to structure our line of credit and I had to race home to get my personal checkbook to cover $30,000.00 in payroll expenses. The payroll would be more than $100,000.00 the following week. I prayed to St. Jude, the saint of hopeless causes (who'd become my best friend) and kept going. *Remember*, I thought, *don't give up!*

The next week new funding sources were put into place and finally the life-line commenced. This abundant contract ended up being double the amount expected. Money flowed in quickly, bills were paid, and there was hope that perhaps this storm had passed. It had, temporarily. As this contract wound down, another lucrative contract was about to begin. Staff members jumped in wherever needed and often took things off my desk so I could be on the road to develop the business, shake hands, and get us in new doors.

We learned very quickly that the government is an unpredictable animal when suddenly our new contract was cancelled. I did what most kids would do—cried to my mom. Why was this happening? I'd expected to have sold the company and be immersed in a career in integrative medicine by now. As always, my mom held my hand and said "you have everything you need to be successful, and you *are* successful. Don't let this time in your life make you forget all the good, and always have faith." I picked my head up and drove back home.

I made a decision to cut salaries at the leadership level right before Christmas. It was irresponsible for me to continue to write personal checks to cover executive salaries. I actually felt liberated at that moment, because the Bank of Betsy had closed, and anyone used to me carrying the load couldn't have their hand out anymore. I began to extricate myself from business relationships that held me back. I was finally speaking my mind and saying "no!" and it felt healthy.

## A New Perspective

The year 2011 started slowly, until one day two policeman and a priest showed up at my home and dealt a blow that would forever impact my world. My dear brother Tommy, a Roman Catholic priest, had passed away in his sleep. We lived ten minutes apart. My world instantly turned upside down as I did the hardest thing I've ever had to do in my life—call my siblings in New Jersey to deliver the devastating news. They then told my mom.

His loss rocked the worlds of so many people yet, as time passed, our family found a way to look for the silver linings. We all moved forward, together. We know Tommy is forever present. My business challenges became minimal compared to the magnitude of his loss, and I quickly put my life into perspective.

Back at work, the following three months brought more disappointment and a sense of hopelessness. Completely worn out, I just needed some consistency. I'd climb into bed at night and cry for my brother, but I knew deep within there was a message here to which I really had to listen.

In early March, the epiphany came. I experienced my first time ever anxiety attack. I sobbed to God to get me through my grief, help me find my way back to a normal life, and to let me get to the other side of this economy in one piece. My life partner Susan recited the serenity prayer and I repeated it over and over again until I calmed down. She held me as I prayed. We turned out the light and I repeated the prayer until I fell asleep.

When I woke up the next morning, I had hope in my heart! God *had* granted me serenity! I put on my best suit and checked my email to find a note from my brother David cheering me on. I went in to work and started to forge my way through lists of sales calls.

It felt like divine intervention as I started to find an inner voice and light that I'd never felt before. I could feel Tommy on my shoulder every day. It became easier to say no to people who drained my energy. I threw their accountability back at them as I realized it was never mine to carry. As I got rid of excess baggage, the business came back.

As I continued to put it all into perspective, yoga, meditation, and church remained key parts of my day. Absorbed in my tennis league, I had the best season ever. When I'd get down on myself for losing, I'd stop and think about what I'd just lived through and I'd zip the ball past my opponent!

A year later AdNet is on a solid path of healthy growth. Our amazing employees helped restore the organization to its integrity and financial wholeness, through their grit, passion, and joy. They continue to inspire me every day.

Today, I know I am not my career or my wealth. Only when I found my inner light did I rediscover my courage and wisdom. It took almost having it go out to discover that my soulful light had always been there waiting patiently for me to turn it on!

As I shifted dysfunctional relationships, trusted my intuition, took risks, and stepped back, I was able to surrender to my faith. And it's my faith, and the knowledge that, after this, there's nothing I can't survive, that's the key.

**ABOUT THE AUTHOR:** Betsy Cerulo is the founder and CEO of AdNet/AccountNet, Inc., with offices in Columbia, Maryland. The company was started in 1990. The organizations focus is in the placement of Accounting, Financial, Administrative, Healthcare, Human Resources and Information Technology professionals. AdNet was most recently recognized by the Baltimore Business Journal as Top 25 Temporary Staffing Firms in 2010. Betsy has a MS degree in Integrative Medicine from Capital University of Integrative Medicine in Washington, DC. She blends her experience as a business leader and her ongoing growth as a healer to positively shift the energy of the workplace.

Betsy Cerulo
AdNet/AccountNet, Inc.
www.adnetaccountnet.com
bcerulo@adnetaccountnet.com
410-715-4035

# The Deeper Truth

## Nicole Glassman

I remember those desperate days like they were yesterday. It was a Friday night. I was twenty-three. My roommate was out partying in Miami while I submerged myself in a warm bathtub filled with lavender oil, desperately trying to dull the pain in my stomach, despair in my heart, and hopelessness in my head. All of it. Drown it out. Figure it out. Make *something* happen.

I graduated from college with a major in journalism and pre-law and when a promised job fell through, I felt as though I had no direction. I had a few jobs after graduation, but they weren't careers. I worked in the immigration department at an international school, taught English as a second language to adults living in Miami, and found employment at the Miami Chamber of Commerce.

But in the end, these jobs only left me bored and apathetic. I was looking for my passion, my calling, my direction, but everyone told me "just get a job, your hobby can be something else." In my heart, though, I *knew* I was destined to love my work.

So I tried everything—searched online, attended job fairs, scheduled informational interviews, revised my resume, and sent out cover letters—but the stress of it all left me anxious and in constant emotional distress. I spent the days pursuing my elusive calling and the nights crying in my bathtub, hoping to somehow soak away my distress.

This became my routine over the next year and eventually my health began to suffer. Weight gain, depression, hormonal imbalance, and digestive issues took their toll. Soon my priorities shifted from job hunting to my own health, and I enrolled in an international education graduate program at New York University. But my hobby, otherwise known as my health, consumed me, and it wasn't long before I transferred into a nutrition program.

After graduation I started my holistic nutrition practice slowly, seeing clients at home. I enjoyed the sessions, but the idea of strangers in my home freaked me out. Not yet ready for an office—afraid to take that leap, deal with rent, and market myself—I also still struggled with a few remaining health issues.

But one muggy June evening the universe pushed me forward in a very uncomfortable way. On a first date, I had two glasses of wine—a lot for me—and when I rose from the table I felt something sharp in my back, but dismissed it, figuring it was my shoes, or maybe somehow the alcohol.

Later that night I awoke at two a.m. paralyzed with pain. My back was on fire. In agony, and clueless about how to help myself, I crawled out of bed and got into a warm bath, which turned out to be one of the worst things I could've done. My back further inflamed, I really couldn't move. After visits to the chiropractor, and tons of lab tests, turns out it was related to my remaining digestive issues.

I spent the entire summer on my couch watching horrible TV, trying to figure out how to stand up straight enough to button my pants. I went from a twenty-six year-old to an eighty year-old hunchback virtually overnight. Convinced this was the worst summer of my life, I cursed my body, my health, my existence.

## "There's More Wisdom in Your Body Than in Your Deepest Philosophy" - Friedrich Nietzsche

Although I could barely walk, my back changed the course of my life. I spent most of my days at the chiropractor's office or at home crying in pain, but little did I know that each time I visited there I created a vision for my future.

I would sit in the waiting room and look around in awe. *Wow, how lucky she is to have an office in which to see patients, a receptionist to answer her phones, and a place to display products,* I would think. *My* products sit in my linen closet! I would quickly dismiss my thoughts and tell myself I wasn't ready yet. I didn't have the money, the clients, or—in truth—the guts. But still, at each appointment I would dream.

Months later I was stronger and my chiropractor connected me to a trainer named George. He and I would discuss my career and talked about how much I loved it, and how I "fell" into it for a reason. But each time told the story it sounded almost like a script recited from memory. I would use the same words: *calling, passion, fulfilled*—knowing they were far from true. I would smile, as if on cue, and act elated, when I knew I wasn't and that something was missing. But I had swallowed my emotions, pushed them down so deep I couldn't access them.

Then one day I had what felt like an out of body experience. George asked an innocent question and I heard a voice that didn't sound like mine begin to vomit up all of my buried emotions. I couldn't believe the words coming out of my mouth! How I was bored with nutrition, hated the awful isolation of working from home, and I *knew* there was more for me. I had kept this disappointment locked away and told myself my health issues had led me to my career and that it happened for a reason—to help others.

Mortified, I started to cry. Moments later came the terrifying questions. Wasn't I fulfilled by helping others? If I didn't love nutrition, then what? Back to the bathtub? Had it all been for nothing? Do I start over again? WHAT DO I DO NOW?

It turns out, after self-imploding in front of George, he became a great help. He connected me to the owner of the gym who had a small office for rent. It was perfect! The night I signed the lease I received a flyer in the mail about training on electrodermal screening, the tool ultimately responsible for my dramatic health improvement. I had considered this training already, but felt I wasn't ready.

But I knew this was my chance to do even more to help others, and to feel challenged in a new way. Still on my path, I just needed to veer off to make it my own. I began to understand that my back injury had been one of many moments when my body spoke to me. My back acted out to tell me that something wasn't right. Although it made me feel helpless and alone at the time, ironically it actually empowered me, and forced me to look inward to explore what truly made me happy. But this wasn't where it ended.

### *"Faith is a Passionate Intuition" - William Wordsworth*

Fast forward four years—I'm settled in my office and routine, but once again something isn't right. I'm attracting all of the wrong clients, I had hired a very difficult employee, and—most importantly—I didn't feel inspired. I complained incessantly, and was so wrapped up in my own misery that I couldn't see how far off my path I had strayed.

The turning point came when I called my mom crying *again*, griping about my day as usual. She said something at the time that sounded so harsh, but I needed to hear it. "Nicole I worry about you. Are you *ever* going to be happy?" Her words stung my heart, flooded my head, and shook me to my core.

What a horrible thing to say—I haven't *always* been miserable! Defensive, I hung up abruptly. But after I calmed down, I sat quietly and realized she was right. The past two years I *had been* miserable. My mother's harsh words lit a fire in me and I wanted to disprove them. I knew it was time to take control again.

I made a decision to *finally* be happy, and my desire for change led the way. I truly believe that when you're open to change it will meet you where you are and guide you. For me change came in the form of Justine, a reflexologist and spiritual healer. If she'd come into my life a few years earlier I would've thought she was a wacko. But ready for a deeper, more connected life, her messages resonated with me. Through her I developed an ideology that let the universe know I was open to all of life's possibilities, and I learned how to connect with my core, ask for what I want, and to dream. This was all new to me.

Justine taught me how to choose my words wisely, and the importance of speaking from a positive perspective. When I changed *"I have the craziest clients"* into *"in the past, I had the craziest clients,"* I became a magnet for positive change. She encouraged me to end my sentences with "yet," if it was something that hadn't materialized, but could. So, *"I haven't found my passion"* became *"I haven't found my passion—yet."*

For the first time I actually felt I had control over my life. I never realized the role I had played in some of my own negative experiences. I had always blamed my circumstances on bad luck, or played the victim, and of course the outcome would always be the same—negative.

I began to explore even further with books, spiritual teachers, and healers. I learned more about the importance of expressing gratitude and the influence of negative thoughts and words on the path of my own life. I learned how to envision my future and started making lists of my ideal clients' traits, my perfect apartment, my ultimate schedule—basically anything I wanted! Through vision boards and affirmations, I watched my life transform.

As a result, I attracted a ton of new clients whom I adore, my relationships improved, and I rediscovered fulfillment in my career—but not because I focused on the positive and expressed gratitude every day. Those things are important, but true joy came when I *heard* my own voice.

Based on the rollercoaster of discovering and rediscovering my own passion, I designed emotional exercises to help clients uncover their own joy. Career, relationships, friendships, balance, or spirituality—you name it—we work on improving these areas in combination with my health packages. It's not therapy by any means, but it really opens people up, not only emotionally, but to life itself.

The positive change in many of my clients is unbelievable! A huge part of a person's health journey starts from within, and I've discovered that I absolutely love helping clients find their own sense of inner peace. I love tending to their nutrition and detoxification needs as well, but incorporating the emotional work is what completes me.

Today, my work is diverse, rewarding, and ever-changing. I've learned that detours in life reflect our own growth and transformation. I made my career my own again and again, and now I can honestly say—not on cue, not with a fake smile, but authentically—*I love what I do!*

**ABOUT THE AUTHOR:** After completing a Graduate Degree in Food Studies at New York University, Nicole Glassman was one of the first practitioners to achieve certification in Dr. D'Adamo's Blood Type course. She is a graduate of the Institute for Integrative Nutrition, and is certified in Holistic Health Counseling and in Bio-Energetic Assessment. Nicole has presented on holistic health at numerous corporations, including the Ethical Culture School, Hostos Community College, Colgate Palmolive, Chelsea Movement, Therapy and AMC Theatres. She runs a successful private practice in Manhattan specializing in holistic nutrition and detoxification.

Nicole Glassman
Mindful Health
New York, NY
www.mindfulhealth.biz
212-245-3129

# Married to the Job
## Victoria Guerrero

Deeply engrossed in my work, I was roused to attention by a quick knock on my office door. The door opened, and standing there was the new boss' assistant, Rob, who'd been sent to get me. "The big guy wants to see you," he told me.

Fear seized me as he spoke and my world spiraled into slow motion. My surroundings faded, and suddenly everything became very quiet. The only sound I heard was my own breathing until I looked up and Rob came into focus. I realized I was about to become their next hit.

I flashed back to that gloomy day in January 2010 when the previous mayor had divorced me. Our relationship survived two administration changes, but on that day, termed out and unable to run again for office, he took his leave of City Hall and left me behind. And on that day, although I'd worked for this forward thinking, visionary for seven and a half years as an executive, I became the property of the newly sworn-in mayor.

The new marriage never really jelled. In the four months following his swearing in, the workplace environment became a nightmare. The new administration used massive layoffs—under the guise of balancing the budget—as a way to terminate or eliminate positions. Work transformed into a place where people lacked morals, turned on each other, and consistently distrusted. Some were laid off because they supported the previous mayor and were from his administration; others simply because they refused to take part in office politics.

I was in both batches. I'd always made it a point not to align myself with any elected official, as I knew many of them would turn against each other. I also made it a point to remove myself from politics and to take the higher road, and focus on my performance instead.

However, doing the right thing cost me my job just the same.

The new administration and unions had resorted to following executives and videotaping them in the hope of catching one in a questionable act that would lead to their termination. Some were caught, displayed in the media, and promptly terminated. Others avoided capture, simply because they never did anything wrong. However, this didn't stop the relentless "hunts," and sooner or later all executives from the previous administration were terminated and replaced with individuals that supported the new leadership.

Back in my office I packed in disbelief. This was the first time I'd ever been laid off! I wasn't sure if I felt relieved, upset, sad, or scared, so I just stood there for what seemed a long time and looked out the window. It was a gloomy, dreary, rainy day—lightning and thunder had flashed and boomed off and on since my commute into work.

I tore myself away from my reverie and began to gather my belongings. Into the box went all of my awards, certifications, congratulatory cards, one by one, and the whole time I wondered, what am I to do now? My box of belongings in my arms, I turned back to look out my office window and view the city's landscape one last time. Then it was time to say goodbye. I closed the blinds, turned back around, and walked out of my office forever.

### *The Work Ethic*

I'm what they used to call a miracle baby. Born to a thirty-eight year old mom in the 1970s, I was a very rare event. Two years old when my parents divorced, my two sisters were eight and fourteen. My mom, who'd come from Cuba during the 1950's—years before Fidel Castro's revolution—determined to make a life for herself and her daughters.

Growing up in the '70's to a divorced mother of three young girls was an enriching experience. Although we never had the luxuries other children did, we never felt we struggled to survive, which is a testament to how well my mom brought us up. Always resourceful, my mom excelled at stretching the dollar and made sure we had all that we needed. She worked various factory jobs and often brought work home with her for extra income.

I remember my sisters and I sitting in a makeshift assembly line at the dining room table, as mom handed each of us certain sections of these key chains we had to make. We'd spend nights creating these liquid-filled cylinder key chains with floating seashells in them.

One by one, we'd give the finished product to my mom, who'd then glue it all together with a glue gun. To this day, I still remember the smell of that hot glue gun and the sounds of the key chains clanging together as we piled them one on top of the other.

At a very young age my sisters and I all learned the importance of being self-reliant. We learned this from observing our mom and from the life lessons she passed on to us. For this I am grateful, as these lessons have shaped me into who I am today and will always be with me.

Growing up we all began to work as soon as we could. I knew I wanted to go to college so I focused on my academics and on volleyball. After graduating from high school I attended college on an academic and athletic scholarship, and received my B.A. in Communications Arts, and an M.B.A. (the first in my family) in Business Administration.

My mom taught us as young girls, not only self-reliance, but also resourcefulness and determination. In business, I'd always thought it's about what you know and how well you do it, so I prided myself on those things. But at my city job, it was about who you knew, and about aligning yourself with who's in power. I look at that now and think *whoa, that goes against everything I believed...*

### The Divorce

Walking down the long, dark corridor I realized I was traveling into the unknown. For the first time in my life, I didn't have a plan. I didn't know what my next step would be. I heard the clicking of my heels echo against the cold marble floor. As I made my way towards the elevator the few people I saw avoided me, glancing down or to the side as they walked past.

The elevator ride was lonely. No one got on, and it was as if everyone had disappeared, like a ghost town. Left alone to my thoughts as I walked through the lobby, I realized I no longer had to come back to this awful place; this prison-like environment that had drained my spirit. Everyone here, once so full of life, had been reduced to walking zombies who went through their daily motions with no purpose other than to collect a paycheck. Yes, maybe it was a good thing this happened to me.

Driving home I realized how entrapped I'd been. Although afraid of what lay ahead, I knew deep inside that I'd be all right. I consciously made the decision to see my lay-off as an opportunity to step back and re-evaluate my life. I was given a second chance to decide what I wanted to make of myself.

Still, I'd been married to my job for almost eight years, and having it all suddenly ripped away made me feel as if a part of me had died. And soon I'd be left to cope with the after effects.

Fortunately, I'd incorporated my own consulting business in 2006 with the intention of leaving the city to grow my company. However, my loyalty to the city, and fear of making such a bold move, led me to decide to continue with my full time employment. I'd ignored that inner voice that'd been telling me throughout the years to venture out on my own and fulfill my dream of having a successful business.

It's funny how things happen, it's almost as if the universe shifted itself so that I'd be placed in a position that gave me the opportunity to follow my dream. That shift happened that day in 2010; I was free at last to fulfill my dream! Grateful to finally fully embrace my opportunity to establish a successful business consulting company, I now focus on helping both businesses and business professionals grow.

I had to go through this journey to understand what's important in life.

My priorities have now changed, and I realize now that it's not about how far up the colloquial "ladder" I go, or how many things I acquire, because none of that truly makes me happy. What's important to me is that I remain true to myself, surround myself with loving family and friends, and give back to others and to my community. I've learned that it truly is the small things in life that are the most valuable, we just have to slow down enough to notice and appreciate them.

In short, I no longer wish to be married to my job! I now understand that all-important elusive word "balance." I needed balance in my life to be truly happy. I've had to look inwards for that balance; to understand what it meant, and in doing so I've made conscious decisions about how I plan to live the rest of my life.

I used to believe that we all have a pre-destined future; that all is written in the books for us. Today, however, I believe that we make our own future by living consciously and understanding that for every action there is a reaction for which we are accountable. Instead of waiting to see what life has to offer, I've now reconnected with my true self and am living consciously.

I'm a strategist, a problem solver who helps organizations and business professionals grow by analyzing their strengths and weaknesses and then developing opportunities. I challenge them to reinvent themselves when needed, to expand, and to reach out for more—in essence to restrategize and grow. I provide them with the strategies and resources needed to help them achieve their goals.

I've now learned to be my own strategist, and the CEO of my life, not just my business. I now use my skills to carve out my own future, to make conscious decisions in order to achieve my goals and lead the life I've always wanted to lead—one of happiness, love and balance. Through living consciously, I've been able to find myself again and by being responsible and accountable for my decisions and my actions, I've actualized the life I've always wanted. Forced to divorce my job, I came to understand true happiness blossomed only when I married my life!


**ABOUT THE AUTHOR:** Victoria Guerrero, a strategy implementation expert and founder of the Academy for Business Professionals, is considered by many their business solutions partner. A natural born leader and problem solver, Victoria provides peace of mind to business owners by developing and implementing customized business solutions and training programs tailored to address their business challenges. Professionally she is a business management coach and consultant specializing in strategy development and implementation, organization development, change management and human resources management. Victoria holds an M.B.A. in Business Administration, a B.A. in Communication Arts, and is a certified Florida Supreme Court Mediator.

Victoria Guerrero, Founder & CEO
Academy for Business Professionals
www.academyforbusinessprofessionals.com
info@academyforbusinessprofessionals.com
305-420-6578 / 888-697-9566

# My First Ten Years as a Survivor: The Real Story

### Gilda Farias Healy

I looked out the window and saw a commercial airliner slice like a knife through hot butter into New York's World Trade Center Tower One. I'll never forget the feeling of New York World Trade Center's Tower Two swaying in a sudden updraft. Ordinarily, there was no reason for the tower to sway.

That beautiful, calm, sunny day was the day the world stood still and my new world renaissance began. September 11, 2001 is now my second birthday, though I was born on January 31. Named Gilda after my Portuguese aunt and the tragic heroine of the Italian opera Rigoletto, I am no tragedy.

Rather, I am a proud survivor. On 9/11, I evacuated from the thirty-sixth floor of Tower Two around eight-fifty a.m. I ignored instructions from the Port Authority to return to my desk, and joined the rushing sea of humanity down the stairs and out into the streets of downtown Manhattan.

"*Never* return to an evacuated building without a fire or police department escort," a New York City fireman whom I'd met during my college days in the 1970's once told me. The fact that I remembered his advice is the reason I am a good statistic, along with fifty thousand-plus other people, who walked out of the Trade Towers uninjured. That advice and the hand of God kept me moving that day as I exited through World Trade Center's Tower Five.

En route, a falling chunk of glass tumbled from the tower and barely missed me before it crashed to the ground. I took it as a personal message from Al-Qaida, one for which I gladly did *not* accept delivery. Although I couldn't avoid being held hostage by modern technology when my cell phone refused to work, no way was I willing to become a serious casualty of Al-Qaida!

I found safe refuge with a former boss who still had his corporate headquarters in the downtown area. From there I was able to call my husband Michael and let him know what had happened, and that I was safe. He told me to stay put where I'd be safe. I told him that I loved him, and would be home as soon as possible.

At ten-thirty a.m., World Trade Center Tower Two crashed to the ground and created a giant monster cloud that consumed the side streets of downtown New York. As I looked out the window from my old boss's office, I shuddered at the thought that we were witnessing a dress-rehearsal for the end of the world. That day I left the New York I grew up in, and it's never been the same since.

Finally back home in New Jersey that night, my husband and I went immediately to my mother's house. Her phone rang nonstop that day with inquiries from family and friends about my safety. I knew it was imperative that I *show* mom that I was okay. An only child, I was all she had. Once there, she insisted that Michael and I share with her a simple dinner she'd prepared. It was understood—in accordance with my Italian heritage—that we had to dine at her house and "break bread" together, or we couldn't leave!

During the meal, I told mom the two things I'd learned that day. The first was to get out if you see an airplane go through a building that's in front of you. The second was to make sure you go to the bathroom before you start your work day! Mom laughed until she almost cried, and congratulated me for my sense of humor, after all I'd been through.

Upon our return home, my mother-in-law, who was waiting outside our house for our return, came up to me, threw her arms around me, and said "I'm glad you're okay, you're tough like your mother-in-law!" High praise indeed!

In 2003 I finally attended a 9/11 support group because I needed to relate to others who'd been through and understood what I'd experienced that day. I learned from this group that when you step back from a difficult situation, the answer will find you. Right after I started the support group, I began having flashbacks. I still saw the plane slicing through the tower. I felt the Tower sway all over again. I smelled burning debris even though I was safe at home in my husband's warm embrace.

## *My New World Renaissance*

Professionally, my world had already begun to change in January 2001. When my employer, a one hundred year-old New York conservative insurance brokerage firm, changed management from an employee-owned company to a privately-owned one, the new owners began the Machiavellian process of corporate house cleaning. By 2001, I'd given them twelve years of my life. Fortunately, I survived the first of many waves of corporate house cleaning.

The signs of corporate America's "24/7" philosophy had already taken its toll on my health. Nine years before 9/11, I was diagnosed with the big three for a heart attack: Type 2 diabetes, hypertension, and high cholesterol. I'd heard all the horror stories about colleagues in the insurance industry who'd dropped dead at their desks as a result of a massive heart attack from all their job stress, and that wasn't for me—I wasn't interested in being a statistic then either.

As a New York licensed broker in property, casualty, personal lines, and baggage insurance, I was assigned to the fine arts department as a broker in 1998, and got to work with museums, art dealers, and art galleries. I loved my new assignment—with it I attended exhibition openings and partied with all sorts of very interesting people!

In 1999, I decided that it was time to try a new career. I'd seen an advertisement in the New York Times for the master's program in museum professions at Seton Hall University and was accepted three weeks after I applied. I loved the arts and wanted to reinvent myself without the burden of corporate America's stress. It didn't hurt that the people I was trying to escape were helping me to do just that by reimbursing me for the cost of the tuition!

I maintained my sense of humor with all the stress of working full-time and going to school part time. I remember when I threatened co-workers that I'd quit my job in the insurance business and get a job in the New York City Sanitation Department because, after all, I was good at wading through trash and corporate house cleaning...in the meantime, I worked in New Jersey as I diligently concentrated on my master's degree.

I sang in my Catholic Church choir and as a cantor—one who leads the congregation in song. I loved doing this because it provided me a safe place between the turmoil on earth and the heavens above. I learned that singing praise to God helps me to heal myself, and others as well. But it was a long time before I could sing—or even listen to—*The Star Spangled Banner, God Bless America,* or *America the Beautiful* because it reminded me of how much pain this whole nation endured.

A gentleman with an impressive resume, armed with a five year contract, was hired to work with me in May 2002. He and I worked together for a year and a half before he found an excuse to get rid of me. I survived a few more waves of corporate house cleaning until the day before my birthday in 2003. The pressure of the Machiavellian house cleaning process was too much for him to bear, and he suddenly resigned in May 2004. That same year I became a New Jersey licensed property and casualty producer out of necessity so I could continue to work in New Jersey. Now I could sell insurance from the Canadian Border to the shores of Cape May...

Finally finished with my masters at Seton Hall in 2007, I trail blazed by writing my thesis about disaster recovery and then designed a disaster recovery plan for the Trenton City Museum during my internship there. My mom, an avid supporter of me as a woman and as a trail blazer, died very suddenly in July 2009. She knew that I'd applied for my plan's copyright. I received notice from the Library of Congress that my disaster recovery plan received a copyright in 2010.

The last full-time position I held was with a small main street insurance agency in northern New Jersey. The three agency owners—more interested in taking vacation than in the business—lost seven hundred thousand dollars in income in 2008 at the start of the recession. They laid me off the day after Christmas.

### Epilogue

In the end, I was glad. I didn't want to be held hostage any longer by corporate America. Corporate America is digging its own grave and I don't want to be buried yet! A survivor, I'm now trail blazing while I volunteer for both the National Guard Museum as a collections management coordinator/consultant, and for The Center for World War II Studies and Conflict Resolution as an archivist.

I think I found the answer for me in this ailing economy, and that it was there all the time. I am about to embark on a new venture as a consultant. With all this experience under my belt, I have a world of love to give, along with expertise in insurance, fine arts, and disaster recovery, and I'm just getting started!

I'm also a member of a 1940's era musical group called *Down Melody Lane,* part of the Center's Commemoration Committee. In December 2011 I sang *God Bless America* in public for the first time since 9/11 and brought down the house. I hadn't gotten over the painful memories that song evoked from that tragic day, but singing it helped reinforce that I'm still here, I'm still standing. People think, *yeah get over it*, but I didn't sing it because I wanted sympathy, I sang it because I want people to know—I am a survivor.

**ABOUT THE AUTHOR:** Gilda Healy is a lifelong resident of New Jersey who holds a B.A. with honors from Marymount Manhattan College and an M.A. in Museum Professions from Seton Hall University. She is a resident-licensed property and casualty insurance broker in New York and New Jersey. Using her insurance and museum professions backgrounds, Gilda loves all aspects of her work - for the National Guard Militia Museum in Sea Girt, NJ, in Collections Management and as an Archivist at Brookdale Community College for the Center for World War II Studies. Gilda is launching her own business as a consultant for Property, Casualty, Fine Arts Insurance, and Disaster Recovery.

Gilda Farias Healy
Gilda Healy Consultants
www.linkedin.com/in/gildahealy
gildacanhelp@gmail.com
732-495-3102

# How I Learned to Love My Life
## Wendy M. Kennedy

I escaped into the solitude of the greeting card store that rainy day at the mall and breathed a sigh of relief. I felt the tension slowly leave my body as I took my time looking around the store. As I read the birthday cards for daughters, my eyes welled up with tears. With a rush of emotion I remembered it wasn't only my daughter's birthday the following week, it was also Debbie's daughter's birthday.

I'd attended Debbie's funeral earlier that day. The past week was an emotional roller coaster—in addition to Debbie's passing, my father-law had undergone multiple heart by-pass surgery. I wasn't ready for reality yet. But my daughter's birthday was eleven days away, and I wasn't sure when I'd be able to get back to the mall again.

My boss and friend, Debbie had died suddenly at the age of forty-seven, after emergency surgery due to circulatory problems in her legs. She'd undergone planned surgeries before, and we'd feared she might lose one of her feet. We never imagined she'd lose her life.

I pictured Debbie's face as it lit up when she spoke about her family, and my heart filled with sadness for the daughter who wouldn't have her mom on her birthday. I couldn't imagine what it would be like to not be there for my daughter and son.

Like me, Debbie's extended family was an important part of her life. In addition, this was a small community and she'd known most of our staff and clients her whole life. Debbie was the type of person who cared about everyone else, and now it was clear she'd neglected her own health. She'd worked so hard for so long, and even though she'd told me shortly before her death she was beginning to take her life back, now it was clearly too late...

We'd split up Debbie's responsibilities at work and waited to see what happened next. I ignored my own symptoms of grief—there was too much to do. Besides, if anyone deserved to have time to grieve and needed support, it was the people who'd worked with and known Debbie longer.

The following months passed in a blur. After returning home from his by-pass surgery, my father-in-law suffered a heart attack. As he recovered slowly, both he and my mother-in-law came down with pneumonia. Since my in-laws live down the street and my husband Errol is their only child living nearby, they've always been close.

I made myself available to staff and clients during the day, and wouldn't be finished with one thing before I was on to the next. Often, on the nights I'd plan to stay late to work or to see a client after hours, my evening would be cut short by a phone call from Errol—he needed to do something for work or to check on his parents.

Exhausted, still I couldn't sleep without waking up thinking about everything I had to do. Too often it came down to a choice between spending time with the kids or doing housework, and usually the kids won. But my patience wore thin, and I'd find myself snapping at them or at Errol. Overwhelmed, I soon felt like I couldn't do anything right. I desperately needed more balance in my life!

That fall a new manager was hired. I stopped working late and learned the word "no." My mind began to clear so that I worked smarter, not harder. This was when I learned a valuable lesson: I didn't have to work so hard! By slowing down and setting boundaries, I was able to accomplish more and feel more appreciated.

### There's No Place Like Home

Even so, I began to notice that something was missing. *Is there something else I'm meant to do?* I wondered. *Who am I? What do I even want? What's important to me? Do I have a purpose? Is there more?*

In January I received a gift when our babysitter told us she planned to join the military. Babysitters were hard to come by and Trish was our third sitter in the past three years. I asked the kids if any of their friends had babysitters close by. That was when they asked me to quit my job and take in some of the other kids. I told them I'd think about it and talk to their dad.

Excited at the prospect of spending more time with Hanna and Andrew, Errol and I decided to give it two years. By then, they'd be old enough to spend some time home alone, and I'd gain the opportunity to figure things out about my next job.

That Christmas my dad was diagnosed with cancer and told he needed surgery, radiation, and chemotherapy. Grateful that I'd stuck with my decision to quit my job, I could now leave early on Friday's to make the two-hour drive to my parent's house and be there to help. My dad has always been there for me, and I couldn't imagine life without him. I found comfort in books and the wealth of information contained within them. As I began to research cancer, nutrition, and meditation, it led me to further exploration of mindfulness and the mind/body connection.

By this time the children were tired of sharing their mother, Errol had wearied of his loss of privacy—some weeks children came and went from seven a.m. to five-thirty p.m.—and he missed being able to come home for lunch to a quiet house. Ultimately, I found babysitting was even less flexible than my job had been.

In addition, I'd ignored my own health for a long time. I stopped babysitting when school let out for the summer, and discovered my thyroid was part of the reason for my exhaustion. Now I had the summer to regulate it, see other doctors, and to spend more time with my dad.

## Who Do I Really Want to Be When I Grow Up?

Still in limbo when September rolled around, I'd discovered during summer that I had polyps on my uterus after an ultrasound. Their removal in October led to a biopsy that was negative, but now I'd need minor surgery before Christmas and then another biopsy.

Forty years old, I decided that it was time to figure out who/what I wanted to be when I grew up. Both children would attend middle school the following year, and I could go back to work without the added worry of childcare. I knew I had to make a conscious decision to live my life more authentically.

In addition, one of my mom's best friends—who'd been particularly supportive when my dad was diagnosed—received her own diagnosis that summer. Little did we know that we'd be saying goodbye to Peg the following January. Once again, I found myself surrounded by grieving people and wished I could do more.

Peg's passing was difficult to comprehend because she'd been so full of life. If there was something she wanted to do, she just did it!

She took courses, traveled, always found time for her friends and family, and lived her life with joy. Now, she became my new inspiration.

Always able to easily manifest a job without even realizing what I was doing, I vowed this time would be different. This time I wanted to consciously *choose* the direction in which I'd go. No longer content to let life just happen to me, I didn't want to throw away another opportunity to find out what it is that I was *really* meant to do...only I had no idea where to start. I knew that I wanted to make a difference and to add more joy to my life. Above all, I desired to find like-minded people, and be able to balance time for family and myself.

Through it all I continued to find comfort in books and listened to Hay House Radio and podcasts. Inspired by many of the Hay House authors, including Louise Hay, I grew to believe that I had the power to create my own reality and that I was going to be ok. I also knew that in order for that to transpire certain things needed to change. It was up to me to identify these things and to change them.

When I no longer blamed others or played the victim, and began to take responsibility for my own feelings and actions, I was amazed at the positive outcome. Changing my own thoughts changed *me,* and I believe the work I did on myself at that time helped me to release much anger and resentment. My new positive outlook of forgiveness also contributed to the success of my surgery and second biopsy, I believe.

Shortly after, I learned about Heal Your Life® Workshop Leader Training. I was eager to attend. What an incredible experience! Amazed to be in the presence of so many other like-minded people, and surrounded by such unconditional love and support, I realized it was time for me to stop putting others needs and desires ahead of my own. I learned that, though it had been easy for me to worry about everyone else in the past, I deserved to take care of my own needs first. That way I had more to give to the people that I love.

I returned for Heal Your Life® Coach training. I was thrilled to make a new friend who also attended both trainings. He introduced me to the Grief Recovery Institute, and their training turned out to be the perfect complement to my Heal Your Life® work and exactly that for which I'd been searching. This accelerated my own journey toward high consciousness and helped open up many possibilities that I had not allowed myself to receive previously.

I continue to learn and grow as I begin to coach. I enjoy the fun and laughter that's returned to my marriage and the relationship with my children. I found what I was missing—*me!* I see now that when I love myself it's easier to live my truth, take care of myself, set boundaries, and bring balance and joy in to my life, and how this also benefits my children. I am very proud as they mature into loving individuals who see the value in family and in helping others.

When my thoughts stray to Debbie and the possible shortness of life, I am encouraged to continue to live my life this way because I believe if I don't live authentically, I might not be so lucky with my health next time. Now that I've learned to love my life, I recognize the importance of my gratitude and how it allows life to love me back!


**ABOUT THE AUTHOR:** At forty Wendy reinvented her life and is excited to see where the journey will take her next! Her mantra has been the George Eliot quote "It is never too late to be what you might have been." This is probably why she was so inspired by Louise Hay's story. This inspiration led her to become a licensed Heal Your Life® Coach and Workshop Leader. She is also a Certified Grief Recovery® Specialist. Wendy's desire is to empower people to live more balanced, joyful lives!

Wendy M Kennedy
OverJoyed Coaching
www.overjoyedcoaching.com
wendy@overjoyedcoaching.com
506-470-7985

# How a Mom of Eight Built a Million Dollar Business

Shifra Lefkowitz

Overcoming challenges is what motherhood is all about, and as a mom of eight children—ages seven to twenty-one, and the oldest of ten siblings, God bless them—I discovered how challenges can help you achieve SUCCESS!

I see obstacles as a way to grow and, empowered with this gift to overcome barriers and achieve success, I've learned how to juggle both work and family at the same time. Despite all my responsibilities, each child's milestone is celebrated! Between attending Faigy's first grade book party, preparing for Tami's eighth-grade graduation, readying Shmul for sleep away camp, and my daily business schedule, there's never a dull moment! Particularly the day my daughter Esther came home with a signed contract for her first position as a fifth grade teacher!

I looked at my daughter with pride and realized it felt just like yesterday when I'd received my first teaching job back in June 1987. I was so excited to be entrusted with innocent second graders. During the following four years I experienced the special satisfaction of teaching and molding my precious students daily. How rewarding to watch the children grow and mature and feel like I made an impact!

When I gave birth to my first child—a beautiful nine-pound baby boy—and became a mother on June 11, 1991, I felt so special! Shortly afterward, my principal called me to wish me all the best and to ask my plans for next year. I offered to come back to teach, but told her I'd need extra salary to pay for a babysitter. Why give forty-five percent of my earnings to a babysitter and forgo being with my baby, I reasoned. Unfortunately she could not accommodate me. It was then that I made the decision to stay home with my son. Bitter at first, it wasn't long before I focused on motherhood and more pressing issues.

Four weeks later, I returned with Mordche to the pediatrician. Like every first-time mother, this visit to the pediatrician was a milestone. Disappointed when the doctor put Mordche on the scale and discovered he'd lost a pound since birth, I became distraught. A baby normally gains an average of two pounds during its first month, but not only had Mordche not gained, he'd dropped weight! No wonder he cried and fussed constantly. *What kind of a mother am I,* I thought to myself, *when I can't even nourish my baby?*

"Your baby is really hungry and doesn't look good," the concerned doctor told me. "You must give up breast feeding and put him on formula."

I held back my tears as I begged the doctor to give me a chance—just one week—to fix the problem. He agreed reluctantly—I think he took pity on me. I had no idea what I was going to do, I only knew one thing: giving up was not an option! For the next twenty-four hours I researched different solutions. In the end I purchased an array of nutritional products, including a shake that came with a 100% money back guarantee.

I consumed these vitamins twice daily as I desperately tried to salvage my thus far catastrophic entrance into motherhood. *Will I be a successful mommy?* I worried anxiously.

One week later, I hoped and prayed for a miracle as I returned to the pediatrician on a beautiful sunny day. "Yes! Mordche has gained one pound!" the doctor said happily. "He's back now to his birth weight of nine pounds." *Thank goodness,* I thought, *I'm not a failure after all!*

Excited, I realized that these amazing food supplements provided me with the essential nutrients—nutrients I'd lacked—to properly nourish my baby! The entire following year Mordche continued to gain weight—a happy and healthy baby, he weighed twenty-seven pounds by his first birthday. I could hardly carry him!

I quickly recognized a double benefit: instead of buying formula, I invested in nutritional products for myself and soon realized I felt very different. I no longer needed my midday nap with Mordche, had lots of energy—even for the dinner dishes!—and my frequent colds had disappeared, I was amazed.

I realized I'd made a huge discovery. When my close friend Lea, expecting her first baby at the time, complained that her doctor was dissatisfied with the baby's size—it seemed too small in utero and two months behind—it occurred to me that if these nutritional products had helped me while nursing, they could probably help her baby too. I recommended she purchase the same products for thirty days—after all, she had nothing to lose and so much to gain since it was 100% guaranteed!

When she visited her doctor one month later, he was in awe. "Your baby is doing great, and the size is exactly right," he told her. Wow! It felt really good to be able to help my dear friend. What happened next totally surprised me. I received a check in the mail! I called the company to inform them of an error, but they said "that was a reward for sharing our products with your loved ones!" I was blown away! I'd never received a check from any company or store that I recommended to someone else! As I shared my story with more of my close friends and relatives my monthly checks grew bigger.

### The Grace of God and One Anonymous Soldier

I trace my roots back to Hungary, where the Holocaust almost annihilated my grandfather, along with so many others. The shock experienced by American soldiers in the 157th Infantry Regiment who first set foot in Dachau Lager on the morning of April 29, 1945 cannot be measured or adequately described by historians. When these soldiers marched in to liberate Dachau Lager, one of the oldest and most notorious concentration death camps in Nazi Germany, they spotted a line of approximately forty railway cars on a siding near the camp's entrance.

To their horror, they discovered that each railway car was loaded with emaciated human corpses, both men and women. Hastily, they searched both trains and barracks for signs of life among the hundreds of lifeless bodies. Inside one of the barracks lay my grandfather Sandor, emaciated and unconscious.

Rescued by an anonymous American soldier, Sandor emerged into consciousness six weeks later with no idea how he'd gotten to the hospital. He asked the patient next to him to read his chart aloud. "You weigh sixty-five pounds, and received eighteen blood transfusions to keep you alive," his roommate informed him. At the young age of twenty-five, with no family around him, he knew he'd experienced a miracle from God, and that God wanted him to LIVE!

As the eldest grandchild, I instinctively knew there is a reason and a purpose for everything and that I must take responsibility to carry on my grandfather's legacy. I also knew that only a big caring heart could carry out such an impossible task amidst all that horror!

*How can a human being bring himself to do such grueling work—to check all those railcars and barracks for life between dead corpses?* I often wondered. Yet, that is *exactly* what this special, anonymous American soldier did that day! My heart is forever grateful to this special soldier, as it was he who played a role and preserved my family's line.

But how can I thank him when I don't know who he is? In what way can I show gratitude for such an enormous good deed carried out by such a selfless person? I realized that all I can do is take this lesson along with me and have it serve as the epitome of GRATEFULNESS! Even though I was only twenty-four, I knew in my heart I wanted to give back, make a difference in people's lives, and leave a mark for future generations!

### Paying it Forward with Gratitude

As the enormity of my discovery unfolded, I realized it presented an opportunity that could transport me far beyond my imagination. The seed of consciousness planted through my incredible experience left me with the belief that I could make a difference—one family at a time!

At that point I was a busy mom with three children, and had achieved a good measure of success. I'd helped several people improve their health with the nutritional products I was using provided by #1 natural nutritional company in the U.S., and was presented with the opportunity to live my life consciously.

Thus began my journey. Believe me, it wasn't a smooth ride—it had lots of bumps along the way, but I didn't allow anyone or anything to throw me off track. *Follow your heart,* I told myself. *Go where it leads you, there is a reason for it.*

My *mission* was clear: I will teach and educate moms how to live a healthier and better life, one family at a time. It was unbelievable—moms were eager to learn how to take steps toward bettering their health and that of their families, and sought advice from me about everyday health challenges. Here I was—teaching again! Not second graders, but moms of all ages.

I worked from the comfort of my home, and it was incredible. I discovered my passion and I loved it! Soon I realized that I faced a challenge. How could I reach a larger audience? It didn't take me long to recognize the power of social marketing and the benefits of recommending a good product or service to anyone. I could teach other moms to duplicate what I do—kind of create competition for myself which would have a ripple effect! Competition isn't an issue in social marketing. Conventional business is different because competition can hurt others. But social marketing provides a forum where the more people you help, the greater the rewards as they spread the word. This very unique concept makes it possible to earn a living with integrity.

Since 1995 I have partnered with powerful women just like myself who take my lessons and continue to share the message of better health and freedom with thousands of women! The result has been my creation of a million-dollar business. My family has had five bonus cars and traveled the world, all expenses paid by my company. You don't need to choose to *do well or feel good*—you can do both at the same time!

Much of my success in building a business I inherited from my father, who got it from his father—rescued that fateful day at Dachau. My rationale behind it all is to give back to humanity the chance that I've been given to live and to build a family. In honor of both my grandfather and the special American soldier that saved his life I must carry on the legacy, continue to give back and, in doing so, inspire other women to overcome and grow from their challenges...

**ABOUT THE AUTHOR:** A health and wellness guru for two decades, Shifra a MOM of 8 children built a million dollar business, while teaching and mentoring women to improve their health and their finances. One of the top 131 Leaders with #1 Natural Nutritional Co. in USA! Shifra is an accomplished woman, she has reached 12,205 women via social marketing and has enabled them to live a better life, through marketing the best natural products—that carry a 100% guarantee! "If your health and financial freedom are important to you, reach out to Shifra she can help you achieve the impossible!"

Shifra Lefkowitz
Your Health and Wellness Coach
www.ShifraLefkowitz.com
info@shifralefkowitz.com
718-744-4543

# A Woman Divided
## Angela Vanegas

Throughout my twenties I was a bona-fide workaholic—that's right, a card-carrying, dyed-in-the-wool corporate maniac. You know the type: young and hungry. One of those newbies who worked overtime to prove I could be depended upon to deliver the impossible.

One manager referred to me as a future rain-maker. My special talent was to consistently over deliver and "add-value" in my area of expertise, computer technology. Fast-tracking through one position and on to the next, I was awarded ever-increasing levels of managerial responsibility in my field.

When my husband and I decided to start a family, I plugged away straight through my pregnancy, and drafted strategic plans, created budgets, and hired new staff. The idea was to position myself for assistant director of my department upon my return from maternity leave. I had it all planned—I'd step out momentarily to have the baby, take a little time off, then jump right back into the professional jet stream *better than ever!* Little did I know that transformation awaited me.

When my first born son Andres arrived, I was dumbstruck by my overpowering emotional reaction. No surprise that this tiny, sweet smelling creature turned my world completely upside down! My experience with him played itself out in text-book fashion. I fell head-over-heels madly in love with this baby and his incredibly intense aura. He and I were—and still are—totally in tune with one another.

To this day, Andres speaks aloud my very thoughts and I, at times, can feel his physical discomforts well before he is able to inform me that he is ill or in pain. It's been this way since his birth. Apparently, intuition or "insight," as some call it, runs rampant throughout my family tree.

My son's birth turned out to be the starting point for an important journey that required me to take note of my intuitive gifts and listen to my inner voice. Now that Andres was here I experienced a colossal paradigm shift; the consciousness surrounding my purpose in life transformed instantaneously.

All of my intense focus on climbing the corporate ladder to secure my future was usurped by my need to be present for him *now*. I was ready to trade my day-to-day scrambling in corporate America for a more peaceful existence that celebrated the stillness of the moment. Now that he was here, I recognized he'd experience only one childhood and I wanted to be with him to celebrate it.

### Exit Strategy

So, how would I break the news? How would I walk away from a career that I'd worked so hard to achieve? After all, I had seen this scenario played out a dozen times before. In fact, I had been in the room and seen the looks exchanged among men (and women as well) when other well-credentialed female colleagues had sent emails proclaiming that—after an already lengthy maternity leave—they'd "made a life decision " and "would not be returning," yada yada yada...

I didn't want to be branded *that* woman—another meteoric fall from grace in the eyes of the type-A denizens in the shark-ridden tanks of corporate America. I decided not to tell anyone yet, and convinced myself I could somehow juggle both roles with equal vigor—super manager by day and super mommy by night! I told myself this was just another challenge that I needed to step up and conquer. On the inside, however, I struggled constantly.

Months later, returning to work right on schedule, I went through all the usual motions of a full-time employed new mother—juggling work projects, managing drop-off and pick-up time constraints, and attending work meetings on merely three hours of sleep.

What remained, however, was an inner discord that spoke to me very subtly. *This is great, but you should be at home with your son,* it said. And I knew my inner voice was right. My life had a new context. For the time being, I would keep my sentiments to myself and press on further at the nine-to-five.

When my second son Sean arrived four years later, the entire cycle began all over again. Now Andres was a pre-schooler and there was no way on earth I saw myself stealing away from both of them on a daily basis to work outside the home with the ever-increasing demands of a corporate career.

This time, however, I was better prepared to address the conflict and decided to make my feelings known. When I explained it all to my husband, Ernesto, he was supportive but struggled with the concept of reducing our income so drastically. After all, we'd established a lifestyle for ourselves that was now dependent on dual incomes. A beautiful home in a community we loved, private school tuition for Andres, daycare expenses for Sean—it seemed impossible to remove my now substantial salary from this equation.

For now, we merely dreamed of a new and different future, but I was ready to do whatever it would take. I'd done the math, and I knew that, in my heart and mind, my kids would be small for only a short time. The time for me to be present for this experience was NOW. My husband, however, wasn't quite there yet.

*So, Angela, what are you going to do to fix this problem?* I wondered. After all, I was a corporate problem-solver by day. That's what I did best! I began to mull over the wildest of possibilities. How could I achieve what I wanted, stay at home with the boys, and be able to continue the lifestyle to which we had become accustomed?

### Getting Down to Business

It was time to seriously enact Plan B. That's "B" for "Business." I'd always wanted my own business. In fact, I'd dabbled in, and been quite successful with, several previous smaller ventures. I knew from my core, that in this moment my dabbling days were over. If I was to have any stake in my own future success, it was going to have to come from a venture of my own creation. Something into which I could sink the same passion that I'd exhibited to previous employers over the years. This was it, my time had arrived!

Still enormously frustrated with the demands of juggling work and family life, I remember telling my husband clearly that I was determined to launch a business. What I realized I had not explained to him was that I meant RIGHT NOW.

I spent every waking minute in between work and parenting responsibilities to research business concepts, the steps involved in launching a startup, and the revenue-generating possibilities of a dozen different business models. I worked through lunches, sitting at red lights, and pulled my fair share of all-nighters.

Finally, I made my decision. I announced that I was planning to empty out my 401K retirement account and buy a coin-operated Laundromat. True story! I'd run all the numbers and determined that I could probably make a decent living from a carefully chosen laundry facility location. I was driven and moving forward with or without cheerleaders.

Until now, Ernesto had only casually entertained my wild notions of beginning a business as an exit strategy for, and an on-ramp to, financial freedom for us. Let's just say that now I finally had his attention. Clearly not interested in helping me run a Laundromat, he asked if we could sit down and talk it out.

It's amazing what happened next. Three weeks later—now working as a team—we'd joined forces as two eager entrepreneurs, totally in accord. It's truly remarkable how the universe responds in kind to the types of energies you put forth. It was as if, because we'd united with a decisiveness to be open to new truths and new realities for our lives, the universe responded in similar fashion. Everything seemed to happen in a chain reaction, and literally only a few short weeks later we had a business concept fall directly into our lap.

At this time in our lives, now balancing our jobs, the kids and this monumental side project of researching and investigating new business ideas, we had even less time than usual to tend to the mundane task of routine household maintenance. So, we decided to hire a cleaning service to help out.

Sorely disappointed by both the quality of cleaning, and the substandard customer service received with the first company, we tried service after service looking for good quality work and positive customer service. Most were decent enough, but still left our homes overwhelmed with the smell of cleaning chemicals. Because Andres was especially allergic to fragrances at this time, and Sean was only a year old, we were hyper-sensitive to the type of chemical solutions used in our home by these companies.

We looked high and low for a service that could accommodate our desire to use natural, gentler cleaning agents in our home and were astonished to find that none existed in our area. Looking back, it was a remarkably dramatic and pivotal moment when Ernesto and I looked up at each other, bright-eyed and incredulous, and said nearly simultaneously "maybe this is what we could bring to market!" Both passionate about wanting to live a green, natural lifestyle, we wondered, *could this be it?*

After performing the usual due diligence to determine that there was room in the market for this concept, we set out to form our own company that summer. A few months later The Green Maid, Inc. was launched. This was it! It was actually happening. Our new future was beginning! My plan to live consciously, and be present for my children and my family, was finally coming into existence.

Five years later, our business has grown according to plan, and we employ more than twenty people, many of them long-term employees who have come to see our business and each other as a family. I have used my experiences in corporate America and my frustrations as a working mother to inform the culture that we have created at The Green Maid.

It's a culture that is truly family-oriented and considers the challenges that working parents face every day. What's more, this business now gives back to me everything I have ever put in to it. Most importantly, I see a future that is brighter than ever, and in alignment with my personal truth. My children deserve to have parents who are present and truly in balance with life and with them. We have discovered that living in acknowledgement of this lifestyle choice, we are happier now than we have ever been in our lives. I am grateful that I am no longer a woman divided...

**ABOUT THE AUTHOR:** Angela Vanegas is an Author, Entrepreneur and Technology Consultant. She is also President, CEO and Co-founder of The Green Maid, Inc., a trailblazing eco-friendly cleaning service and sustainable business based in Chicago, IL. As a working parent with two young children, she was The Green Maid's first client and has lead the brand management, website design and marketing efforts for her business since its launch in 2007. She has also been featured in various print and online publications centered around entrepreneurs and their successful startups, including Crain's Chicago Business, Jean Shatzky's Blog and Reader's Digest.

Angela Vanegas
Entrepreneur
www.angelavanegas.com
hello@angelavanegas.com
312-267-2265

# The End of Innocence
## Carol Walkner

I stepped onto the cushioned stool, grasped the polished wood railing with both hands, and slowly leaned forward as one lone tear fell with a silent *plop!* on the gleaming parquet floor far below. *I've got to jump,* I thought to myself.

My life was in ruins...my heart felt as though it'd been through a shredder...my soul was nothing but a pile of ashes. *I can't go on! I might as well jump and get it over with. But with my luck I probably won't die—just break my neck and be in a wheelchair wearing diapers for the rest of my life. Oh God!*

Who knew I'd feel like this, when eighteen months earlier, I had *the* perfect life. I lived like royalty in my luxurious, newly purchased, to-die-for condo. Surrounded by friends, my social calendar was filled, and I loved my job as an executive in a large, well-respected company that had chased me, hired me, and moved me from New Jersey to Cincinnati. It was magical and I was like a princess in my very own fairy tale.

The fairy tale didn't last long. One morning without warning—as I sat in my large corner office and the sun streamed through the windows—my boss and the human resources lady walked into my office and shut the door. Hmmm, had I missed a meeting?

The boss scowled nervously and the HR woman clutched a tote bag as if she wanted to strangle it. My heart flip-flopped, and for a moment I stopped breathing. "We're going to have to let you go," said my boss.

*What?* I thought to myself—I mustn't have heard right! "But why, sales are up, we all went to lunch just yesterday—what changed since then?" I ask.

"This has been coming for while—we're restructuring the whole company and altering some of the departments" my boss replied.

My mouth felt like the Sahara Desert, words flew around in my head like a hurricane, but when I opened my mouth, I heard myself croak "why me?"

"You're so creative and talented," said the Nazi from HR, "maybe you want to go into real estate or something where you can better utilize your people skills."

*These two must be from Mars, I thought, what is she talking about? I've been in this industry for over twenty-five years, why would I want to do something else? And, if I'm so damned creative, why are you letting me go?*

"Can't we work something out? " I plead, desperate. "I'll take a cut in pay, work part-time, whatever you need..."

"The decision has been made!" The HR Nazi helped me pack my personal belongings to ensure I didn't steal one of the company paper clips, as the tears ran down my face and I turned away. I won't let them see me cry! Oh, how can the sun still stream through these windows when my world is dark and I was just cut into little pieces and fed to the sharks?

Pushed off the corporate cliff with no safety net, one minute I was flying my jet high, and the next I was in a tailspin! I came crashing back down to earth, broken, unconscious, and wrapped in a cocoon of fear. In complete shock, smothered in insecurity, I thought *what am I to do now—with no income, a mountain of bills, and all alone?*

### Appearance Vs. Reality

Later that year I met a fabulous woman, and knew immediately we'd be great friends and possibly business partners. We complemented each other in many ways. Both of us were creative—Marsha in a more artistic way, I as a visionary with a head for business.

Marsha's thriving marketing company needed a shot of business sense and someone to help her fill in the missing piece of her marketing puzzle: promotional merchandise. Luckily, that was my area of expertise, so of course I figured together we had it made! *This* could be my *forever* job—I was sure I'd found the perfect business match!

Marsha's company appeared, from the outside, to be successful, and her database of more than three hundred clients surely worth the money I invested. I was a dreamer who dreamed big! So what if she seemed flighty, totally disorganized, and unable to concentrate on the day to day work? So what if she had the annoying habit of continually clearing her throat? I had the foresight she lacked, the imagination, creativity, and strong relationship-building skills. With my business expertise and her clients list, how could we lose?

Then why did my hand shake when it came time to sign our binding business agreement? I soon realized why. Her client list was built on quicksand—many of them had been out of business for years! Her business *appeared* to be prosperous but was put together with super glue and paper clips. Marsha was in debt up to her pretty little innocent eye balls! By the time I woke up, learned that everything was in her company name and that what I'd invested was long gone, I was devastated!

"Your client list is nothing more than an outdated database of non-existent companies!" I confronted her.

"Well of course it is!" she admitted with a derisive cackle. "You were really stupid to assume that any marketing company could have three hundred active clients! You *think* you're such a smart business woman—I really got *you!* Ha! You don't know anything! We're done!"

"We're done alright!" Head high, I walked toward my desk to clean it out and realized that not once during our conversation had Marsha cleared her throat. The lies were no longer stuck there— she'd finally told the truth!

I began to realize that much of my shock and devastation stemmed from the fact that I'd been deceived and betrayed by a woman. Women have always been important to me—female friends and family members have been there for each other since the beginning of time—when they were in caves, and the men were out hunting. Women stick together for safety's sake, like my mom and her circle of female friends. I viewed Marsha's deceit—I'd *never* expected a women to betray me!—as ruthless, and was all that much more shocked, devastated, and angry!

I'd thought we were two halves of a whole, and I'd handed her my power on a silver platter with a smile on my face. I wondered how I could have been so stupid. In addition to having been betrayed by an unethical woman with no honor, I'd been betrayed by my own naiveté. Like a baby in a three piece suit—outwardly I had all the trappings of a savvy business person, but inside I was like a kid without a clue—I was ready to follow whoever offered me the safety and security I so desperately sought in the business world.

And so it was that the Universe presented me with yet another opportunity to re-invent myself. *Why not start my own promotional business? I have twenty-five years experience in the industry, business savvy, and before I leave I'll bet I can convince Noel, that new salesman we'd just hired, to come with me rather than stay with that unethical ex-business partner of mine.*

Noel was the best door opener I'd ever met and I knew I needed him. He was awful at long term client relationships, but that was my job anyway. I believed I couldn't do it without him. We made a great team. Nothing could stop me...stop *us* now.

But something wasn't right. Sometimes when I was with him, I thought I could see something beneath his constant smile—something rotten, ugly, hot and putrid. When that happened, I'd squirm deep inside. He was like the proverbial wolf in sheep's clothing. But I pushed these images aside and convinced myself that we made a great business team. He made initial contacts with ease, and I followed by quickly establishing bonds of trust, empathy, and good will. Our steadily growing client list included some of the top companies in the city. They trusted my business suggestions and they liked *me!* My resilient, creative light was shining brightly!

### When Reality Bites—Bite Back!

One day I walked into my showroom with several orders in hand after a great meeting with our most prestigious client. I couldn't believe my eyes. The showroom straight ahead—usually filled with expensive jackets and shirts, award and recognition pieces—was empty! And the office furniture—gone!

Bewildered, I dropped my briefcase and ran back to my office. The room was a shambles and my computer was missing. I ran back to my front desk where Noel usually sat. I could have sworn he told me he'd be in that day. His files, phone, fax machine, even our client lists...*gone!*

I grabbed my purse and dug for my cell phone. My hands shook so hard I dropped it on the polished hardwood floor. My mind raced through all the possibilities—had I been betrayed, deceived? *Again?* Panicked, alone, powerless, my deep-seated security issues bubbled to the surface.

"Are you all right?" A voice from the doorway shocked me back to the present. It was Beth, the pretty blond, saleswoman I'd hired to start that day. *Oh my God! I'd completely forgotten about her!*

"What the hell happened here, anyway?" she added as she walked through the door.

Immediately, she dropped her briefcase, helped me up, and stood beside me. Beth stayed with me through the police visit since she'd seen Noel loading my computer into his car. She called him and told him if the computer wasn't back in this office by four p.m., he'd be very sorry!

He must have believed her because he brought it back. Who was this enthusiastic woman with the can-do attitude, and confident smile? Not flighty, not a wolf in sheep's clothing, no—a real, forthright woman. That is the angel called Beth.

Although Noel owed my company a lot of money, and stole my top two sales people, he didn't have time to steal the client list. My clients, who'd seen him for who he really was, rallied around me when I told them what had happened. Many of those original clients are still with us today and Beth and I remain both business partners and close friends.

Now, far from that wooden railing of years ago, I realize that then I was someone who didn't own my power, didn't follow my heart authentically. Everyone in my life has been a mirror, and when I'm mired in fear and anger, I attract those who prey upon my insecurities, and who cut me off at the knees every time. But when I am conscious of my own power, I meet the right people—like Beth. The road has been long, hard, and sometimes disappointing, but my journey—from naiveté to empowerment—has landed me safely at the end of innocence...

**ABOUT THE AUTHOR:** A trained public speaker, workshop leader, and group facilitator, Carol Walkner applies her forty years experience as a certified writing teacher and marketing executive to help those in transition/crisis better express themselves. Through her experiential program *The Dragon's Way* she teaches others how to successfully retreat from the brink of an emotional cliff, access personal safety nets, and conquer fear, so they can move forward with clarity, passion, and power. Carol, who holds a B.A in Journalism and an M.A. in Expressive Arts Therapy, develops writing circle programs that assist hospice nurses /social workers in crisis, and help seniors write memoirs.

Carol Walkner
LifeSpring Consulting LLC
www.thedragonwriter.com
carol@thedragonwriter.com
513-328-1038

*PART FOUR*

# Conscious Spirituality

*"Simply that everything we do
is motivated either by love or by fear."*
*~ Marianne Williamson*

# How I Healed From the Disease to Please

Jennifer Connell

I sat in the same row of our catholic church every Sunday morning for the first seventeen years of my life and perpetuated an ongoing internal dialogue riddled with questions about the sermon, the existence of God, and the meaning of life—of *my* life. Never truly satisfied by what was being espoused from the pulpit, and uncomfortable discussing my feelings with my parents and friends, I felt I never really fit my parents' image of what a daughter should be.

My father's parents came to America from England and Ireland via Ellis Island with only eighth grade educations. Both of my parents grew up with and maintained traditional Christian values, principles, and beliefs—marked by clearly defined roles for males and females—diverse and emotional expression and independent thinking weren't highly encouraged in our home. For example, crying was met with *"Are there broken bones? Are you bleeding? If not, there's no reason to cry!"*

In a more illustrative exchange, I recall telling my father one day that I wanted to go to college. "Why do you want to do that, honey?" he responded. "Won't you just get married and stay home and raise children?" The idea of women attending college was foreign to him. Women barefoot and pregnant was a much more familiar concept.

Over time, I learned to comply-to behave in ways that were acceptable to them—with the exception of a few mischievous "right of passage" incidents. All the while my soul screamed from behind my mask *there's more, there's more for you to be and do!* I simply didn't know how to respond to this voice.

Adept at pushing the pain away, the double life I lived became more and more intense. The more time passed, the more it became clear to me that I was living an unfulfilling and miserable existence. I longed for more fulfilling relationships, and craved a stronger sense of connection and acceptance. I wanted to feel whole within myself. I believed that fulfilling these desires would make me happier and more engaged in life.

Then one day I woke up with excruciating pain in my hands and weakness from my shoulders to fingertips. My limbs and joints appeared normal, but the pain brought tears to my eyes. Turning faucets was near impossible and holding a blow dryer or mug became a hardship. When I looked at myself in the mirror, nothing had changed on the outside, but inside I felt like an old woman, limp, and peppered with debilitating pain. Embittered by thoughts of "why me?" I was exhausted.

After numerous office visits and various traditional protocols the rheumatologist concluded I couldn't be helped by traditional methods. *Oh great,* I thought, *what then?* "I'd really like you to see a colleague of mine to whom I send people on rare occasions when my protocols don't work," Dr. W. told me. He explained that he thought my case was beyond the scope of allopathic medicine. "We're going to address you from the inside out."

And so I was introduced to Ed.

### *No One Can Make You Feel Inferior Without Your Consent!*

Meeting Ed was pivotal. During a lengthy intake, he gathered quite a bit of information about me—my upbringing, lifestyle, etc. Our conversations revolved around the introduction of new ideas that challenged many of my previous ways of thinking. Ed suggested that the physical pain I experienced was likely attributable to the fact that I'd been seduced and hypnotized by the belief that I wasn't good enough, and that I'd spent years seeking validation from my relationships.

I recall thinking, *Whaaaat? It sounds like he's suggesting my thoughts and feelings have an impact on my physical health...what a preposterous idea! Ahem...um...could there be some truth to this?* My ensuing discoveries simultaneously inspired and frightened me.

The first conscious step on my personal expedition began with a dive into my *self*, a scary place in which to venture, and ultimately I learned that my habitual patterns were indeed marked by worry about "doing the right thing" to evoke responses of love and acceptance from others. The by-product was that in my effort to cultivate fulfilling relationships, I'd fostered superficial ones rife with validation-seeking behaviors.

In short, I was infected with what's known to some as the "disease to please." I perpetuated a cycle of approval-seeking behaviors that, when met with responses that didn't match the conditions I defined as appropriate, would send me reeling into feeling rejected, sad and humiliated. This only fueled an unhealthy and vicious cycle. I had allowed the actions of others to dictate my happiness and feelings of self worth, and when I went reeling, I blamed them.

Armed with this new insight, I made a conscious commitment to break this cycle. I put myself under the microscope and, as I gained clarity, slowly became more and more self-aware and skilled at recognizing when I blamed others for my own feelings. During this process, I adopted and used as a mantra the wise words of Eleanor Roosevelt: "No one can make you feel inferior without your consent!"

During the next five years I lost twenty pounds, created my own job description, received a promotion, and—best of all—became pain free. The job creation and promotion proved to be another turning point, and had a profound influence on me. Living in London and in a commission-only sales position with a U.K.-based firm, I worked for a demanding CEO and sales director who, rather than support or develop people who continually produced lackluster results, chastised them. They showed no interest in the employees' well-being unless they were one of the sales "rock stars" (translation: generated big profits!)

Their behavior perpetuated an "us versus them" milieu, and after working there successfully for only a few months, I noticed the low level of morale and energy among many of the steady performers. Their enthusiasm had waned, and complaints and absenteeism increased. Only if they'd had a great week, marked by closing a big sale, were they paid any attention or offered professional support. In addition, the company seemed to contain a revolving door through which people came in with big dreams but left shortly after because they felt completely discouraged.

I felt in my heart I could make a difference for those uncared for professionals, and approached the CEO with an idea. What if the company offered its salespeople training and development? Then they'd start off their employment in this organization with a foundation which, over time, would reduce turnover and increase morale on the sales floor. This in turn, would increase sales.

I proposed to design and implement a training program to coach existing salespeople and onboard new salespeople. The intended outcome would inspire and equip them for a successful sales career in this organization. He agreed to a pilot, and within a couple of months the communication between leadership and staff improved, the salespeople became more engaged, and ultimately they evolved into a sustainable, high performing team.

Along with the success of the program came a new title, an enviable salary, and frequent travel between New York, London, and Amsterdam, as they asked me to introduce a formal recruitment and development program in their New York office.

Once riddled with physical illness from the perceptions of judgment, I felt freed from the unhealthy vice-like grip that blocked me for so many years. My confidence began to soar—I felt empowered!

My work continued to focus on helping others tap into their potential. This required care, concern, compassion, empathy, and support towards others—and I noticed that all of these traits flowed from me naturally. Many women shared how they were inspired and felt loved and safe in my presence during our consultations.

### Little Jennifer

Paradoxically, although I'd received myriad validations, and believed I elicited a positive response in others, I still couldn't escape that judgmental voice in my head. It continually chastised me: *You're not doing well enough! Your recent bout with success is only a fluke—don't expect it to continue! You're really not smart enough to sustain success! Don't let others see your vulnerabilities, and don't ask for help!*

Taken aback by the intensity of my inner dialogue, especially after all I'd learned and practiced over the past few years, I realized how the voice in my head continued to incapacitate me and interfere with my daily life. That I had to dive deeper within myself to meet yet another part of me became obvious.

The most recent and profound turning point to date occurred one day when I heard a soft voice during meditation: *"Hi Jennifer, remember me? I'm the little girl you abandoned many years ago and have been living inside you all this time. I feel ashamed and angry, and I don't want to be in pain any longer."*

Followed immediately by flashes of childhood memories that included judgments, messages of unworthiness, reprimands for expressing emotions, and subtle ridicule of my dreams, this message was emotionally overwhelming. Despite the care, concern, compassion, empathy, and support I showed others, I recognized how I'd spent my entire life rejecting myself.

I'd packed up those self destructive memories in a box long ago, never to be opened again. However, in the process, I ended up treating everyone else in my life better than I treated myself! My reaction to this *aha!* moment was visceral, and I instantly realized that to attain the internal wholeness I was missing, I had to stop the judgment and embrace "Little Jennifer," who was frightened and convinced she was unworthy and unloved. I had to commit to cultivating a loving, compassionate relationship with the little girl inside, with *me*.

So, I learned to consciously practice acceptance of all the thoughts, feelings, and emotions that ride through me, and to give myself permission to have and feel them all. The best thing about this is that when I give voice to those emotions that need air time, they lose their grip or dissipate completely and I am then able to replace them with feelings of self love.

I wish I could report that this relationship transformation happened overnight, but in truth, like my overall journey of self discovery, it's been an evolution. On occasion, it's a struggle to process my feelings, and my happy place gets rocked. Other days it's easy to embrace them and to find my place of peace and acceptance. Yet, when I recall how I once longed for fulfilling relationships, to fit in, and to feel whole within myself, I realize now that I have all of this and more. Happily engaged in a fulfilling life, healthy in my body and mind, I'm still evolving, but now it's by conscious choice since I learned how to heal from the disease to please.

**ABOUT THE AUTHOR:** Jennifer Connell thrives when she serves in a consultative role, supporting individuals in developing their internal capacity to lead, adapt to change, and achieve new heights of success. She earned her Masters degree in Organizational Systems and integrates her multi-disciplinary professional and personal experience with integrity, humor, creativity and passion. Jennifer's entrepreneurial spirit is boundless. After building and then selling a successful nutrition and exercise center in New Jersey, Jennifer moved to Florida, where she thoroughly enjoys her non-profit philanthropic service, teaching yoga and meditation, spending time with family, and assisting people who welcome growth and change.

Jennifer Connell
Jennifer Connell International
www.JenniferConnell.com
Jennifer@jenniferconnell.com
904-252-7935

# From the Inside Out
## Cindy Cox-Ruccolo

Divorce was out—*uh uh, I'm not doin' that,* I'd think to myself. I wanted to leave but, with the negative social stigma about divorce embedded in my brain from childhood, I hung in there. My family didn't believe in divorce and looked down on divorced families. You stuck it out and made it work—for the kids.

So I hung in there when he criticized me, pointed out my faults, and made negative statements like "you can't cook," "you're a bad wife and a bad mother," "you're fat," and on and on. I knew it was a horrible situation. I also knew there had to be more to life than living with someone who did not respect me.

One day I confided in my reverend how I felt about this divorce thing, and that I didn't want my son to come from a "broken home," as my mom called it. I'll never forget how she looked me in the eye and said matter of factly, "sweetie, the home is already broken." That's when the light bulb went on and everything shifted.

It was after a devastating breakup from a man I'd loved very much that I met and quickly married Jose, whom I barely knew. Also a bodybuilder, it was mainly a lustful, physical attraction. At least we had the bodybuilding in common. We competed in national bodybuilding shows together and were extremely competitive, even with each other. Two people dieting, taking steroids, and training for shows in the same house did not a good combo make!

It was an intense relationship, and we'd be on again off again. During our hiatuses, we'd date others, but always come back to each other. It was during one of our time out's that I found out I was pregnant with his child.

We decided to have another go and become parents to this little soul. Initially very happy about being a mommy, by the seventh month I knew he and I were done. He wasn't nice to me, deep down didn't respect women, and never treated me as an equal.

I was just beginning to grow spiritually and to learn how to love and respect myself, and fill the empty void inside, and I didn't like the way any of it felt. As I started to learn how to love myself more, I realized this was *not* ok.

Shortly after that conversation with my reverend, I woke up one morning, realized I was worth more, and started to fight back. I was not going to live like my parents and stay even though I wanted to leave. I was not having co-dependency in my own life! I decided I wasn't going to take it anymore, we were done, and he had to go...

### *The Wild Child*

My parents had me in their forties and joked I was an accident. I'd always felt in the way growing up, like I wasn't really wanted. The youngest of four, all separated by seven years, my sisters and brother teased me about it and treated me like a step-child. I never felt like I had a "real" family.

I'd been the wild child—what my parents called "a handful," much more of a challenge than my two older sisters and brother, who never got into trouble. My dad would snap at me in his usual controlling, impatient, too tired, too busy way, and punish me. My mom, co-dependent, always played the peacekeeper and never wanted to upset my dad. She'd ask me to apologize even when I hadn't done anything wrong. "No way!" I'd scream, the strong willed brat.

They argued a lot, often about me. Deep inside I'd wonder why they didn't really love me. My friend's families were so much closer. They'd look out for each other, stick up for each other, protect each other, spend quality time together, have more patience, gentleness, and—most of all—unconditional love.

I wanted attention and, if I couldn't get it positively, I'd get it negatively. Always wild and in trouble, I was the kind of kid other parents would never let their kids hang around. The leader of the gang, I snuck into bars at fifteen. I'd steal my mom's car and go joyriding—a lot. One time I stole it, wrecked it, and parked it to make it look as if she had scraped it up—and let her get the blame.

I'd torture the neighbors. One day the cops came and knocked on the door several times because I'd taken everyone's mail and swapped it to the other mails boxes on the block. Another time they came because I was throwing rocks onto Interstate 95.

There was the time I ordered a huge pest control job to a neighbor's house, and the company came and did the job. When the parents came home and saw the bill, they asked their daughters (who'd been home alone) what it was. They said they didn't know, they'd just let them in. When the company played back the message on its voice mail, it was me ordering it on a crank call.

The icing on the cake came when my parents went out of town and I stayed at a neighbor's house. I broke into my own house, threw a big block party, and stole the car. The neighbor's mom told my dad, and I caught hell—not good to be a trouble making, drinking, drugging, juvenile delinquent when your dad's a retired cop, was one of the first sky marshals, and a U.S. Customs officer.

## Too Late to Say I'm Sorry

My father died suddenly of lung cancer—I was only twenty-one and stationed in Hong Kong in the Navy. I'd matured a lot in the Navy, and wanted so much to tell my dad I was sorry about all the hassles I'd put my parents through, and to make things right. To tell him that I really did love and appreciate him and all he'd done for me; to ask his forgiveness. I felt deep regret I'd never be able to do that.

Home now, I managed to secure a transfer to Key West, only three hours from my mom. Married for forty-two years, her whole world had revolved around my dad, and I worried that she wouldn't handle his loss well at all. On all kinds of medication, the doctors just kept writing her prescriptions for everything—she had a pill to wake up, calm down, sleep, breathe! I knew all these pills couldn't be good for her.

Her health issues included high blood pressure, heart disease, and spastic colitis, not to mention stress and nervousness. I tried to get her to eat healthier and become more active, but to no avail. If it didn't have to do with taking care of us or her home, she wasn't having it. Mom never did anything for herself. I don't think she knew how. I always thought in the back of my mind: please do not let me end up like that. Help me to be an independent, strong woman.

I planned a trip home one Friday afternoon and spoke with mom that morning to tell her I'd drive down to see her after work. At three o'clock I got a call from my brother. Hysterical, he blurted into the phone "Mom just checked out!"

"What?"

"Mom's dead! She had a heart attack in the shower—you have to come home, *now!*"

It had been only eight months and I—hardly over one parent's death—was forced to bury the other one. My lack of real relationships with my sisters and brother left me feeling scared and alone for the first time in my life. They were grown up and living their lives. I was twenty-one, and felt like an orphan...my parents were really all I had.

*I'm screwed,* I thought. I tried to kill the pain with alcohol and partying. I thought if I buried it, it would go away. There wasn't a bottle big enough into which I could crawl. I drank and partied in every country, all over the world, with the best of them.

And all the time I felt guilty—guilty for not being the model child I should have been, guilty for not having made amends, first with my father, and now with my mother.

## The End of the Cycle

After the death of my parents, a bad marriage, and a bitter divorce, I found myself a single mother working three jobs. I'd begun the process of serious self discovery before my marriage, when I felt a real longing to search my soul and find out *why* I did what I did and what made me tick; I'd wanted to fix my broken self.

Now I knew there had to be even more; that I was capable of becoming a better version of me. Thank God I had the gym and working out, but it wasn't enough. I started going to Unity Church and counseling and read just about every self help book I could get my hands on. I began making major changes, and started down the path of real self love and spiritual enlightenment.

This was not easy, because all the while I was raising my son. I still made mistakes, but finally I knew what I *didn't* want and *wouldn't* stand for. I tried consciously not to repeat the same mistakes my parents made with me and to raise my little boy in a different environment—one of belonging, love, safety, positive reinforcement, feedback, with no anger, no abuse—and to give him a strong sense of self. I wanted him to know he was wanted, that he mattered, and was an important part of the family unit.

I realized that my attention-seeking behavior—the partying, drinking to kill the pain, bad decisions, promiscuity, steroid use, bodybuilding competitions, all of it—had been my way of seeking attention, love, acceptance, and validation outside of myself to replace what was missing within. And it wasn't until I realized that all of my outside behavior was just bullshit and distraction—I could get my outside body together and still be a mess inside—that I stopped looking outside myself for answers.

It was only then that I discovered how to truly end the cycle. I'd made my share of mistakes, but they were my life lessons and *finally* I got the message. It took courage to quiet my mind, go within, and listen—to trust myself enough to understand that the answers were inside of me. Now, when my mind is right, my body follows. When I learned to love my whole self, fill my *own* voids with healthy behaviors, everything totally shifted for me, and I really began to live.

I raised an amazing son, who's in school on an almost full academic ride, created the life of my dreams—including marrying my soul mate—started two successful businesses, furthered my education, and changed my health for the better. A lifestyle coach, a certified fitness trainer, and certified sports nutritionist, I teach women everywhere how to truly love themselves *from the inside out.*

**ABOUT THE AUTHOR:** Cindy Ruccolo, as seen on NBC 6, is a powerhouse! She is a Certified Fitness Trainer, Certified Sports Nutritionist, Author, Motivational Speaker, and a Mindset Mentor. Cindy has created a proprietary program that helps others get "Fit from the Inside Out". As a National level Body Building Champion, Cindy holds many first place titles, so she knows first-hand how to help individuals get in shape and stay that way. Cindy works with people around the world both in-person and via Skype. She is in the business of changing lives one body at a time and helps people Eat Clean and Get Lean for Good, NO EXCUSES!

Cindy Cox-Ruccolo
Certified Sports Nutritionist
Certified Fitness Trainer
www.cindyruccolo.com
954-242-2580

# The Fire
## Tonya S. Coy

I didn't ignore the call that came from my neighbor Princis that Tuesday afternoon in November because she never calls unless it's important. And what she had to tell me changed my life.

"Your house is on fire!" Princis finally said, after I questioned why she kept saying I needed to come home immediately. I grabbed my pocketbook and coat, told my boss I had to go because I'd received a call that my house was on fire, and ran out. As I left, I saw missed calls on my cell from my neighbor's son, my daughter at college, and my son at school in New York.

Princis talked to me on my cell the whole ride home. When I pulled up to my street, she and another friend met me at the corner. They instructed me to get out of my SUV, and the friend parked my car as Princis put her arm around me and walked me to my home. The rain poured down, and several fire engines, police cars, and spectators blocked my street. By the time I arrived, the fire had destroyed my house. I broke down in tears.

As I left for work earlier that morning, I'd walked our dog Max to his cage and told him I'd see him later. As usual, he'd look up at me with his big brown eyes, so innocent and trusting, and went obediently into the cage. "Goodbye sweet Max!," I'd called as I flew out the door a little earlier than usual to take my dad to work first. On my way to his house, I noticed there'd been a fire around the corner from me. Several buildings had burned and the street was blocked off.

Now several officials greeted me and began to ask questions. What time had I left home? Was anyone at the house? Did anyone live with me? Did I leave anything on the stove? Did I have any candles burning? I answered their questions, and kept asking "Where's Max?" but it seemed no one could tell me.

The firemen continued to go through my home as police officials stood nearby, and friends, family members, neighbors, and even strangers gathered in front of my house. Many offered me their condolences, and expressed concern and support. But still I didn't know about Max.

It wasn't until my stepdad and mom arrived, and he and I walked over to my neighbor's adjoining yard that I saw Max's cage in our yard. Instantly, I knew he was gone. Overwhelmed by the thought of him locked in a cage while the fire raged around him, I burst into tears again. I kept thinking how he must have fought for his life and struggled to get out of his cage—like when I came home from work and he scratched to get out as if to say, *hurry up and let me out, I know you're home!* I was crushed.

How was I going to tell my children Max was gone? Max, who'd been with us since he was a month old, and was a family member we loved and cherished who'd just turned twelve. Half Pomeranian and half terrier, Max thought and acted like he was human, and sometimes we did too...

The dreadful moment came. I told my son David over the phone, and when I heard him cry I broke down again because—as the eldest child, now a young man—he's usually the stronger one. In college for several years now, Max was used to him being gone for long periods of time. But whenever David came home, he'd grab his leg ready to play, because he knew David would wrestle with him on the floor.

"Where's Max?" was Jasmin's first question. She sobbed as I told her the awful news. Max was her baby, her buddy. He followed her everywhere. He wasn't used to her being gone for more than a night or two, and it was hardest for him when she left for her first year of college. One night, no problem, two nights, not so bad, but when she didn't return he would face the front door, waiting. He looked at that front door for almost two solid weeks. He would go and sleep in her bed. I even took a picture of him there and sent it to her. The caption read: *I'm chillin' in Jasmin's bed until she gets back!* It took him another week to realize she wasn't coming. But when she did, he'd get *so* excited.

As for me, while the kids were gone, he kept me company, even though I wouldn't admit it to my family and friends. Always feisty, Max would follow me everywhere I went in the house and not let me out of his sight for long. He used to get on my nerves, but I think he thought I was going to leave too, so I'd tell him "I'm not going anywhere, I'm just going upstairs!" But he'd be anxious, especially when he realized the kids had gone to school. He didn't care what I said because I'd always bust him sneaking to see where I was. When we lost Max, we lost a family member.

Eventually, I was told he died of smoke inhalation and was asked if I wanted to see him. I declined. He was taken away by animal control and again, I cried.

### There But For the Grace of God Go I

Both of my children wanted to come home the day of the fire but I asked them to wait until the day before Thanksgiving, as originally planned. I needed some time alone to think and to process what had happened and what would be my next steps. I also wanted to be strong for them emotionally.

When we finally came face-to-face, it was an emotional moment.

The following day was Thanksgiving Day. My plan was to put the fire aside and enjoy the holiday with my family. Able to enjoy spending time with my uncle, cousins, aunt, mom, stepfather and my children, I had a great day. I laughed so hard I almost went to the bathroom on myself. We played UNO, ate, shared jokes, talked, and just had fun. I needed that day. My children needed that day. Being surrounded by family gave me great comfort and peace. It was a day full of love and joy. By the end of the night, stuffed and exhausted, we returned to my mom's.

The Sunday after Thanksgiving, my mom, my children, and I went to church. That day, church service was different. The week before, Bishop Jenkins had explained that when you're in a crisis, you don't run away *from* the church, rather the church is where you should run *to*. During this service, he spoke about my loss and called me to the altar. I appeared, my children by my side. He asked the congregation to give an offering on my behalf. Overwhelmed, my eyes filled with tears as people came forward and placed money at the altar. I wanted to run, but instead stepped off to the side. I couldn't believe the financial support I received—the congregation's generosity really took my breath away, and I felt so blessed!

After the offering, I returned to my seat. The stage was set up to look like a talk show set with two chairs and a small coffee table. Bishop Jenkins had invited a guest speaker, a friend of his in his mid to late fifties, to come onto the stage and talk about his testimony to the congregation.

His testimony was a powerful one. At nineteen years old, he'd had half his stomach removed and endured a multitude of surgeries over the years. He continued to experience medical issues to this day. Blind in one eye and deaf in one ear, he stated that he wasn't supposed to be here, but his faith in God was stronger than ever.

Listening to this man's testimony, I experienced a true *aha!* moment, and I knew I was going to be alright. Here this man lost his sight in one eye, he's deaf in one ear, and he's had all these physical ailments since he was nineteen years old—how can I complain? All of my clothes, furniture, etc., can be replaced, but my kids and I are here, *we're ok.* That was something to me, and it was humbling to listen to somebody else's story.

The kids had the majority of their clothes, which made it easier for me—I had to worry only about my own clothing. And I'd salvaged our photo albums, realized a great support system, and had the foresight to purchase good homeowner's insurance. I walked away thankful for my good health, and the health and safety of my children. Even though the loss of my home and pet was tragic, I couldn't find it in my heart to complain about my situation, as it did not hold a candle to this man's journey. After his testimony, we gave an offering for him as well.

Those things in mind, my faith in God grew even more. So now, when people say, "you sound good," I always refer to Bishop's friend's testimony to help them understand from where my true strength comes. The loss I experienced left me with a greater understanding that people and things that I love can be taken away at a moment's notice, and that I am not immune to personal tragedy. Now I slow down, treasure my life to its fullest, and try not to sweat the small stuff. I maintain my faith and trust in God, and know that He will see me through.

And He has. He's shown me that I am truly loved and highly favored amongst those I've helped throughout my life. On the day of the fire, I found myself surrounded by so many people whose lives I've supported, helped, or touched in some way, be it big or small. And for that, I am truly grateful. I always try to help others in any way that I can without looking for anything in return. And God returns the favor.

I have persevered through my struggles by giving it to Him. The fire is just one of many life experiences that makes me who I am today. Instead of looking at these challenges fearfully, I treat them as an opportunity to focus my life's direction toward what is most beneficial for me, which is what led me to create *Empowering Your Success, LLC*, a coaching business to inspire, empower, and motivate others to live the life they desire, with purpose.

**ABOUT THE AUTHOR:** Certified as a Life Empowerment Coach, Tonya created Empowering Your Success to inspire, empower and motivate individuals to overcome barriers and create a more balanced life both professionally and personally through coaching, workshops, and motivational speaking. For over 15 years, Tonya has been working as the Director of Operations for a non-profit organization. She volunteers for Heart to Hearts, Susan G. Komen for the Cure, and Literacy Volunteers of Mercer County. She holds a MS in Human Resources Management and is the proud mother of two children, David and Jasmin. Her motto is *Live Well, Laugh Often and Love Much!*

Tonya S. Coy
Empowering Your Success, LLC
www.empoweringyoursuccessllc.com
tonya@empoweringyoursuccessllc.com
609-851-8036

# The Unkindness of Strangers
## Madeline Ebelini

The judge started to scream at me, and it was as if time stood still. In the courtroom full of attorneys waiting for their cases to be called, my opposing counsel and I stood before the judge during what started out as a fairly routine hearing.

The opposing attorney had been flouting the rules of the court for months, repeatedly refusing to provide documents he was duty-bound to disclose. As my client's legal advocate, I stated our position clearly and professionally. I stressed my client's entitlement to the requested documents and noted the obvious misconduct of the opposing attorney.

As I spoke, something in the judge snapped. His face turned beet red and his voice shattered the air like a crack of thunder. He boomed that I had "yelled" at him. "How dare you yell at a magistrate in a court of law!" My heart stopped beating. I stood there, frozen. What happened? I hadn't yelled or done anything remotely inappropriate.

What unfolded next was beyond my comprehension. During his seemingly endless rant, the judge even threatened to put me in jail! Ultimately, he stormed off the bench toward the office door behind him. By this time I'd sunk into my chair at the counsel table. I felt as though I'd left my body and was hovering over the scene as I tried to make sense of it.

In shock, I didn't notice that everyone in the courtroom had stood up when the judge flew off the bench. Slowly, I re-entered my body and realized I was the only one in the room still sitting down. The judge stood at the door, glared at me from the corner of his eye, and waited for me to stand in his honor.

As if in a nightmare, I slowly rose to my feet. Only then did the judge open the door and disappear. It was a stunning display of rage and irrationality, and I'd been its sole recipient.

I didn't return to work for several days. At home, I sobbed uncontrollably, incapable of functioning. How had I been so long part of a system that left me feeling crushed, inauthentic, and empty? Where was my resilience in the face of unkindness?

Not the only incident I'd experienced of this nature, it was surely the most dramatic. After practicing law for twenty years, this episode highlighted my inability to withstand unkindness, and eventually helped solidify my decision to leave the legal profession.

But first I had to go down a very ugly vortex of stress. Day after day I internally rehashed my anger toward people who'd been unkind or unfair to me. I experienced insomnia, chronic pain, anxiety attacks, and a case of shingles, and swung between irritability, hopelessness, and sorrow.

My twelve year-old son repeatedly urged me to see a doctor. "I'm too busy," was my standard response. Eventually I began to see his handwriting on "Post-It" notes around the house—in the kitchen, on the bathroom mirror: "Go to the doctor!" This finally convinced me. I described my symptoms to my doctor and mentioned how unbearable my job had become. "I think you're depressed," she said, and suggested I leave my job. I did.

### Silence is Golden

Around this time, a close friend invited me to a yoga class. The inner peace I experienced in that hour of yoga was something I hadn't known for years. Lying on my yoga mat, I actually fell asleep at the end of the class—blessed relief from my insomnia. I was hooked!

The experience spurred me to read everything I could get my hands on related to yoga and meditation. I tried to meditate, getting up early each morning before my family. It was difficult, but I kept at it.

After a few months of yoga, I signed up for a yoga teacher training program—at age forty-seven! I also enrolled in a master's program in transpersonal psychology—the study of the mind in the context of ancient spiritual traditions and modern psychology. I devoured every book, article, and lecture, and embarked on a path of learning and transformation. Eventually this inspired me to establish a regular and deep practice of mindfulness meditation and yoga.

My growing interest in mindfulness led me to a weeklong silent meditation retreat. I'd never meditated for so long—six hours each day. My very first night I experienced an explosion of vivid and intense dreams.

In the first dream, I argued with my mother, and physically felt decades of anger boil and rise inside me like a volcano. My heart pounded wildly, and I sat up in bed, screaming out loud at her. Mortified at my middle of the night outburst in the "silent" dormitory, I thought *what happened? Did anyone hear me?*

When I fell back asleep, a barrage of intense symbolic dreams followed. In the next dream I received a telephone call from someone who informed me that, unbeknownst to me, I'd given birth to a child I'd never met! I excitedly told my son that he had a brother or sister. I then found myself in a public place—possibly an airport. An anonymous and faceless woman appeared in the distance pushing a stroller toward me. As she approached, I knelt down to see the face of this child, who I believed to be mine. Instantly I realized with a shocking jolt that the little girl in the stroller was me!

In my next dream I walked through an amusement park, and came upon a girl of about seven or eight. She lay motionless on the ground, unconscious, apparently having wrecked her bicycle. Her body lay twisted—her head, shoulders, and torso faced backward, while her legs remained astride the bike.

No one seemed to notice her lying there, despite the large number of people in the park. I roused her and helped her back onto her bike, only to discover that the bike was outlandishly huge in comparison to her small body. She couldn't reach the pedals, and the handlebars towered over her head. "You can't ride this bike!" I exclaimed. Determined to continue on her way, she replied, "I have to," as she struggled to ride off.

It was difficult to integrate the painful personal truth of these dreams. I'd sensed from an early age that, for reasons unknown, my mother and I seemed never to have truly bonded. I'd spent most of my life trying to figure out why.

My mind struggled for years to understand the reason. Was it postpartum depression? Was it because, having been born with a birth defect, I spent months in a heavy cast, making it difficult for her to lift and hold me? As a child I believed it was because my birth caused her ugly Cesarean scar, or because I wasn't as beautiful or as smart as she. Whatever the reason, somehow I'd always felt inferior and painfully alienated from her. That unconditional connection other girls seemed to have with their mothers did not exist in my world. In the emotional sense I often "mothered" myself as a youngster, a reality starkly validated in my dream about the child in the stroller.

## My Mother's Soft Spot

I wonder now what my mother's childhood was like. I knew little, though she recently shared that her grandmother gave birth to twins when her mother was little. Both babies died a few days after birth. Did my young grandmother blame herself for the deaths of her siblings? Did this—or some other factor, such as her own mother's grief or depression—create an unconscious pattern of self-blame and anger that she projected onto *my* mother during her childhood?

And was this dynamic repeated between my mother and me? I remember my inner relief when I discovered, during my pregnancy, that my only child would be a boy. On some level, I must have been afraid I'd repeat the same pattern if I had a daughter.

These dreams marked the beginning of my awakening to the truth of my early life experience. Always the overachiever, seemingly independent and unafraid, I was the girl driven to ride the bike that was too large. I functioned at a level beyond my years, focused on earning love and acceptance, but afraid to stop and feel the pain of its absence. I drove myself to excel, to keep going, but to *where*, for *what*, and for *whom?*

My verbal outburst during the first dream was the release of subconscious anger I'd suppressed most of my life. I believe I subconsciously projected this suppressed anger onto others, who directed it back to me. Because I was less than whole, I had no effective way to cope when this happened. Working in an adversarial, ego-heavy legal system didn't help. When unkindness hit, I'd flounder in that vulnerable, wounded place born of disconnection—disconnection from my mother and from my authentic self.

This is what Tibetan meditation master Chogyam Trungpa describes as our "soft spot." Each of us has one—that place so wounded in childhood that we subconsciously spend much of our lives trying to protect it from being bruised. Our habitual and often destructive patterns of thought, emotion, and behavior become a suit of armor to protect and defend our soft spot. This suit of armor is a "false self" which becomes our "identity."

Both ancient and modern philosophers identify the "soft spot" as the source of our sorrow, anger, and fear, but also the birthplace of our authenticity, compassion, and connection. My meditation practice, and these dreams, brought me face to face with my greatest fear—that I was unlovable in the eyes of my mother. I had to consciously realize and face this fear in order to integrate the lost pieces of myself, and transform my fear into wholeness and compassion.

This marked the end of my search for reasons, and the beginning of forgiveness and growth. I know now that my mother always loved me, but found it difficult to give and receive affection. This saddens me for us both, but my mindfulness practice allows me to step out of the old pattern, and to transform it. I made a strong effort to connect with my mother and began to say "I love you" at the end of each phone call. She's responded in kind, and this is now a tradition.

Now that I've left the legal profession and embarked on a second career as a mindfulness-based stress reduction educator, my mother is one of my biggest fans. I trust that our relationship will continue to grow in authenticity and whole-heartedness. I may never know the true nature of her "soft spot." I only know that she suffered when I was young, and that she never intended to hurt me. I also know that her love is real and that she, too, longs for connection. Today I can only let her know that my heart is filled with love for her.

**ABOUT THE AUTHOR:** Madeline Ebelini, MATP, RYT, founder of Integrative Mindfulness in Bonita Springs Florida, holds a Masters in Transpersonal Psychology, and teaches *Mindfulness-Based Stress Reduction (MBSR)* and Yoga. Her graduate work explored mindfulness, meditation, growth-fostering relationships, and integral practice. She completed professional instruction in MBSR with senior faculty at the Center for Mindfulness in Medicine, Health Care and Society at UMass Medical School. Madeline is a member of the teaching faculty at eMindful.com where she teaches *Mindfulness at Work.* Her mission is to create the conditions for transformation through health-promoting and life-enhancing programs utilizing mindfulness to explore our human potential. www.IntegrativeMindfulness.net

Madeline Ebelini
Integrative Mindfulness
www.integrativemindfulness.net
Madeline@integrativemindfulness.net
239-390-1113

# My Special Tool Box
## Brenda Ernst

I pulled Charlotte out from the get go, and made a conscious choice to practice each day. Charlotte is my cello, built in 1860, with which I've spent many an hour, but had neglected since work took over my world.

Charlotte is just one of my tools.

Several years ago my dad gave me a toolbox when I moved out on my own. The tools within the toolbox are a hodgepodge—some are rusty, others shiny, some are useful, others novel. Along with the toolbox he imparted immeasurable wisdom. One thing is for sure, the toolbox helps me in times of need.

I found myself in such a time of need recently, when my office announced an upcoming acquisition. It was then that I started to do things a little differently—not because of the acquisition, but because my life was out of balance. I began to limit the number of days I actually took home my laptop (quite honestly, I could log in from my home computer). I stopped working on the weekends (except until Sunday night or if there was an emergency). I cut my work day down to no more than eight hours.

In short, I tried to incorporate more fun and balance into my life. I was burned out. About six months before, I'd vacationed in one of my favorite places: the north woods of Wisconsin. On this particular journey "up north" I stayed in Stone Lake, which is like a little bit of heaven to me.

Fortunate enough to be able to escape to the north woods a couple of times a year—sometimes with friends and sometimes with family—there I'd wake up to the loons, drink my morning coffee by the lake, walk through the woods, swim in the lake, fish, read, and visit with good friends and family. To say that I love it up there would be an understatement! Up north I can relax, and I always have a difficult time leaving.

I was burned out and exhausted before this particular trip. A director in charge of technology programs, my work was non-stop. In the process of rolling out a new technology program with limited resources and tight deadlines, the stress mounted. I worked hard, and yet it was tough to get even a simple "thank you" from those around me.

I remember one particular day during the summer—blue skies and perfect weather—that marked a turning point. I'd planned to attend my nephew Lake's baseball playoff game, but walked out of work knowing that I could go to the game and risk having a meltdown there, or I could have my meltdown in the privacy of my own home. I drove home and missed the game.

During that trip, I envisioned working someday in a setting like Stone Lake. Prior to my trip, I found myself repeatedly saying "I want out of these walls!" The walls confined me, even though I had a window! My dream was to have a desk by a very large window that overlooked the lake, where I could listen to the loons and drink my coffee. I'd travel back to civilization every now and again, knowing that I could return to my little bit of heaven. I kept this vision in my head for months. I would tell people about it. It was a beautiful vision. I can see it still.

### Transition Time!

Then one day it happened. My company laid me off—I was a causality of the acquisition. Finally, I was in "transition!" How I love that word! I'd actually mocked up a picture of myself a few months earlier getting significant time off from work—not vacation—where I continued to be paid. My wish came true. Three days prior to the layoff I dreamt that I was politicking for my position. In my dream, when they told me my services were no longer needed—although my emotions were mixed—my eyes were smiling.

I went home that day, gave myself a day or two to feel sorry for myself, and then said *no more*. Time to make lemonade out of a lemon, right mom?

Still feeling mixed emotions—I was sad, depressed, and embarrassed—I didn't want to think that people might talk about me. I knew that any transition has its stages, and that transitional events can be seemingly negative or positive. The loss of someone close, the end of a relationship, marriage, the birth of a child, a major move—all carry with them stages or phases. Eager to work through them quickly, at the same time I realized that I mustn't rush the process.

Each day when the alarm went off I'd be out of bed and ready for a new day. I started journaling my thoughts and daily activities. Each day I grew stronger in my consciousness. Quickly I became centered, calm, happy, and at peace. I listed all of the things I wanted to do. And then I did them.

The warmth of Key West took the chill off the Illinois winter and brought fun, relaxation, and a chase from the coast guard after my friend Karen steered our paddle boat out to sea instead of along the coast!

This time spent in Florida with Karen allowed me to be me—to relax, and fully let go. She and I have had great times together, good laughs, and we always create terrific memories. It's times like these that I really value and appreciate my close relationships—I'm the luckiest girl in the world when it comes to my friends and family! I overflow with gratitude for those who are in my life.

Exercise, while always part of my daily routine, had never included yoga. But now I embraced it because I knew I'd have to remain conscious and present in that practice. Some days are easier than others, while some days I fall all over the place and hope no one is watching! It's a great mind-body experience that unites me physically, mentally, and spiritually.

### The Greatest Gift

Slowly I realized that I was becoming more conscious, and it didn't take long before I understood that my lay off had presented me with the biggest gift. Aware of that, I didn't want to waste a minute—every day became precious, every moment a gift. Each day I worked on me, and tried to stay conscious and aware in every moment. (At least I tried for every moment!)

Of course the reality is that sometimes I'd fall to pieces anyway. When something crossed my path, I didn't want to miss it. As I look through my journal now, I see the daily events that occurred and how they brought me to the next place. I worked on the house (Target and Home Depot became my two favorite hot spots), met with my coach, and volunteered my time. Basically I kept moving, stayed conscious, and tried to utilize the information I received.

I write now every day. Staying conscious, present, open—that's how I came to write this chapter, as I seized the opportunity when it crossed my path. Since "transition" became a description of my state of being, I'd told a friend that I should write about it. And here I am, doing just that...

Charlotte and I joined a community orchestra once again, and there, together, I feel more complete. Playing in the orchestra presents me with another exercise in staying conscious and present. If I don't then I'm behind the score!

Reconnecting with my music soothes my soul and touches me very personally. In my quest to reconnect with my musical past, I attended the recital of my first Suzuki cello teacher with all of her students. Dr. Shinichi Suzuki, a violinist, educator, philosopher and humanitarian, pioneered a method called "talent education," through which he advocated the teaching of music to nurture loving human beings and to help develop each child's character.

As I listened to twenty-five cellists perform a finale of Pachelbel's Canon (preceded by *Twinkle Twinkle Little Star*, of course!) and heard them so lovingly coax resonant, mellow sounds out of each of their cellos, it brought me such joy and peace. So familiar to me, there's no better music to my ears!

In addition, I've created my own toolbox. I appreciate all my tools and savor all of their memories, as I continue to consciously put tools into the box and take others out of it. The box contains things like gratitude, yoga, friends, coaches, family, Charlotte, faith, presence, nature, meditation, journaling, and fun. I've removed the things that no longer serve me: some friends; paperwork; and old thought processes. Like the one my dad gave me, my toolbox helps me in my hours of need. I like to think that I create wisdom and memories too.

And in my mind, I am always "up north," but physically I'll be there in the spring or summer. I sit here at my desk now, looking out the window and writing. The desk and window are not the ones I envisioned on Stone Lake—rather the desk is a café table at the Morton Arboretum, the window is twenty times the size of the window I envisioned, and the lake is Meadow Lake, with trees and blue skies all around. Not quite baseball season yet, but you can be sure that I'll be at the playoffs next summer!

The future is a mystery, but I am confident, centered, open, happy, balanced, in alignment, empowered, and conscious. I embrace each day as a new day and each moment as a gift. I feel more like "Brenda" than I have in a long time. I thank the transition for these gifts.

ABOUT THE AUTHOR: Brenda Ernst spent many years in the field of information technology, where she developed her strong business sense, built dynamic teams, and mentored others. She is committed to coaching individuals as they move through personal transitions and explore their individual passions. Based upon her belief that individuals can align their lives with a personal vision; embrace their uniqueness; and strive for balance utilizing their own personal "toolbox," Brenda was led to form Blue Adagio...a coaching and consulting company specializing in transition. In Brenda's spare time she enjoys playing her cello "Charlotte," spending time in the "north woods", dabbling in endurance sports and practicing yoga.

Brenda Ernst
Blue Adagio
www.blueadagio.com
brenda@blueadagio.com
630-730-0500

# The New Rules
## Lynda Flowers

My jaw dropped and my stomach churned as I turned my pick-up truck into my gravel driveway and saw two men loading my couch, chairs, TVs, grill, pictures, lamps, tables, and more onto two trailers, one enclosed and one flatbed.

"Mommy," my three year old son Brett asked "Where are they taking our stuff?"

I tried to remain calm and composed in front of my children so they wouldn't see me either explode with anger, or collapse into the chasm of my heart's pain. I think my lips moved and my mouth spoke some words, but I have no idea what I said. My heart pounded ferociously, and before I could park and get out of my truck, the men jumped into their SUVs and made a fast getaway through the front yard.

I felt violated. And stupid. My estranged husband Kevin and I agreed that we'd discuss who takes what possessions. In fact we were supposed to meet that day at eleven o'clock, in fifteen minutes, after the kids' swimming lessons. He knew I wouldn't be home until then. He waited for me to not be home so that he and his brother-in-law could clear out the house. I'd played by the rules, honored the agreement, and once again, I lost. I shook my head, thinking *not again, not again...*

As the kids and I walked into the now mostly empty house, sparsely furnished with only a few toys and some trash strewn about, my mind flashed back nine years to my first divorce. After the long drive home to Illinois from my cousin's wedding in Michigan, my eighteen month-old daughter Allie and I were looking forward to coming home to our own beds.

I noticed the echoing hollow sound as I unlocked my front door and we stepped into the foyer with our bags. I held Allie's hand tightly as I reached for the light switch and quickly flipped it up. My cute townhouse, overlooking the lake, was empty of all but a couch and a loveseat!

Stunned I stood there, paralyzed, scared, and lost. Had someone broken into my home? As I looked around, I realized my husband Bill had cleared out all of our possessions, leaving behind only a few things. How could someone who once professed such love be so cruel and cunning?

Only a few short months later, as I walked down the front steps of the courthouse, my feet felt like fifty pound concrete weights and I could barely breathe. Even though my eyes were open, I couldn't see anything. It was almost as if I wasn't even in my body. I couldn't tell if the pain was so great that I'd gone numb, or if I'd simply shut my heart's door to all feeling. I felt so alone, homeless, friendless, broken, and mostly so empty, that I was drained well past ever being able to feel full again, as if my life had been completely sucked out of me.

Like some sort of mechanical robot, I'd found my car and driven to my parent's home, where I lived  temporarily in their spare bedroom. It took every ounce of energy for me to step out of the car and walk into the house. When I arrived, my dad wanted to know all the details of the court session. We sat down at the kitchen table and I explained how the judge ordered me to release my daughter into her father's custody for his visitation, even when he drove up so drunk he couldn't find the car door handle and make it to the front door of the house.

My daughter was the last thing I had left. How could I possibly let her go into that danger? My heart filled with fear. My father was filled with anger and frustration at the court system and the judge. I couldn't understand how, even though I'd played by the rules, I still lost everything at the hands of such a discompassionate court.

I'd been a good wife. He'd been abusive and cheated numerous times. The judge had given Bill the house, both cars, and the business I'd started, which included my income! As I gazed out the window, I wondered how much more I could take—or rather lose. What's the point, I thought. Not only was my dream of marriage shattered, my whole being felt slashed to the core.

As the days blurred by, I grew angrier and more bitter. I begged and pleaded with God for justice, then blamed Him when I lost time and time again in court. I questioned the existence of a God, and finally turned my back completely. I figured it didn't matter how much I tried to follow the rules, I'd never see justice.

### Dancing Out of the Fog

I snapped back into the present as my son and daughter walked over to me. "Mom, what are you staring at?" my five year-old daughter Jenny asked as she gazed up at me. I stood in the middle of our family room looking at the emptiness. All that remained were a few scattered toys and an empty soda can on the floor. My older daughter was at a friend's house playing, and I was thankful that she didn't have to experience this event twice in her life.

Once again, I wondered where God was and why I continued to play by the rules when nobody else seemed to follow them. Why, I wondered, did I always seem to come out on the losing end when I tried so hard to do the right thing and be a good person? Out of nowhere a small voice inside of me said "go find God. See what He has to say."

As a child, I went to church with my family every weekend. The sermons were long, boring, and an exercise in how long I could sit without fidgeting or falling asleep. As I grew, I followed what I thought were the Ten Commandments: I tried to be a good person, a straight A student, to always have a job, to please those in authority over me.

My parents raised me to believe that you always tell the truth, don't lie, don't cheat, and don't steal. At the same time I was very sheltered—I grew up thinking that everyone was like me, serious about telling the truth and not cheating.

Then there was my low self esteem. I had an older brother by nearly two years, and I pretty much ruined his life when I was born, in his opinion. Everything revolved around what was good for Kurt. Seemed like everything I did just wasn't good enough. I'd get an A and it was "ok, good," but my brother would be rewarded with money or gifts for each and every A he earned!

When I'd share my emotions and tell my parents I felt like they didn't love me, their response was, "oh no, that's not true, you're wrong, of course we love you..." There was never any, why do you feel that way? It was always that I was just *wrong*. I think I lost touch with myself and my intuition. Some of it was probably also related to my mom's issues from her own upbringing—she'd walked in the shadows of her older sister her whole life.

I was shocked that Bill lied and cheated during my first marriage, but I rationalized it away thinking he deserved compassion and sympathy because he'd had a hard childhood and a tough life. Still naive and devastated by my first marriage, I delighted in the fact that somebody was interested in me as a woman. I just felt so low, like such a failure, that when Kevin came along and expressed interest, I jumped in...

It was when Kevin left to serve in the army in Iraq, and one of his co-workers invited me to his church, that I began to attend regularly once again. The pastor there had heard that Kevin was shipping out and reached out to me to ask what he could do for me.

I soon realized that, even though I'd been raised going to church, I never really knew God. As the days and months passed, I began to experience a newfound curiosity. I immersed myself in church and bible studies, and counseled with the pastor, and Nancy, the wife of one of the elders.

Each week Nancy, another woman named Brenda, and I met at a local restaurant. We talked and prayed. My bible study leader Janet called me nearly every day to pray with me or just check in and see how I was doing. They all taught me, loved me, pushed me, stretched me, and invested their time, energy, wisdom, grace, and love in me.

Eventually I realized I'd been taught to treat God as if he was a vending machine, or some kind of genie—I'd ask for forgiveness for small transgressions, and he'd grant it. When I found myself in situations where God didn't seem to listen or answer my prayers, I questioned if he was really there and if he cared about me.

Five years later the judge granted me a divorce. There was no fighting. There was no fear. There was no sadness. As I walked out of the courthouse and down the concrete steps, I felt light, as if I had finally danced my way out of the fog. That chapter—that *whole book*—of my life was now closed.

## *Epilogue*

I determined that my next book would contain *my* rules. For most—if not all—of my life, I'd been trying to live by everyone else's rules in order to be the good daughter and the good wife. I allowed others to tell me how I should behave, what I should do, like, dislike, and who I should be.

It simply didn't work. It didn't honor who I was made to be, unique, and beautiful. When I truly found God, through the friends at church, and the three women who invested weekly in me, I came to understand that God made me in a special way to have my own dreams and desires. And, in honoring myself, the creation that God made, I am in a sense, honoring God and allowing Him to use me in positive, creative ways that enriched me, as well as others around me.

Today I lead a group of ladies in a bible study community group. My life is full and overflowing with my children and friends, I've travelled to Nicaragua twice as a part of a medical missionary group, and my heart is whole. My purpose, which honors God—and me—is clear.

**ABOUT THE AUTHOR:** Lynda Flowers is a Registered Nurse, Certified Professional Coach, consultant, author, motivational speaker and Energy Leadership Master Practitioner. She empowers women to nurture the 'Me' in motherhood, helping women to reconnect with and honor themselves, and as a result, become great moms! She invests in women and her community as a Bible Study leader, 4-H leader, Scout volunteer, and coach. Lynda travelled twice to Nicaragua as part of a medical missions trip. She and her three children live on a farm, show Quarter horses and are active in sports. Lynda is an avid reader, quilter and gardener.

Lynda Flowers
MomMeRX, Inc.
www.MomMeRx.com
Lynda@MomMeRx.com
630-277-0110

# The Bridge
## Carla Forsyth

I remember the exact moment my journey began. Lying in bed next to my drowsy husband one night, I heard myself say "I want to be more spiritual" just before drifting off to sleep. The words didn't come from my mind, they just fell from my mouth, and it sounded as if someone else had spoken with my voice.

I now know those words came straight out of my heart, and that I heard my *true* voice for the very first time that night. Even my bewildered husband paused. He instinctually sensed a shift, as did I. We knew our static existence was about to change dramatically and forever.

The spark that triggered the change was my lay-off from a high paying job at an e-commerce software company in 1997. A thirty-eight year old new mother at the time, my corporate career ended abruptly, which shook the foundation of my secure world. One day, on line at the N.J. Labor Department, I met a man who recommended the book *Many Lives, Many Masters*. This book—about people who became aware of their past lives—prompted me to read another book by the renowned psychic Sylvia Browne.

An exercise in Sylvia's book described how to telepathically contact a loved one that's passed on. As per her instructions, I closed my eyes and imagined entering a round room with nothing in it but two chairs and two doors. I explored the room and noticed its detail and décor. Surprised by painted off-white walls and ornate woodwork of the French provincial style—not a décor to which I'm usually attracted—it nonetheless felt authentic to me.

Long open windows framed with flowing white silk curtains waved in the warm comforting breeze. Ocean waves broke in the distance outside, and the sun hung low in an orange and purple haze. Very little furniture inhabited the room, and flames danced from three white candles held on wall sconces. In the center of the room sat two opulent red and gold upholstered chairs.

Before beginning this journey, the book had instructed me to choose one of the chairs to sit in, and to wait to see what happened next. I chose the chair on the left and glanced at the door to my right because I heard it move. It opened slowly on its own, and a ball of white light floated into the room.

Frightened at first (I'd expected a human form to enter), I sensed almost immediately there was nothing to fear. The only human feature about the ball of light was its two eyes, which I recognized as belonging to my father. First the ball of light floated in front of me, then hovered over the chair to my right. When my father spoke to me telepathically I had difficulty understanding his words, but saw his eyes so clearly! He looked at me with complete and total love—immediately I knew he wanted me to know he's always watching over me...

Sylvia was right! I *could* contact those that had crossed over!

### *Discovering My Higher Self*

Another time, as I sat in my favorite maroon leather reclining chair next to the fireplace in my living room reading *Sacred Contracts* by Caroline Myss, I suddenly experienced a spontaneous vision. A very tall Native American woman with intense dark brown eyes and a plain brown dress spoke telepathically to me. "You will do what *she* does," she communicated, meaning the author, Caroline Myss.

Astounded, I thought, *what could she possibly mean?* I didn't understand at the time which way to turn. I later realized she meant I was to be a spiritual healer and teacher, a connector between worlds both physical and spiritual.

At this point I developed an insatiable thirst for knowledge. I read so many books on mysticism, sacred geometry, etc., I couldn't count them all. I joined a shaman's circle, where I experienced many life altering realizations. I also found two of my dearest friends and companions to accompany me on this spiritual journey.

I began my spiritual practices by meditating five minutes per day. That's all my loud, busy, hectic mind could muster at the time. I built on that until I could focus for longer periods. Eventually, I was able to step back from my thoughts and observe them. That was profound for me. Once I could observe, I realized that the observer in me was separate from the thoughts I was observing. That is when I understood the concept of the *higher self.*

The observer was my *higher self,* while the producer of my repetitive thoughts and beliefs was my *ego self.* From that point forward I began to study energy and energetic healing. I relentlessly pursued my desire to understand how all of this was possible.

My next teacher, Drunvalo Melchizedek, taught me the importance of entering the sacred space in my heart, and how to live completely from that place. Vitally important because the sacred space in the heart is the place where we are connected to source, Drunvalo showed me a mediation that led me to realize that my ability to effect change was part of my own energetic nature—not just in the physical world, but in the energetic world as well.

I spent years compelled to explore what seemed like random healing modalities and obscure esoteric studies. At times, I almost believed those around me who said I was wasting my time pursuing these bizarre subjects, and not making enough money. My inner guidance told me to continue, no matter who objected.

Introduced to Transference Healing® by my one of my friends from the shamanic circle, I was particularly attracted to this method of healing because it was a heart-based technology that incorporated everything I'd focused on for the past twelve years, and more. I knew I'd found the place I belonged when I travelled to Sydney, Australia to receive my practitioner and teaching credentials from the founder, anchor, and channel of Transference Healing®, Alexis Cartwright.

A few years later I attended the first level of the 7th Golden Age Mystery School, created by Alexis Cartwright, and it was during that time I remembered much of the knowledge that had been buried deep inside of me my whole life. Amidst innumerable revelations and new experiences came two significant initiation events that changed me forever.

During the first initiation I felt like I was suffocating and wasn't sure I'd live through it. Terrified, I heard myself say "let go, know that you are safe and held. Have faith that you'll be okay, no matter what!" I took that advice from my higher self and let go. I was shocked when others told me about their wonderful experiences during the same initiation!

### Past the Stars and the Planets

When the next initiation began I became aware that significant symbols where being energetically embedded into my hands, feet, and main chakras. I took this to be a healing and felt supported by it. Suddenly, I began to float outside of my body and at the same time became aware that my arms were rising. My physical body began to levitate, as my consciousness travelled far into the universe past the planets and stars, at a rapid speed. I stopped suddenly and became aware of feeling absolute, unconditional love!

This had been a goal of mine since my spiritual awakening began—to embody unconditional love! It simply flowed in all directions into and out of me. This moment of joy was so profound and so fulfilling that the idea of problems and the physical world no longer even existed. After enjoying just *being* love for a while, my energy shifted. I couldn't believe what came next.

My energy body began to travel, and once again I journeyed past the stars and planets and launched into a non-physical dimension. I could see and feel everything that was happening on earth and in the universe simultaneously! I knew I was one with *everything* at the same time.

I felt incredible compassion and love for everything to which I was connected. This is *I Am* presence. I am home! Finally, I knew what I'd been searching for all of those years. I wanted to experience being one with source energy again! As *oneness*, I felt compassion for all life, everywhere, because I knew myself to *be* all life everywhere.

My perception of everything changed and I now know who I am. I felt the inner peace equivalent to those who've come back to life from clinical death. I stopped sweating the small stuff because I realized such "problems" are merely circumstances set in our path so that we can experience ourselves, and that we are more than we know.

Now I feel compassion for others when I see them act in a way that isn't for the highest and greatest good of all. I also realized what the ascension process—experienced currently by the earth and all of humanity—is all about: raising our frequency so we can live in the unity of consciousness.

I began to teach others how to live from their own sacred space, and to utilize the energetic healing so they can move through their ascension process with ease and grace, rather than resisting the flow of change. I clear the energy of people's homes, companies, and business projects, and work with individuals as well. Since everything we do, everywhere we are, and everything we create, is an extension of our energy, healing and ascension can be achieved in all of these areas.

As I work with others to help them live more consciously, I receive the blessing of the energy that comes through for them and flows into me. That makes offering energetic healings a win/win scenario. It's the perfect fifth dimensional business model—I engage in work that's for the highest and greatest good for all.

The healing work I do requires me to channel through from spirit what procedures the particular client needs at that moment. I explain to them at the end of their session what issues were addressed and what they may need to focus on in their life.

There are a lot of people who still aren't there yet, and I tend to work mostly with those who are just waking up and looking for answers. Sometimes I work with people who aren't awake yet, but there's something in them that feels the pull. I call myself an ascension facilitator, and people are drawn to me because they want to go through this ascension process without the struggles they currently experience in their lives.

This is the future; I am a connector between a world being created now with every thought, action, belief, and feeling we experience, and a world in which we communicate telepathically, listen, and live from the heart, in order to enjoy the peace and love of higher dimensional consciousness. I am a bridge.


**ABOUT THE AUTHOR:** Dedicated to spiritual, esoteric, and mystical studies for the past fifteen years, Carla Forsyth possesses mastery in many healing modalities, including Reiki, Pranic Healing, and the energy and frequency alchemical healing technology Transference Healing®. Carla assists people to remember how to be self-healers and achieve self-mastery. Carla guides people with ease and grace through the ascension process, which the earth and all of humanity are in the midst of now. Carla shares the blessing of Transference Healing® with all those that resonate with this profound, loving energy as a practitioner, teacher, and 7th Golden Age Mystery School initiate.

Carla Forsyth
Heartself Healing
www.heartselfhealing.com
carla@heartselfhealing.com
973-320-3815 ext 111

# Into the Fire

## Lisa Jenks

It was two a.m. by the time I dropped the boys off and pulled into my apartment's parking lot, very tired. Focused only on how few hours were left before my alarm would go off for work, I barely noticed another car had pulled in a few spaces down. *Someone else is out late,* I thought, as I walked towards my apartment door.

Suddenly grabbed from behind with violent force, I tried to scream, but a man's hand covered my mouth tightly as something heavy pounded my head. I tried to struggle and fell to the ground with him on top of me. My own wet, warm urine soaked my pants as my body entered panic mode. Within a few seconds, he'd handcuffed me and tied a blindfold around my eyes—all the while holding me down to the cold ground. In the next few seconds, he shoved me onto the front passenger floorboard of his car and we drove away. I'd find out later that his name was Michael Riley.

Shortly before, my ears still rang with the incredibly powerful sounds of Bruce Springsteen and the E Street Band's performance as I drove home from his concert with my boyfriend Mitch and my brother Steve after seeing Bruce play for the first time on March 4, 1981. We'd listened to Bruce's music all the way back from Lexington, Kentucky, to Cincinnati, and sang along to make the ninety mile trip go faster. "The sky was falling and streaked with blood; I heard you calling me then you disappeared into the dust; Up the stairs, into the fire; Up the stairs, into the fire," we sang with all our heart and soul.

Now I lay shivering with terror. Blood oozed down my face from the wounds on my scalp. I knew I faced huge danger. In less than a minute, I'd lost complete control over my life. Something inside me knew that I had to maintain control over my own thoughts and emotions if I had any hope of survival and escape.

To help quell my hysteria, I focused my attention on where we were driving. *Right onto Beechmont Levy, stop at a light, drive several minutes, right turn. A quick left and then another right. Right into a driveway, and then a garage.* As my mind concentrated, I became a little calmer. It dawned on me that the more details I gathered, even with a blindfold on, the greater my chance to help the police (if I ever got that chance...)

Riley guided me into the house, and proceeded to rape and beat me repeatedly for the next twelve hours. He made me feel his gun, and told me over and over that he was going to kill me. He took out an instamatic camera, and forced me to pose naked in various positions as he clicked away.

Meanwhile, I made as many mental notes as I could. *Bathroom— down the hall on the right from his bedroom—steps are across from the bathroom.* During certain periods despair set in. Afraid I'd never see my family or boyfriend again, I hoped my parents would at least find my body so they'd know what had happened. Physically and emotionally spent, my body and head throbbed from the beatings.

### Count to One Hundred...

The concert now seemed light years away. Everything safe, normal, and happy seemed so far away. Bruce's words "may your strength give us strength; may your faith give us faith; may your hope give us hope; may your love give us love" resonated in my head. I didn't have much strength or hope, but I did have faith and love. That man never took those from me.

Not only did I grasp at as many details as I could, but I quickly realized what an insecure human being Riley was and I worked on telling him what he wanted to hear. He told me that, if he did release me, my boyfriend would never touch me again once he found out what had happened to me. I adamantly admitted that I'd never want to tell my boyfriend about what Riley was doing to me. He told me my parents would think this was all my fault, and I agreed with him. "I never want my parents to find out about this," I told him.

At one point, he asked me if I thought I would have gone on a date with him if I'd met him in a "normal" way. Every cell in my body wanted to scream *what a disgusting, filthy excuse for a human being you are!* but I stayed emotionally calm and told him what he wanted to hear. I convinced him that I wouldn't tell anybody what had happened, and that I actually liked him. This very possibly saved my life.

Eventually, he drove me to a field by the Ohio River, sat me down, unlocked the cuffs, and told me to count to one hundred and then take off the blindfold and walk home. I sat there, my heart pounding, positive he was tricking me into sitting still so that he could shoot me in the back of my head. There was nothing I could do to prevent that. Instead, I heard his car drive away. I stumbled to a nearby house and asked them to call the police.

The police were able to quickly catch this monster, in large part because of the details I provided. They narrowed down where he lived and got blueprints of all the homes in that area, which helped them figure out which homes had layouts similar to what I'd described. Evidence in the house indicated that he'd attacked numerous women and killed several. I testified at his trial, and testify before the parole board each time he comes up for review, despite his telling me that if I went to the police he would track me down and cut me into hundreds of pieces. Thirty one years later, Riley is still in prison for what he did to me.

Very few of us go through life without any emotional traumas. Each of our traumas is different. For some, it's the premature death of a loved one. For others, it's the divorce of our parents or our own divorce. For all too many, it's sexual or emotional abuse. We have very little, if any, control over these hardships sent by life. I believe, though, that we have total control over how we allow those hardships to affect us.

For twelve hours, Riley had complete physical control over me. He could have killed me and I couldn't have stopped him. He weighed about eighty pounds more than me, I was handcuffed, and he had a gun. However, Riley never gained emotional control over me.

Since that day, I have not allowed his sick, violent behavior to define who I am. I went on to medical school, married, have three beautiful children, and many close friends. I have loved and been loved. I enjoy life, expect the best from people, and do not live in fear.

Each March 4, I take a long walk and celebrate the fact that I chose to become a survivor after Riley attacked me. So often we give our power over to negative people and events in our lives. I could have spent the rest of my life wallowing in fear and hatred because of what he did. That would have made me a victim, pulled me down into his world, and given him the ultimate victory. I'll give him the battle, but I am not about to let him win the war.

## Forged By Fire

Growing up my father used to tell me that each person needs to develop a place within their core that nothing and nobody can hurt. I call that place within my soul "God." What's important to me about God being at the center of my core is that He allows me to tap into a greater strength, peace, and joy than I'd have known if my core was only me. It's been said that there's not enough darkness in all the world to put out the light of one small candle. Likewise, there's not enough hatred or violence or sadness in all the world to put out God's light within me.

After the police arrived at the home to which I stumbled after my release, they took me to the emergency room where I received numerous stitches, x-rays, and a rape work-up. After all I'd gone through, I then had to spend another four hours at the police station. Finally, exhausted, physically beaten and emotionally wrecked, I got to go home.

For close to a week I did nothing except lay on my couch, eat ice cream, cry, and take hot baths. It was three weeks before I was back at work full-time, and close to two months before I could sleep by myself. Slowly, my body healed.

Each day I tried to focus more time and energy on celebrating that I was alive and less on my physical and emotional injuries. At that point, Riley was still loose and I was confronting the fear that he might be stalking me. However, working almost daily with the police department and a private investigator empowered me.

As I acknowledged my pain and trauma, I recognized how important it was not to dwell on—or choose to define myself by—the events that had happened to me. I did spend time with a therapist, took long walks, and gave myself time off before getting back to my regular schedule, but I knew it was as healthy and crucial for me to do those things as it was for me to return to my "normal" life.

I could choose to allow my pain and sadness to control me, or I could control my pain. Emotional survivors are those who don't allow their grief to control them long-term. In order to do this, one has to compartmentalize one's feelings. In my case, I could tell myself I was angry and hurt and scared because of what one man had done to me, but *not* turn into a person who was angry, hurt, and fearful towards all people, in all situations.

Sharing our stories is a vital part of the healing process. That allows each of us to process our feelings, and helps us to understand how many others have experienced similar situations. As word spread about my attack, the number of women who came to me to describe similar experiences astounded me. We need to remember that we are not alone—that extending a hand to others as role models is reason enough for us to rise above our own crises and come out as survivors. I know my children and my dear friends will all endure their own traumas. I want them to draw strength from having watched me survive my foray into the fire.

**ABOUT THE AUTHOR:** Dr. Jenks graduated from University of Cincinnati's College of Medicine and then moved to Colorado, where she practiced emergency medicine until becoming a full-time mom. In 2007, she returned to medicine by opening Genesis MedSpa, which she owns and directs. Genesis has won multiple awards, including the coveted Better Business Bureau's Excellence in Customer Service Award. Dr. Jenks has volunteered countless hours with various non-profits in her community. In her spare time, she enjoys road biking, hiking, traveling and the company of her three grown children.

Lisa S. Jenks, MD
Genesis MedSpa
www.genesis-medspa.com
lisa@genesis-medspa.com
719-579-6890

# Lily Dale

## Pat Jones

*"Pat, can you believe these women who stay in marriages when they're not really happy?"* The question came from a woman I knew casually from town, just as I'd walked into her store to purchase some goat milk soap for my son Josh.

My knees buckled, my jaw dropped, and I felt a rush of electricity run through my body—the same kind of intense energy I'd experienced when my inner voice had yelled at me to *get to know* Jeff, the man who became my husband. "Yeah, can you believe that?" I stammered in response. I felt like I'd been hit with a two-by-four. I purchased the soap and left quietly.

So that was it. I knew that I had to listen, I could no longer live in what felt like a lie. That night, although I knew it would break his heart—and my son's as well—I asked Jeff for a separation. How did things get to this point, and would I have the courage to follow through?

Actually, it'd been a full year since I felt the change in our marriage, but since I couldn't understand it, I didn't want to listen to the truth of it. Probably one of my greatest fears about living an intuitive life is that the guidance I receive can require sudden, radical changes in my life. Usually I find the courage to follow through, but this time was different—this involved my family!

All I knew for sure was that it happened during a weekend trip to Lily Dale. Something that, to this day, I can't fully explain. I just know that I changed profoundly, and that when I returned I was no longer connected to pieces of my old life.

Lily Dale, in upstate New York, is one of the oldest Spiritualist communities in the country. Home to many psychics and mediums, it's well known for its paranormal activities. Eight of us went that weekend as part of the Personal Transformation Program I was running—we were all sensitive to the invisible realm of subtle energy. As the group's teacher, I felt responsible to make sure everyone could handle whatever occurred there.

About five miles from the entrance of town we started sensing its energy field. Liz was driving, I was in the passenger seat. All of a sudden I felt overwhelming waves of grief and tried to breathe through them. Liz started to experience what I can only describe as "transformational belching!" It was very absurd, and we both felt it was completely out of our control. I'm surprised she was able to drive.

As we made our way into the town, it all looked so innocent and quaint. Little houses nestled among the trees by a beautiful lake and yet, by the time we pulled up to our hotel, I was actually wailing! I didn't know what to do, other than surrender to the experience. I strongly sensed that Liz and I were being used as some kind of channels for the energy held there in the land.

The owner of the B&B came out to meet us. While the others lined up behind our car to create a barrier between us and the owner, they explained we were having a "small problem" in the car. Liz was still engaged in this outrageous belching, when someone opened my door and I literally rolled out of the car and landed flat on my back on the ground. It felt like high voltage electricity was running through one side of my body.

As I laid there crying and wailing, I suddenly sensed my guides come in and put on me what felt like lead boots. Immediately, everything calmed down enough so that I could walk into the place, with the help of some of the others.

That was our arrival, and that was just the beginning. Many illogical, intense energy experiences occurred that weekend, and we did our best to understand them and ride the waves in whatever form they came. I dare say, everyone had some kind of personal transformation that weekend!

### *You Can Never Go Home Again...*

Home again, I noticed that something had changed drastically. The cord that I'd always felt between Jeff's heart and mine was no longer there. Where did it go? What happened? Confused, I felt betrayed by my inner guidance and perceptions, and refused to listen to what my experience was telling me for the entire next year.

Married to Jeff for nine years, in many ways, it was a very solid marriage. We always talked, enjoyed each other's company, and participated in many fun, family adventures. When I first met him I thought he was a canoe salesman, and only later realized he was an actuary who had a very comfortable lifestyle, but kept a low profile. We ended up moving to Saranac Lake where we built a house together.

Very unsettled and deeply unhappy after my return, I kept feeling like something was now missing, and I didn't know, didn't want to know, what to do about it. But if I was going to be responsible for "breaking up" my family, then I was going to make darn sure that I exhausted all possibilities of reconnection. I spoke openly with Jeff, and we tried various ways to reconnect over the next year. We tried counseling, renewing our vows, and various energy therapies, but nothing seemed able to reconnect me to him.

My son Josh was only five years-old when Jeff and I married. They'd bonded quickly, and within that first year of marriage Jeff proposed adopting Josh, even though his biological father was still very much in the picture.

I discussed it with Josh's father, Paco, and he agreed. A year and a half later, Paco was diagnosed with cancer and passed away only ten months after that. Ultimately, through the exploration of parallel lives, we came to believe that the souls of Paco and Jeff had been friends in another life, and that Paco had brought Josh to Jeff to raise as part of their soul contract. We also discovered that part of my role in this lifetime was to bring Josh and Jeff together.

Through it all—Paco's passing, Jeff's later heart attack, and my bout with cancer, we'd always had that strong connection. Always gentle, and supportive of my healing work, he'd embraced my journey into a four-year intensive course of study only a week after we'd married. Used to talking to each other openly, I was shocked when, upon my return from Lily Dale, all that seemed changed.

## To Thine Own Self Be True...

The day finally came when my inner guidance yelled at me, the same way it yelled at me to get to know Jeff originally, that I could no longer ignore what I knew to be true for me. If I thought asking Jeff to agree to a separation had been difficult, it was nothing compared to sharing the news with Josh.

I think there's a maternal instinct that prevents you from willingly hurting your child, and I felt I was going against it. It was just a few weeks before his thirteenth birthday and I had a trip planned to Sedona with a group of friends. The timing of everything was just horrible. I meditated for quite awhile and asked for guidance on whether or not this weekend was a good time to talk to

Josh. I heard "he will be ok."

I thought the message meant he'd be ok this weekend, but looking back now I realized it meant in the long run. Naively I went into the conversation assuming he'd "be ok"—talk about having blinders on! I remember him crying and screaming "no, no, you guys are my whole world!"

Jeff kept saying "this can't be right, this just can't be right!" and the intensity of my pain forced me to leave the house. *If I'm causing all this pain then I need to leave,* I thought. I drove down to the lake in the middle of an intense thunderstorm, sat in my car, and cried. Confused, I didn't want to hurt anyone, least of all my son!

If I didn't follow through on what felt like my guidance, then how could I ever teach others to do the same? If I ignored what felt like a "big" message, then how could I live with myself? Maybe I was interpreting this all wrong. I demanded clarity! I pounded on my steering wheel and yelled out to Spirit, "If I am to leave my family and cause all of this pain, then I demand a concrete sign right now!"

Suddenly, through the thunderstorm, the clouds above me parted and some rays of sun shone through. Holy shit! No denying that! I felt a certain calmness settle in, while at the same time a different kind of dread settled into my heart. I prayed for the courage to follow through with what I knew I had to do, even if I didn't know all of the reasons why. I prayed for grace and support for Jeff, and especially for Josh. It was the most difficult action I've ever had to take.

### Epilogue

It would take some time for all of the wounds to heal, particularly with Josh. He was pretty angry for about a year, understandably so. Jeff and I were able to draw upon our very strong desire to be loving parents for him, and found our way back to the friendship that had always been between us.

Our commitment to Josh was so strong it really forced us to deal with any of our own stuff that interfered with being there for him. Every day, for many months, I sat in meditation, bringing forth the love that I felt for Jeff, and setting the intention that what was most loving in our connection remain intact. I am so very grateful that it did.

To this day, I don't know why it all played out the way it did. However, I do know that there's a place you can learn to live in, where you feel the bittersweet grace of walking alone with Spirit, being called to act in ways that are painful and confusing, and yet somewhere underneath all of that you trust it's for everyone's highest good. When I feel the waves of guilt come through, that's where I go, and I sit in the love that I feel for those dearest to me— even if we're not living in the same household anymore.

**ABOUT THE AUTHOR:** *Healing Adventures* founder Pat Jones' passion is to help guide energy-sensitive individuals to a more joyful life—one filled with clarity and ease. The creator of *KIA Reiki ™*, a unique form of healing from the level of one's core, and the *5 Spiritual Body Types ™*, which helps people understand the energetic and spiritual dynamics of their relationships, Pat assists individuals to understand and tap into their body-mind-spirit connections. Available for private sessions, lectures, and classes, both in person and long distance, Pat has locations in central and northern New York, and facilitates a worldwide Personal Transformation Program.

Patricia Lee Jones, BA, CSH, CHt,
Healing Adventures
www.healingadventures.com
pat@healingadventures.com
518-524-3422

# Happy for No Apparent Reason

### Victoria Milan

Glass of Cabernet in one hand, snacks ready to be devoured in the other, I settle down for my uninspired evening of CNN, ready to let the embers of another day fade uneventfully away because I don't know what my dream is anymore.

Who I am and what I want are recurring questions these days. It seems that all my certainties have long gone, each having lived out its natural life. Children grew, businesses changed, markets crumbled, and elders passed. And I am left without a mission statement or the architecture upon which to rebuild a recognizable semblance of the life I used to know.

Surveying the current landscape, I don't like my options. Where there was once a brilliant career, there is now only a lackluster job. Where there was once financial might, there is now only a paycheck. And where there was once passion, now I only go through the motions. I have no new-and-improved edition of what my fifty-something life will look like, and to be honest, I'm too weary to know where to start. This is not what I had planned. Scared and barely breathing, my life tilts precariously as I watch the ground shift beneath me, leaving little room for joy. I'm losing hope at an alarming rate—and my health along with it. I am at the breaking point.

In an effort to rekindle my natural exuberance and innovative spirit, I remind myself that I did a great job raising the kids. They're happy and thriving in college. But now what? Unconvincingly, I repeat the hollow declaration that I have already reached the pinnacle of my career. Yet secretly, I know that in the undercarriage of that statement lies a gnawing sense of dread that maybe this *is* all there is. No, this is no ordinary moon-shadowed winter night.

Stoic silence is ruptured by the exaggerated sound of the doorbell. My fractured thoughts race. Who could be here at 8:57 p.m. on a brittle January night? I get up from my safe nest alongside Gizzy, my opinionated, red sable Pomeranian, to peer through the window. It's my ex-boyfriend of eleven years prior. I don't hesitate. I unbolt the door and invite him in, asking if everything is all right, thinking surely there must be some family emergency to bring him to my door after so many years of separation. He assures me everyone is fine and says he needs to tell me something before it's too late.

Immediately launching into his well-rehearsed monologue, he reveals the intent of his visit, saying he never fully acknowledged his contribution to the failure of our relationship. He describes how he unconsciously kept a pane of bulletproof glass between us, acknowledging that only recently had he come to understand why I left: because love is a dance between two hearts, not a spectator sport.

Stunned by his presence, I cannot feel my body. I sit frozen, like Han Solo in carbonite, unable to absorb the magnitude of the message. He continues, telling me that he loved me (yes, I already knew that), he had always loved me (yep, I knew that too), and he still loves me (breaking news!). He affirms that he'd wanted to marry me, but his fear of commitment got in the way. Pausing just long enough to place his wool coat on the back of the sofa, he gathers the courage to confess he's never been able to replace the love we shared and then, "I just wanted you to know that before it was too late."

Meanwhile, unable to shut off the voice shouting inside my head *you're in your pajamas, go get changed!* I excuse myself and sprint off to change into something presentable—like a Rockette during a timed costume change behind the scenes of a Broadway spectacular. I return to stake my position on my champagne leather metropolitan sectional, only to find that the conversation has shifted gears to polite family updates and current events.

Then, as if the clock had struck twelve, he reaches for his coat, hastily conveying that he'd best not take up any more of my time. I begin to sense the presence of that bulletproof pane of glass, like the automatic window of a presidential motorcade, silently sealing him off from any possibility of furthering the conversation.

My mind screams *what does all this mean?* while my heart laments *can't you stay just a little bit longer?* Wary not to break the plastic, Ken doll exterior that would throw him into an emotional tailspin, I opt to silence my questions as he disappears into the winter night, looking back twice as he walks to his car.

The rest of my night is spent in an impenetrable numbness. What just happened? Does he need closure to finally let go of the past, or is this the start of something new—something good?

My mind races ahead, speculating how this event might magically bring a return to grace—a return to a life I could recognize as my own. Could this be a sign that the recent stream of struggle might finally be getting the cosmic boot?

For the next six days, we exchange lengthy e-mails that unearth parts of our souls, open up avenues of healing, and profess concealed devotion. Then the floodgates open with nearly biblical magnitude, as I come to the realization that I haven't dated anyone for years because I am still passionately in love with this man.

As if held in a state of suspended animation, the love feels as strong as—no, *stronger than*—it did years before. I can hardly wait to tell him the news. We set a date for January thirtieth. Another two-thousand-word e-mail arrives, and I read with delight as we plan our date. Fifth paragraph, line three, I read the words "but you may not want to accept this invitation when you realize I'm currently in an active relationship with a woman I've been dating for eleven weeks."

I don't understand. I can't understand! Who? Why? How can eleven weeks compare to eleven years? None of this makes sense.

The weeks that follow are completely intolerable. I cry at work. I cry in the car. I cry in the shower. I sob uncontrollably. This is not a breakup. This is a betrayal. The devastation is unbearable—until a random comment from a casual friend cracks the hidden code. "Look what he did to you!" she blurts out from nowhere. Defensively, I respond, "No, look what he did *for* me."

Somewhere in that monument of tears, I broke so unfathomably wide open that I had no choice but to become conscious that I alone have the power to create joy, feel loved, feel beautiful. From that place of unimaginable devastation, I made a pact with myself to get healthy, to love my job, and to love myself—regardless of the circumstances. I instantly felt a kinship with Elizabeth Gilbert because I, too, had lived an eat-pray-love experience. Gilbert's book chronicles my story alongside hers. It took a devastating breakup for me to make peace with myself and with my belief about life—a life I remembered I co-create.

And so began my search for wholeness. Like the gravitational pull of the sun, I was drawn to anything and everything that created a sense of self and a connection to source. Gradually, my reality began to rejigger as I trusted my own wisdom and allowed my heart, not my head, to guide me.

I began to feel the distant tremor of a seismic soul shift—the liberation of my authentic truth. What if I relinquished the notion that I need to please everyone else? What might happen if I began to get curious about what I want to contribute to the world with my one-and-only life?

The next thing I knew I had packed the only hippie skirt I could find and my knock-off Birkenstocks and was making the first of many trips to Rhinebeck, New York, to find a slice of uninterrupted bliss. There I began to recognize and heed the messages from spirit: Laugh more. Play more. Seek truth. Fall in love with what awakens you!

Synchronously, I found both yoga and gourmet, nutrient-rich foods. I learned to breathe deeply through meditation, finally getting grounded in my own body. I opened up to the divine presence that I could finally find within my weathered, Grinch-like heart. I forgave others. I forgave myself. Spontaneously, I felt a flood of self-confidence warm my body, mind, and spirit. I shed fifty pounds along with old, limiting beliefs and long-held muscle memory. I was happy and it showed. At work everything changed, yet nothing was different. Co-workers began asking my secret.

Today, I think, act, and create from a different frame of reference. I am no longer willing to mechanically pick up the useless scraps of pain and injury in a futile attempt to patch everything neatly back together. Instead, I let the broken promises of denial fade away, like old sepia photographs, finally releasing me from their obligation. I finally celebrate my personal brand of brilliance and recognize that it's the path to manifesting my heart's desires—to finding my own unique bliss blueprint.

I have learned to listen to the deeper wisdom that so often we shut out and shut up with food, wine, shopping, or any other mood-bending, culturally accepted activity. While I may always be a work in progress, at least now I know what fuels me. I trust my instincts. I honor my heart's enlightened messages. I move toward what brings a sense of wonder and joy. I create a life I fall deeply in love with. I luxuriate in acts of random kindness toward others, and—more importantly—I luxuriate in acts of random kindness toward myself. I honor my body's wisdom by feeding it food that activates my DNA's native ability to heal. I am happy—often for no apparent reason. I have found my own unique brand of bliss, and I live my best life—regardless of external circumstance or judgment. I breathe deeply. I look inward. I crave authenticity. And I don't postpone joy.

### A Prayer

Let the facade fall. Let the divine goddess within be heard. Let our bodies be healed with nourishing foods—the way nature intended. Let the passion of our hearts lead us to what we truly desire. Let us choose to leave behind the useless scraps of pain and denial and make a soulful break for a bold and beautiful future, where our fierce feminine soul illuminates everything it comes in contact with.

**ABOUT THE AUTHOR:** Victoria Milan is a real food advocate and certified holistic health coach dedicated to illuminating the power of nutrient dense foods. She is the founder of Take Back Your Plate, a grass-roots movement to raise awareness and inspire healthy choices, one plate at a time. Vicki is a motivational speaker, trainer, writer and entrepreneur. Her business, BestLife365.com, offers online and private coaching programs that create transformation and healing by blending ancient wisdoms with modern science. Vicki is a graduate of Institute for Integrative Nutrition, a Reiki practitioner and a certified Neuro-linguistics coach. She passionately believes that it's our birthright to live our BestLife365!

Victoria Milan
BestLife365.com
Twitter: @bestfoods365
Facebook: Take Back Your Plate
609-577-9410

# Destination: Fabulous Fifty and Beyond!

## Alisa L. Oglesby

Every Saturday morning as a child, I held school at my imaginary *Innovative Prep School* where the mission was to teach students *how* to think instead of *what* to think. My state-of-the-art school produced some of the greatest creative and intellectual minds of the time!

Much later, I left my small college hometown—now a young college grad in 1985—armed with goals and dreams, ready to take on the world. A goal-setter since my early teens, I knew I'd move to a big city, work for a major company, and climb the corporate ladder. Always excited and motivated each time I placed a check mark beside another completed goal, I thought *wow! I'm on my way!*

I wanted to work in corporate America for twenty years, learn as much as I could, and move on. "Life begins at forty" was a popular saying back then, and I figured that forty would be the perfect time for me to parlay my experience and connections into starting a company whose mission would be to enlighten, empower, educate, and enrich women and girls throughout the world.

But the excitement of corporate life dwindled as each year passed—where did the first ten years go? I knew I'd reached the half-way mark in my long range plans toward my entrepreneurial quest, yet I was at least five years behind on starting my part-time business.

I comforted myself with the reminder that, after all, my goal-setting formula had always worked, and in the knowledge that I had more years ahead of me than behind. I also knew I'd be able to accelerate my plans, get back on track and—once again—feel the joy of placing a check mark next to another completed goal.

It was somewhere at this point of my journey that I realized my soul yearned for something more. Life appeared to be great, my journey was smooth, yet deep down inside I felt empty and unfulfilled.

An avid reader of motivational business literature during this time, I applauded the success stories of others, but the goal-setter in me knew it was time to write my own success story. Not for recognition, but for *self. What am I here to do? When will I live in accordance to my purpose?* I asked myself, since these questions had consistently remained unanswered. It was time to consciously journey toward the answers.

In my quest for purposeful living, I took a spiritual giftedness assessment. I remember that spring Saturday morning as if it were yesterday. I answered each question carefully, straight from my heart. Finally completed, I took the exam into the administrator's office for her to review and determine the outcome.

I sat eagerly awaiting what my answers would reveal. I wondered how the findings would shape or reshape my future. *Would I be obedient to Spirit or would I continue to flow in opposition of my purpose?* I asked myself. *What could I do that would be a natural flow and give me that glow?*

The administrator walked in armed with the results and sat down at the table. "Alisa, your gift is to teach," she told me. Tears started to roll down my cheeks as the obvious was revealed—no, *confirmed!* This revelation was consistent with my life mission statement: To be a channel of enlightenment, education, empowerment, and inspiration to those who are open and receptive to living life abundantly.

### Roadblocks, Detours, Twists & Turns

Armed with my giftedness assessment, I continued my journey and chose the still somewhat smooth route—after all, corporate life was safe, comfortable, and familiar. The thought of life without a steady paycheck, benefits, a company car, and other perks was very scary.

Though I experienced some unexpected roadblocks, detours, and changes of direction along the way, and had to reposition my road map in order to continue to move forward, I held to my vision. Looking back I could justify my delays: I had relocated to another state to work in another industry. Still, happily single, childless by choice, a great daughter, and a fun auntie, I continued to create adventures and enjoy new experiences.

I travelled along the journey of wife and second mom (of three wonderful children), although neither of these roles was listed on my short or long range road map. This was quite an adjustment, but a priceless experience. The teacher in me once again came to the forefront and my *Innovative Prep School* was reborn, as homework, enrichment work, creative thinking, and personal development of the children took center stage in my life.

My goal had been to take online courses and complete a master teacher certificate at my church within two years. However, the demands of work and second-motherhood increased as the intelligent socially active children grew. Thus, I reasoned their growth and development was more important and I placed my goal on hold.

Although on hold, I couldn't simply settle—after all, I wasn't getting any younger and time was quickly passing me by. Perhaps now it was time for me to place a check mark beside my long-term entrepreneurial goal! It had never been my desire to live a life filled with *if only, I wish, I should have, I could have*...now was time for me to make conscious choices and continue along as my journey unfolded.

But what was next? Was I in park, where I could continue to remain in comfortable, unfulfilling situations? Dare I even think about returning to the hurtful, painful people and situations from my past? Maybe I should coast along and simply see what happens, or—*wait, I can drive!* Follow the divine road map towards infinite fabulous possibilities!

I resigned from my job, lived off my savings, and expanded our family as I gave birth to "our baby," a new home care agency business. I nurtured and developed this business by working twelve to eighteen hours a day in addition to transporting three teens to and from their extracurricular activities, while my husband continued to work in the corporate world. Life was great—the new freedom, flexibility, and quality of life made up for the long hours I prospected, networked, and developed business. Happy and proud, I placed another check mark beside a major long-term goal!

I remember the excitement on the children's faces when they found out the company was named KNM Home Health Care in their honor; we were creating generational wealth. In five to seven years we would sell the business, live very comfortably, and volunteer in our community. My marriage was solid (or so I thought), the kids were excelling in school, the business was growing, and the money was starting to flow. Life was wonderful!

### Fueled by Faith

Little did I know that, within four years, my roles as a wife, second mom, and daughter would be memories of the past. Within months, he fell in love with another woman and conspired to ruin me financially, the children left, and my mother passed.

Day after day, during the longest and loneliest journey of my life, I'd think, *wow, Spirit, you really redirected my journey!* The core people to whom I'd been totally dedicated were no longer a part of my life. But even in my darkest moments of heartache, sorrow, and pain, I'd give thanks because I knew deep down inside these experiences would be the catalyst for a more conscious journey.

Over three or more tumultuous years passed, and it seemed like an eternity. Many nights I lay in bed—confused, frustrated, and anxious—and questioned the legal and justice system and why my voice seemed to be ignored or go unheard.

But through my darkest times I held onto my truths, which included knowing that the divine is the source of my *supply*—safety, sanity, money, security—and that the law would prevail. I believed the divine created this road map especially for me and that it was time for me to journey on to greater destinations. *My journey is aligned with the divine, therefore ALL things will work out fine,* I'd repeat to myself daily.

I promised myself that I would see the good in all situations, look beyond the surface to where truth lies, and have faith that in time all things would be revealed to me.

This was the refueling I needed to continue my journey. Although my roles and goals changed abruptly, messages from the divine within assured me that my challenges were preparing me for a more conscious way of living.

Today, as I reflect, I realize I learned patience, demonstrated abundance, tuned up spiritually, and surrendered to the still, small voice within. The more I trusted and surrendered, the more reinvigorating my journey became—and I was able to leave behind the heartache, sorrow, and pain at their appropriate crossroads of my journey.

I turn fifty in 2012, and though I've encountered unexpected road blocks, detours, traffic jams (parentless, childless, divorced) along my road to conscious living, I acknowledge them and quickly focus on the miles of great memories, lessons, and blessings. Even in the midst of the storm, I know my new roles and goals are being put in place by the divine creator of road maps.

In my twenties I had time on my side, but time can be a fickle friend and, as I turn fifty this year, may not be as kind to me as in my youth. But time has blessed me by transforming me into a person of greater quality, possessed of the richness of knowledge gained through my experiences. In the time I have left in this form and on this earth, I know unabashedly I'm ready now to make more impactful demonstrations, enlarge my territory, spread my spiritual radius of influence, and ascend to a higher level of awareness. I am evolving into the teacher/business women and inspirer with a platform far greater than the goals I'd set for myself earlier in life!

As I continue to grow, mature, and demonstrate in accordance to my level of awareness, I realize the smoothness of my journey is in direct proportion to the amount of faith fuel I take along with me.

At this point of my journey, I reflect on the road traveled to arrive at this major mile marker, and I know faith fuels my future. Also, I now view my road map/GPS with wiser eyes. I realize this road map was crafted by the divine especially for me, and therefore welcome any future road-blocks, detours, and traffic delays, as these provide me with the challenges, blessings, opportunities, experiences, and platforms necessary for me to travel beyond humanly imposed limitations. As I continue to follow my Sprit-guided divine road map, I embrace all of the wonderful possibilities of fabulous fifty and beyond!

**ABOUT THE AUTHOR:** Alisa L. Oglesby is consciously moving in the universal flow: to educate, enlighten and empower generations of women and girls about the Universal Principle of "Abundance". Alisa earned a Marketing degree and worked in corporate America for over 20 years. Her entrepreneurial quest evolved with her desire to make a positive impact in the areas of women's issues and senior care. This multi-tasker is an author and speaker, and president of OMG:WomenUnited and ALO:WomenUnited – organizations committed to Women's Rights. Having co-founded a home care agency in 2005, Alisa currently uses her expertise in elder care to conduct Boomer Caregiver workshops.

Alisa L. Oglesby
OMG-WomenUnited
www.omgwomenunited.com
info@omgwomenunited.com
Twitter @omgwomunited.com

# Living Too Small

## Lorraine Smith

I sat in the dining room as my father blatantly smoked a joint right in front of me. Suddenly, he leaned over and kissed me—in a way a father should *never* kiss his thirteen year old daughter. I jumped up, screamed for the umpteenth time how much I hated him, and ran out of the room.

Shocked and disgusted, at first I did not—*could not*—believe what just happened! Was this *my* fault? Had I done something to make this happen? Hurt, confused, and angry at him for causing so much pain, I wanted him out of our lives for good.

My father often drank too much and was frequently abusive. When I was only seven I remember the car swaying all over the road as we drove home one night. I was petrified. When we arrived home, he began to rant in front of the house about meddlesome neighbors and in-laws, and ended up yanking the telephone out of the wall. These sorts of incidents happened all the time.

My early childhood life was chaotic and confusing. While one side of my family was very large—my aunts, uncles, and cousins would throw big family gatherings—the other side was small and isolated. They always seemed fearful and worried about what other people thought of them. But, in spite of the contrast, there was love.

The day my parents told us they were separating I stormed out of the living room and started slamming things in the other room. My father eventually moved out, but visited occasionally. Usually he was really drunk when he did. I knew my mom finally had it with him. So I told her what happened in the dining room that day and gave her the ammunition she needed to divorce him. And that's exactly what she did.

I realize now that it wasn't easy for my mother to raise five kids on her own, but I didn't see it that way at the time. Away most of the time working two jobs and picking up the pieces of her life, she often left us to fend for ourselves. Dishes stacked up high in the kitchen sink, and laundry forever overflowed. As the oldest girl, many of these responsibilities fell on my shoulders. I remember my little brother asking me to help him wash out a pan so he could make himself something to eat.

## The Road to Nowhere

Angry and rebellious, I stopped caring about school and began to smoke and drink. One night, on my way home after hanging with friends, it occurred to me that I could stay out as late as I wanted because there was no one home to notice when I got in.

Alone and scared, I skipped school and turned to drugs my freshman year. A group of us would hang out during the school day with a woman we knew, an addict who probably welcomed us so we'd share our stash with her. At night, I'd hang out at bars—I looked older than my early teens, which made it no problem to get served.

Young, pretty, and vulnerable, guys would buy me drinks or share their stash, no problem. Lonely, I mistakenly confused sex with love. Sometimes I'd black out and wake up in an unrecognizable place—I had absolutely no recollection of how I got there. I remember my current crush gave me the cold shoulder when he learned I'd spent the previous night with his friend. Devastated, I had absolutely no memory of it—nada!

I hooked up with a guy more than twice my age, a Vietnam vet with major ghosts from his past. He was into drugs and sex parties at his apartment—the perfect gig, escape and love packaged into one really sick deal. I didn't care what he encouraged me to do as long as I had someplace to stay. By the middle of my sophomore year, I stopped going home, quit school, and moved in with him.

Tormented, I knew I didn't belong in this underworld, but didn't want to go home. I spent my days feeling sorry for myself, dreaming of "normal" while waiting for the next high. When Mr. Vietnam lost his apartment and had to mooch off his friends, I walked the streets alone in the middle of the night in the dead of winter—drunk and hungry, with no place to go. Home, which was only a town away, was not an option.

Alone in an all-night diner among a crowd of deadbeats, I needed a place to sleep. I knew the apartment from which Mr. Vietnam had recently been evicted was still vacant, so I broke in. No heat, but at least I had a mattress to sleep on that night.

Eventually I hooked up with Mr. Vietnam again who, by that time, had another apartment. I shacked up with him and we pretended to play house. I would go home every once in a while, but was too angry and hurt to stay.

## In Search of Normal

I found employment as a file clerk and soon tired of supporting Mr. Vietnam. I moved to Florida with a girlfriend and had some fun in the sun working for a gas station and car wash. After a while, the fun wore off. The thought of spending the rest of my life chasing the next high became unbearable, and it wasn't until I realized how empty I felt that I *finally* decided to go home.

I blamed myself for the downward spiral that had consumed my adolescence. I'd run away for so many years because I lived in fear that I was destined to be like my father. But I knew it was time to pick up the pieces, that being a victim was a path to nowhere.

I knew I had to find another way.

To this day, I don't know how I avoided becoming an addict. Though I never put a needle in my arm, I certainly put a lot of stuff up my nose and swallowed lots of pills. Thank God I was able to walk away from the drugs and eventually quit smoking.

Back home again, I found employment with a large corporation and steadily worked my way up to a respectable management position. When a coworker introduced me to Louise Hay's book *You Can Heal Your Life,* its impact was tremendous! I then spent four years in therapy letting go of the ball and chain of my past. The rest of my emotional baggage I stuffed into a box and tucked neatly away, determined to create a "normal" life for myself.

When my brother introduced me to a friend who turned out to be kind, considerate, and funny—unlike any other man I'd known—we started to date. I'd built a brick wall around my heart but he made me laugh. I thought *how could someone love me, stained soul that I am?* But David was very patient and, although in uncharted territory, I decided to let him in and we began a life together.

## The Hard Work

So here I was—I'd fulfilled my dream to live a "normal" life—with a wonderful husband, two beautiful children and a great job. Everything I'd always wanted. So why did I still feel so empty? I felt trapped in my own life.

Then, only in my early forties, the carpet was pulled out from under my feet—I went into menopause. Overnight, my body started to change. Still overweight from having kids, I put on even more weight. Without warning, I'd get hot flashes and break out in a full body sweat—in the middle of a business meeting, during the night, while putting on makeup, even right after a shower! Worst of all, my emotions took a roller coaster ride—not the cute little kiddy rides, but the Kingda Ka of roller coasters! One minute I was okay, and the next a raging maniac. My family tiptoed around me for fear the beast would be unleashed.

My life spiraled out of control and I hated the person I'd become. I thought I'd done my therapy years ago, but suddenly those buried emotions from so long ago erupted like Mount St. Helen. Not willing to surrender—not after all I'd been through, I knew I needed to make some drastic changes.

Jeez, did I have *some* hard work to do! Releasing a lifetime of self-criticism and negative talk wasn't easy, let me tell you! I focused on a daily ritual of affirmations to try to stop myself from constantly feeling not good enough. Out came the Louise Hay books and every other self-help guru I could find. I pasted positive notes everywhere and said them aloud constantly. Every morning—no matter what I looked like, no matter how exhausted I was, or how crappy I felt about myself—I'd look myself in the eye in the mirror and say: "I love you...I *really*, really love you..."

It wasn't easy at first. But, little by little, day by day, I began to notice a change. One day I smiled at myself in the mirror and really liked what I saw. Looking back at me was a woman who'd been through it, had a tough start, made a lot of mistakes, but there she was, starting to believe! What a great feeling...

When I was young, my father often accused me of being *too* emotional and sensitive. Usually it was when I was reacting to *him,* but his words convinced me it was a weakness. Recently it's occurred to me that my compassion, empathy, and sensitivity to others have served me well, both personally and professionally. But through the years I've found out the hard way that I can go overboard and fall into the dangerous pattern of doing everything for everyone else and forgetting about me. I realize I'm a better person, and more capable of serving others, when I don't sacrifice my own needs and desires.

I now know I was living much smaller than I am. I also understood that, in order to really let go of the past, I had some forgiving to do. When I forgave my parents and my elders for not being what I thought they should be, it enabled me to let go of the pain and resentment of the past. Most importantly, I forgave myself—the little girl inside of me—and know that she did the best she could.

In learning to love myself I'm no longer buried under all the junk from my past. My journey of self-empowerment helped me open the door to my heart and find true happiness by learning to follow my joy. My life is now simply too big to be living too small!

**ABOUT THE AUTHOR:** A Health and Fitness Coach, Lorraine uses various techniques and strategies to help clients achieve their individual nutrition and wellness goals. Passionately inspired about working with women to help them shed self-sabotaging behaviors and limiting beliefs so they can live the lives they were born to live, Lorraine loves teaching group classes in health and fitness. Her thirty year administration and human resources experience in the corporate arena has equipped her for success in her second career in the health realm. Lorraine's greatest personal triumph is her nineteen year marriage and her two beautiful children.

Lorraine M. Smith
www.lorrainemsmith.com
www.lorsmith.USANA.com
lorsmith@msn.com
732-629-6066

# Into the Light
## Christine Suva

I heard the door slam and the keys fly across the room and hit the wall as he yelled loud obscenities. I'd been cleaning all morning and just taken a load of clothes out of the dryer. I remember the lump in my throat and the hairs standing up on the back of my neck. They always did that when he got volatile.

My whole body shook as I nervously folded the clothes into the basket. Cleaning seemed to be how I got rid of nervous energy when he blasted me with anger and hostility. It was almost a form of therapy for me. Angry, indignant, and ready to unload with both barrels—it didn't matter that I knew he wasn't angry at me—I was about to catch the brunt of it anyway. I usually did.

My thoughts flashed back to when I'd gone to his family's home our first Christmas together. I shook just hearing him come up the steps and wanted to lock the door and hide. I'd had nightmares that he'd tried to smother me with a pillow. We'd argued then too. I remember how, only inches from my face, he'd yelled and punched both sides of the couch on either side of my head, swearing at me because I couldn't commit to working out with him that day with all the busyness of the holiday. It had escalated and, thankfully, he stormed upstairs and slammed my bedroom door.

Angry at his obscene, uncalled for behavior, I stupidly followed him. "How dare you talk to me like that!" I called through the door. "What the hell is the matter with you!" I'd never been talked to that way before in my life, and couldn't believe this was the same guy who, to this day, is the most romantic guy I've ever met! He'd gone to great lengths to sweep me off my feet. I thought he was different from my other boyfriends.

He was—he didn't treat me kind when I was around and tell me what I wanted to hear, then break my heart by cheating on me like they had. No, he was much worse! This man was a walking time bomb! This man would shake me to my very core. The man I thought loved me and literally filled my "tank" with his hugs—would also, for the first time in my life, crush my sense of safety at home.

I'd yelled one more time through the bedroom door "how dare you!" With that, he flung the door open and charged at me, teeth gritted, eyes like daggers that cut through to my very soul, and shoved me with both hands toward the top of the stairs. Thankfully, I didn't fall, and instead turned and went back downstairs—completely shell-shocked and shaking from head to toe.

He'd immediately retreated back into the bedroom, slammed the door, and stayed there for hours. That was the first time he was volatile, the first time he was emotionally and verbally abusive. That was when I should have left him—ten months into our relationship. It was my first window to walk, but...I hadn't.

Now, as he stormed in—ready to blast me once again as I stood nervously folding the clothes—something shifted deep inside of me. I knew I was done. I was leaving. It was over. My life was going to massively change direction and I was going home.

I did go home. In fact, amid a merger and layoffs, my position was deemed too early for the strategic plan and had been eliminated on the same day I was going to sign a new lease! I already had family lined up to move me two days later, so they moved me home instead. At twenty-eight, my relationship, my job, and my living circumstances all changed drastically in the same week!

### Lines in the Sand

That summer in Woodstock was the darkest time of my life. I was like an empty shell at that point, I felt beaten to a pulp. Severely depressed, I suffered from insomnia, and even though I was eating, the weight just kept falling off my body to the point where I had amenorrhea.

Normal body fat for women is eighteen to twenty-two percent. Mine fell to twelve percent. It was not an eating disorder, but I was driven to exercise every day just to get rid of the anxiety, stress, and sadness from years of unhealthy relationships. That summer, I literally *ran* my way out of depression! My heart had been broken repeatedly and it had taken a toll. I didn't know who I was anymore.

My therapist suggested anti-depressants, but I knew my depression was situational, not a chemical imbalance. I'd taught relaxation and stress management for years, and knew that when you're going through a really, really, hard time, it's important to learn to take massive care of yourself. Now it was time for me to swallow a dose of my own medicine. Getting back to myself was a journey I had to allow. I did anything and everything I could think of to make myself feel calm, whole, peaceful, and remind me that life was good.

Meanwhile I contemplated how I, a smart person, ended up with these relationships that kept on hurting me. Relationship ended up being the deepest darkest place in my life. The turning point came when, in the midst of my depression it hit me that I'm better off alone than in these relationships, unless I can learn to trust my judgments.

I tried to be as gentle with myself as I would with a child. I was at that crossroads between believing that a healthy relationship was in my future, and giving in to anger, bitterness, and a complete emotional shutdown. After months of soul searching and brutal self honesty, I realized I'd been raised to treat others the way in which I wanted to be treated. However, somewhere along the line I'd misinterpreted some of the critical life lessons my family and faith tried to teach me by taking them too far.

My home, growing up, was a very safe place, and I began to see how naive and unprepared I'd been for the big, wide, not-so-wonderful world. I grew up with no boundaries in an environment where I'd learned we're all God's children, we're all connected, there's goodness in everything, and love for everyone. To stick up for myself or call people out on bad behavior was somehow not "nice." Saying "no" to things I didn't have time to do or want to do, was being selfish—and selfish was a "dirty" word to me.

As a child I think this all-inclusive love got in the way because I openly loved everybody unconditionally when they may not have deserved it. I had to learn boundaries the hard way by getting smacked in the face by reality. And nowhere was I more selfless than in my romantic relationships. Somehow, I'd managed to maintain appropriate boundaries professionally—but in romantic love, I had none at all. When I gave my heart away, I gave it away completely—to men who taught me those boundaries.

For that reason, I never want to forget those hard won lessons. At this point I made a conscious decision—I realized I could spend the rest of my life feeling victimized by men, or choose faith, trust, and hope. And despite going through hell, I chose to forgive them for taking advantage of my naiveté, for breaking my heart, and nearly crushing my spirit.

I'd gone out into the world with arms open, ready to love

everyone! In those painful relationships in my own life, I finally learned my boundaries. I finally drew that line in the sand.

### The Healing Process

Meanwhile, I remained very clear about my career path, and knew early on that I felt most whole when I helped others lead happier, healthier, more fulfilling lives. Not a dating coach, I work with executives and others to identify where they hold themselves back from achieving their desired goals. So many of my clients want to create more meaning in their lives, but don't know where to start. I help them hone in on their strengths, skills, values, and passions to help them get to where they want to go in life. I not only help others figure out their purpose, but am skilled at showing them how to best achieve their goals.

I continued to heal and work on raising my own consciousness in relationship. When I met Tom, through my best friend and her husband, we both almost didn't go to their party, but we both had an intuitive urge to go. We started talking and I noticed he had the most beautiful green eyes and long eyelashes! But what captivated me most was how he spoke to me. He didn't give me a bunch of lines, put on the pressure, try to impress me, or even ask me out.

Instead, he took genuine interest in getting to know me. He seemed kind, down to earth, humble yet confident, and he made me laugh. In the middle of this crowd of mutual friends, everyone seemed to disappear as we spoke for hours. He didn't push me to go out. He realized I'd been through a lot, he said, and he'd love to get together sometime if I agreed. He then gave me his number and left me to be with my friends. Our first date was two weeks later, on the night I turned thirty.

I love Tom deeply, and my father married us on the hill at his family's home on a beautiful, sunny, summer day! I'd finally stopped my self-sabotage and held on to my faith in the future, my faith in myself, my faith in him, and my faith in us.

When I lose sight of that faith, I center myself again and pull myself back to that place deep within where peace lives. I remember to trust that everything happening at any given moment is part of my journey and is meant to teach me something, to help me grow. When I feel pain, anger, or fear, it's my soul's way of calling to my attention something that I need to learn. Reminding myself of this is what helps bring me back to center.

Now I understand that sometimes from our darkest moments come forth beautiful beginnings! When my world gets turned upside down, it's God's way of showing me there's another path. It's that trust and willingness to walk through the darkness that allows me to come back into the light and appreciate it all that much more when I get there.


**ABOUT THE AUTHOR:** Christine Suva, a Certified Professional Coach, Energy Leadership Master Practitioner, and Founder of THRIVE Coach Services, Inc., is deeply committed to helping others find passion, purpose and success in their lives! She has over 15 years experience guiding thousands across the country to achieve career and personal goals as an Outplacement Consultant and Wellness Professional. Expert certified in state-of-the-art assessment tools; Christine provides customizable group/one-on-one coaching, motivational speaking, training and consulting. She has a talent for getting to the core of who a person is, what they want, what holds them back, and provides tools and strategies for success!

Christine Suva, President
THRIVE Coach Services, Inc.
www.thrivecoachservices.com
630-427-7432

# Acknowledgements & Gratitude

There are many incredible women who have partnered to birth this moving and heartfelt anthology book; and it is the Powerful You! Women's Network members in the U.S. and around the globe by whom this book was inspired. We love you all!

First, to the amazing women who authored these chapters, we have great respect and love for each of you. The archetype you represent by honoring and sharing your truths and wisdom is an example for women around the world who have chosen to step forward and live boldly ... You have raised the bar for all women and have surely inspired their own expression of faith, truth and empowerment though your story.

We have deep appreciation for the experts who have helped to birth this book: our editor Sheri Horn-Hasan, our graphic designer Jodie Penn and our business experts—AmondaRose Igoe, Jennifer Connell and Laura Rubinstein as well as the many other women who have contributed their guidance, expertise, love and support.

Kristine Lackey, a beautiful woman with a loving spirit, along with her husband Skip, have shown us that knowledge in action and love combined with inner work is a powerful combination. We are honored to know them both.

We are grateful to our friends and families who lovingly support our inspirations, projects and unconventional ways of being—with your guidance and love we remain steadfast in our vision for life.

Above all, we are grateful to God and Goddess and to life itself for providing opportunities for continued growth and mindful living!

*With much love and deep gratitude,*
*Sue Urda and Kathy Fyler*

# About Sue Urda and Kathy Fyler

Sue and Kathy have been friends for 23 years and business partners since 1994. They have received awards and accolades for their businesses over the years and they love their latest foray into anthology book publishing where they provide a forum for women to achieve their dreams of becoming published authors.

Their pride and joy is Powerful You! Women's Network, which they claim is a gift from Spirit. They love traveling the country producing meetings and tour events to gather women for business, personal and spiritual growth. Their greatest pleasure comes through connecting with the many inspiring and extraordinary women who are a part of their network.

The strength of their partnership lies in their deep respect and understanding of one another as well as their complementary skills and knowledge. Kathy is a technology enthusiast and free-thinker. Sue is an author and speaker with a knack for creative undertakings. Their love for each other is boundless.

Together their energies combine to feed the flames of countless women who are seeking truth, empowerment, joy, peace and connection with themselves, their own spirits and other women.

Reach Sue and Kathy:
Powerful You! Inc.
973-248-1262
info@powerfulyou.com
www.powerfulyou.com

# About Kristine Lackey

 For the last ten years, Kristine has partnered with her husband, Skip Lackey, sharing with others how true freedom, wisdom, connection, health and grace can be found within. They have dedicated their lives to meeting people exactly where they are and delivering them the tools they may need to wake up to the truth of who they are.

Together they have travelled extensively throughout North America delivering over 1000 workshops and are currently working on their first relationship book, *Standing Naked – A Guide to Creating Conscious Relationships.*

And their latest heart felt passion is the creation of the Mediation Prescription which is a library of modern meditations for people with specific physical and behavioral issues. It demystifies the ancient practice of everyday mediation and brings this scientifically proven technique into your everyday life.

Kristine lives just outside of Boulder Colorado with her husband and two young children, Riley (6) and Ryder (2).


Kristine Lackey
Co-founder of Evolution Unlimited
Meditation Prescription, coming Summer 2012!
www.EvolutionUnlimited.com
www.MeditationPrescription.com
Kristine@EvoUnltd.com
973-680-0271

# Powerful You! Women's Network
# Networking with a Heart

OUR MISSION is to empower women to find their inner wisdom, follow their passion and live rich, authentic lives.

### Our Vision

Powerful You! Women's Network is founded upon the belief that women are powerful creators, passionate and compassionate leaders, and the heart and backbone of our world's businesses, homes, and communities.

Our Network welcomes all women from all walks of life. We recognize that diversity in our relationships creates opportunities.

Powerful You! creates and facilitates venues for women who desire to develop connections that will assist in growing their businesses. We aid in the creation of lasting personal relationships and provide insights and tools for women who seek balance, grace and ease in all facets of life.

### Our Beliefs

❖We believe in the power of connections.
❖We believe in the power of being present.
❖We believe in the power of relationships.
❖We believe in the power of women.

We believe in the power of devoted groups of collaborative and grateful individuals coming together for the purpose of personal growth and assisting others in business and in life.

## We believe in a Powerful You!

Join or Start a Chapter for
Business, Personal & Spiritual Growth
www.powerfulyou.com

# More About
# Powerful You! Women's Network

Powerful You! was founded in January 2005 to gather women for business, personal and spiritual growth.

Our monthly chapter meetings provide a collaborative and comfortable space for networking, connections and creating personal relationships. Meetings include introductions, discussion topic, speaker presentation, growth and success share, mini-mastermind, and a gratitude share.

Member Benefits *(Some available to non-members too!)*

- Powerful You! Learning Center
- Powerful You! Virtual Network Meetings
- Online Social Networking Website
- Advertise with Powerful You!
- Discounts on Meetings and Events
- Speak at Powerful You! Meetings
- Archived Learning Center Recordings 24/7

For more information about Powerful You! visit our website.

## www.powerfulyou.com

Follow us online:
Twitter: @powerfulyou
Facebook: www.facebook.com/powerfulyou

Join or Start a Chapter for
Business, Personal & Spiritual Growth

# Would You Like to Contribute to Our Next Anthology Book?

## Become an Author Easily, Effortlessly and Soon!

Do you have a story in you? Most people do.

If you've always wanted to be an author, and you can see yourself partnering with other women to share your story, or if you have found yourself daunted by the prospect of writing a whole book on your own, an anthology book may be your answer.

We are committed to helping women express their voices. Learn more at:

Powerful You! PUBLISHING
Sharing Wisdom ~ Shining Light

Powerful You! Publishing
973-248-1262
powerfulyoupublishing.com

# Live Consciously Now!

Are you inspired by the stories in this book?
Let the authors know.

See the contact information at the end of each chapter
and reach out to them. They'd love to hear from you!